FROM GURS TO AUSCHWITZ

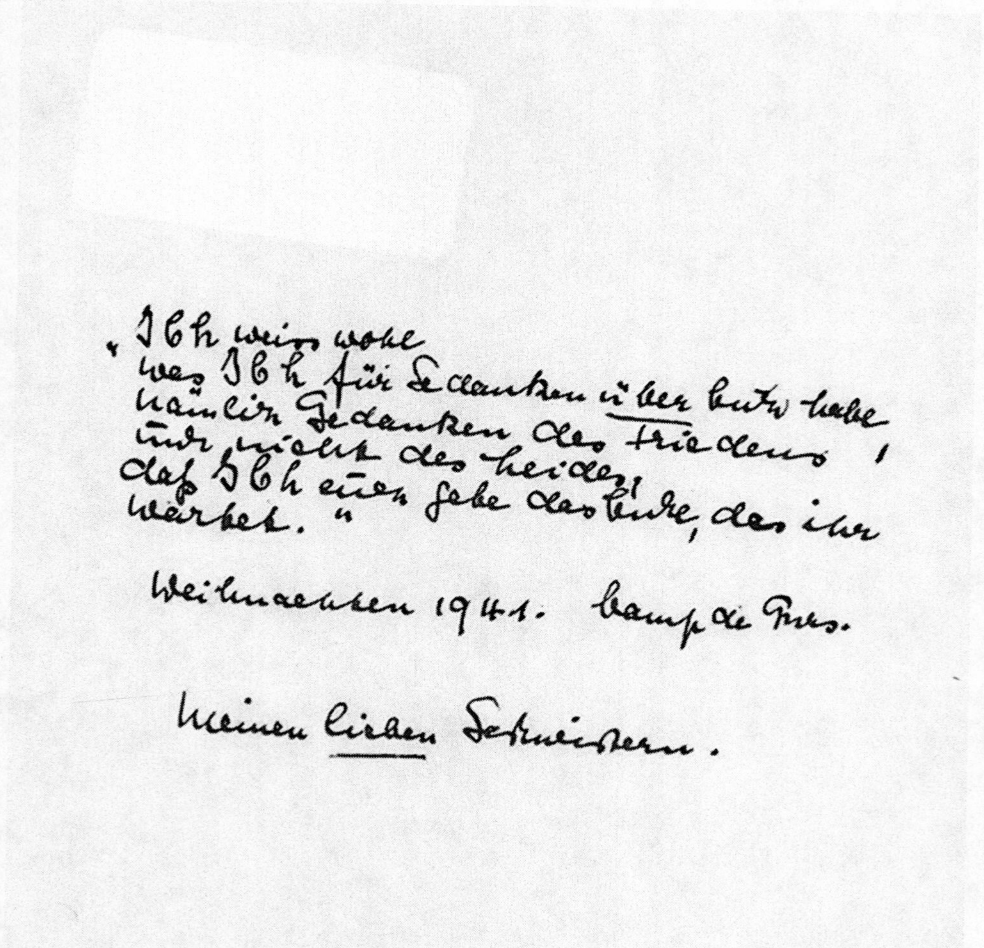

„Ich weiss wohl
was Ich für Gedanken über Euch habe
nämlich Gedanken des Friedens,
und nicht des Leides;
daß Ich euch gebe das Ende, das ihr
wartet. "

Weihnachten 1941. Camp de Gurs.

Meinen lieben Schwestern.

Figure 1: Maria Krehbiel-Darmstädter, text enclosed in a letter to her sister
(Camp de Gurs, December 25, 1940)

FROM GURS
TO AUSCHWITZ

The Inner Journey of
Maria Krehbiel-Darmstädter

PETER SELG

Translated by Matthew Barton

STEINERBOOKS | 2013

STEINERBOOKS
An imprint of Anthroposophic Press, Inc.
610 Main St., Great Barrington, MA 01230
www.steinerbooks.org

Originally published in German as *Maria Krehbiel-Darmstädter:*
Von Gurs nach Auschwitz Der innere Weg
Published by Verlag des Ita Wegman Instituts, 2010.
Translated by Matthew Barton

LIBRARY OF CONGRESS CATALOGING-IN-PUBLICATION DATA

Selg, Peter, 1963–
[Maria Krehbiel-Darmstädter. English]
  From Gurs to Auschwitwitz : the inner journey of Maria Krehbiel-
Darmstädter / Peter Selg.
    pages cm
Includes bibliographical references.
  ISBN 978-1-62148-042-6 (pbk.)—ISBN 978-1-62148-043-3 (ebook)
  1. Krehbiel-Darmstädter, Maria, 1892-1943—Correspondence.
2. Christengemeinschaft—Biography. 3. Christian converts from
Judaism—Germany—Mannheim—Biography. 4. Auschwitz
(Concentration camp) 5. Gurs (Concentration camp) 6. Holocaust,
Jewish (1939-1945) I. Krehbiel-Darmstädter, Maria, 1892-1943. II.
Title.
  BP605.C45S4513 2013
  299'.935092—dc23
  [B]

                                                        2013021003

Contents

Translator's preface ix

Foreword xi

I. "Living in Dignity to the End"

Mannheim 3

Gurs Internment Camp 45

Limonest 127

Drancy and Auschwitz 217

II. "No Separation Where Love of Being and Truth in Christ Prevail"

Excerpts from letters by Maria Krehbiel Darmstädter, 1940–1943 . 229

Notes and references 333

Bibliography 352

Picture credits 354

"It is this we have to learn in our times:
to live with pure trust, without any existential certainty,
trusting in the ever-present help of the world of spirit.
Truly, there is no other way."

RUDOLF STEINER

Translator's preface

The letters by Maria Krehbiel-Darmstädter at the heart of this book reveal a sensibility at work that, to find its true expression, frequently puts language "under pressure" in the best sense. This was necessitated not only by the dire constraints and strictures of her outer circumstances—such as the limited page allowance for letters sent from an internment camp, and the omnipresent eye of the censor—but also by their author's inner wrestling with language to convey sometimes inexpressible realities and experience. In responding to both her outer circumstances and inner commitment to truth, Maria Krehbiel-Darmstädter developed a style of writing that is—like poetry—often elliptical, highly economical and idiosyncratic in syntax and punctuation (see notes 9 and 29).

This is not just "style," though, but a deeply authentic response to her own currents of thought and feeling. The translator faces a challenge here, as in the translation of all poetry: to render the letters, with their unique qualities, in a comprehensible and accurate way, while nevertheless retaining a sense of the ineffable or inexpressible that they frequently invoke.

As far as possible I have tried to keep the sense of immediacy that is palpable in Maria Krehbiel-Darmstädter's often unorthodox or disjointed syntax, with its sudden movements, leaps and abrupt caesuras. In particular I have faithfully retained her use of the colon, ellipsis and dash, the latter highly reminiscent, for me, of the dash used to such powerful effect by one of America's greatest poets, Emily

Dickinson—a unique form of punctuation that many critics regard as intrinsic to the dynamic movements of her creative mind.

Matthew Barton, May 2013

Foreword

In October 1970—the thirtieth anniversary, to the day, of the deportation of Jews from the Baden, Saarland, and Pfalz regions of Germany—there was widespread astonishment when Professor Walter Schmitthenner published 150 letters written by a victim of these events, Maria Krehbiel-Darmstädter (1892–1943). Schmitthenner's edition of these letters[1] documented a more or less unique inner path at a time of persecution and atrocity. Maria Krehbiel-Darmstädter had written to friends and family members from Gurs internment camp in the Pyrenees, then later from near Lyon where she was staying on temporary sick leave, and finally from the detention camp at Drancy near Paris, prior to her deportation to Auschwitz on February 11, 1943, where she died soon afterward. Her accounts were measured, detailed, intelligent and precise but spoke less of the outer circumstances in which she was forced to live than of efforts to preserve her moral and spiritual integrity. She also sent remarkable poems of her own, and asked "Have we not, of necessity, all become poets?"[2] Of her letters she said,

> They are riddled with errors; they're imprecise, sentimental and often self-congratulatory. They are, however, true reflections of my striving and learning I. And may serve others through acknowledgement both of what is too much in them; and too little.[3]

In her book published after World War II, *Job and the destiny of the Jewish people,*[4] Margarete Susman made the following remark on the difficulty of writing anything after Auschwitz: "In relation to these events it is probably true to say that every word is either too much or too little." And Paul Celan began his poem for Nelly Sachs, "Zurich, At the Stork Inn," with words alluding to Susman: "We spoke of the too much, and of/the too little."[5]

Maria Krehbiel-Darmstädter wrote her witness-bearing correspondence at the time Simone Weil died and Nelly Sachs found her poetic voice—and these letters are on a par with the works of Simone Weil and Nelly Sachs both in the expressiveness of their language and their metaphysical and moral power. Shortly before her deportation to Auschwitz, a female friend wrote to say that she would accompany Maria Krehbiel-Darmstädter inwardly by rereading all the letters received from her—with their distinctive thoughts on confronting suffering and death. Maria rejoiced at this. In the last postcard received from her from Drancy, five days before transportation in a cattle truck to the concentration and death camp Auschwitz, she remarked: "The thought that you will read my old letters moves me infinitely. From afar I will add to them, won't I, what I have to experience at first hand."[6]

After the war ended, Walter Schmitthenner, Maria Krehbiel-Darmstädter's godson, collected (with the help of Margot Junod) all the letters and postcards that had survived from the time of the deportation—more than 320 letters,[7] and in 1970 published a little under half of them in unabbreviated form and in the knowledge that Maria had indirectly authorized this in the following passage in a letter:

> There are letters that, however personal they may be, acquire greater universality. Then we can say that they are generally valid because they release themselves from the "personality." You understand me. Letters never ought otherwise to be "published," yet even the most intimate are. When the necessary time has passed and this therefore becomes permissible. Maybe so that they ripen enough to fall from the tree of life and be harvested? True letters intrinsically bear a personal tinge as their color, the nuance of their landscape and origin. But then they can pass beyond this and be more. Because "it" speaks through them.[8]

Publication of the letters met not only with amazement, admiration and veneration but also bewilderment or unease, albeit only after some time had passed. The author's very idiosyncratic and unusual way of writing—also in terms of grammar and syntax[9]— was acknowledged, but the sense that she relativized suffering or even made it taboo in her interpretation of events by trying to "render it meaningful" was regarded as problematic.[10] Maria Krehbiel-Darmstädter's letters passed through the camp censor's office at Gurs, and were likely to be opened several times by the authorities before they reached their addressees, which necessitated a degree of reticence in her formulations. But above and beyond this it was said that, because of her "religious and philosophical thought constructs," the author of these letters had suppressed her sense of grievance until the power of this "spiritual-moral superstructure" grew weaker in the face of her forthcoming deportation to Auschwitz, and finally collapsed altogether, and she *at last* gave vent to an experience of fear and pain, loss, despair and hopelessness.[11] It is true that, compared with other prisoners at Gurs, Maria Krehbiel-Darmstädter rarely spoke of her sufferings, her physical ordeals and afflictions and everything connected with these miseries ("It is true to say, however, that this hardship, the daily struggle for space, or a little light, warmth and freedom of movement, so easily numbs you. Your thoughts soon start to focus just on your own weal and woe, and that of those closest to you in the camp." Else Liefmann.[12]) In fact, Maria Krehbiel-Darmstädter's general silence about such things was the very opposite of an ultimately failed attempt at self-suppression. Viktor E. Frankl, who survived Auschwitz, wrote in 1945 of the possibility and necessity of maintaining spiritual freedom in extreme circumstances. He described the inmate's survival as a task of "turning his merely suffering state into an inner achievement,"[13] growing beyond himself in a real sense. The "courage to suffer," said Frankl, was the imperative need at moments of destiny, rather than giving way to grievance and lament that consumed all one's powers. In his memoir of the concentration camp experience, he quoted Nietzsche's phrase, "One who has a 'why' to live can bear almost any 'how,'" and stated:

In the face of our suffering, too, we have to wrestle our way through to the insight that our painful destiny is unique and never to be repeated in the whole cosmos. No one can take this load from us or suffer this suffering in our place. But a unique opportunity for an unrepeatable achievement...lies in the way we ourselves bear this fate and suffering. Suffering, for us, had revealed its potential for inward labors and achievement—of the same kind that induced Rilke to cry out "How much suffering we must bear!"[14]

With this outlook Frankl survived Auschwitz and three other concentration camps—at the same time supporting fellow inmates who caved in to despair. Maria Krehbiel-Darmstädter thought and acted in the same way, accepting and internalizing her suffering and her human anxieties, and sparing the recipients of her letters *because* she was fully aware of their distress ("And my experience tells me that others often find it harder to bear things than the person directly affected."[15]) and because, in preserving an ultimate inner freedom, she accepted for herself, as Frankl did, the task (or "achievement") of suffering. "For me, she was always exemplary: not only in her capacity to endure suffering but for the inner greatness and dignity that a person is capable of summoning in the midst of tragedy," wrote Gertrude Spörri, former priest of The Christian Community, in a letter to Margot Junod on November 3, 1947.[16]

Maria Krehbiel-Darmstädter not only wrote special letters but was also a special person, a "rare woman."[17] She thought differently from others, and possessed an understanding of herself and the world that exceeded the ordinary, and had tangible effects on her social surroundings. She was tirelessly devoted to her "close companions" at the camp, giving advice and helping those around her to find and maintain their inner dignity. In Drancy the Polish Jews she was locked up with spoke of "Mère Maria."[18] A fellow inmate[19] wrote:

She was an extraordinary person, and she helped many people there in their distress. She herself passed seemingly unscathed through all privations and degradation, always thinking only of others. She emanated a...powerful spirituality.

Gurs signified a trial, an abyss and a threshold in the "mystery play" of the twentieth century:

> It did not matter where you came from or what your past was. Here all that counted was who you were. Here each person had to live by their own strength, prove themselves good or bad, without support or backdrop. Gurs was a testing ground where only the authentic proved its worth.[20]

~

The source of strength that Maria Krehbiel-Darmstädter drew on in her life was, primarily, Rudolf Steiner's Spiritual Science. She did not regard this as some kind of "religious and philosophical thought construct" or "spiritual-moral superstructure" but felt it belonged intrinsically to the substance of her inner being, to the "authentic" reality of her existence. Krehbiel-Darmstädter spoke of Rudolf Steiner (1861–1925) as her spiritual "teacher" and of Anthroposophy as the "most important" aspect of her life. Of all the fields of work and institutions initiated or facilitated by Steiner, The Christian Community founded in 1922 as a "movement for religious renewal" was closest to her heart. She felt herself to belong deeply to its world of sacrament and worship, and spoke of it as "my community."[21] To categorize Anthroposophy as "thought construct" and "superstructure" would have drawn a wry smile from her. Having an intimate knowledge—as she did—of this Spiritual Science and actually practicing the path of meditative schooling, becoming different in the process, growing more mature and entering the domain Schiller described as the human being's higher "I" ("for it is the great task of our existence to seek accord with the immutable unity of this "I" through all changes and fluctuations"[22]) means becoming simultaneously more circumspect and more differentiated in one's evaluations, judgments, and formulations.

The contents of Rudolf Steiner's books and lectures—including numerous texts concerned with the profound challenges and afflictions of the twentieth century—and the path of inner development taught by Steiner, had to some extent prepared Maria Krehbiel-Darmstädter for the travails of 1940 to 1943. She was familiar with Steiner's Christology, and his teachings about Christ's return "in the etheric realm"—in other words our increasing capacity to experience Christ, specifically in circumstances marked by misery and distress[23]—and this formed part of her ongoing studies. Writing in a letter on August 21, 1942,[24] she says, "You know it is the time of his [Christ's] return." We can scarcely understand a way of living and an outlook like that of Maria Krehbiel-Darmstädter without some knowledge of Anthroposophy, its content and implications. The people Maria came to know in Gurs, on whom she made an unforgettable impression, respected the fact, at least, that she drew on a remarkable spiritual source in her actions, words and letters. Rudolf Steiner had spoken of a forthcoming "culture of selflessness" that would draw on capacities of the highly developed "I," its powers of conscience and responsibility; and it was not hard to see that Maria Krehbiel-Darmstädter, in the religiosity and morality intrinsic to her, belonged to such a culture ("We are made of the very essence of devotion. The most profound thing we learn is a fearlessness that we would never, never otherwise have learned."[25]). By no means did she affirm and accept Gurs as such, but she did embrace the fact that the world's outmoded bourgeois ways of life were falling apart, and she had long since recognized that "homelessness" is part and parcel of our existence in the contemporary world and will continue to be so in future. It was necessary, in her view, to learn to live through the pure powers of the "I," out of the inmost Christ or Sun ground of the human being—free despite all threats and the complete lack of existential security:

> For how many years have we no longer had any "safety." No longer free. A state we seem destined for—and that, once resolved after the very greatest battles—allows us to glimpse a new world. The true world of *grandeur*, of the free condition.... Unspeakably difficult to grasp it; since after all it no longer offers any "refuge" as we understand this (such as parental home, mother tongue, name). Even memory "impairs" it. A

wall become transparent—with a clear view to the other world. (Wall in the sense, almost, of the Orthodox Church; except that, instead of the icon, pain-woven veils are stretched across it.)

On the path toward initiation, homelessness is the first "probation" and stage. How hard this is already. But what grace in the fact that today so many people are relieved of this choice and have been "compelled to embark on the journey." The immensity of this is something we can experience at first hand in the way we grow weak and faint. In the laceration accompanied by unearthly protection. In accompaniment by a truth such as this: "in peace I meet the world." Departing from everything—that is, leaving all behind—we have gone forward to meet the "I," accompanied by what is eternal in it, which cannot be lost.

Thus the second world is built; which consists far more strongly of expectancy than the first and—of *a particular* expectancy. (April 11, 1942[26])

There is no doubt, surely, that these are times of initiation. And—you're about to see; what I discovered early this morning (after "reading" it) is really true: we are close to allowing ourselves to be deprived of our "I" while we are still alive. And—what is left for the second death, of the physical body, if "I"-consciousness is already extinguished in spiritual death—and the Christ impulse does not mightily and overpoweringly encircle and storm round us? (September 12, 1942[27])

～

In a letter written after World War II, the evangelical priest Pierre Toureille, who met Maria Krehbiel-Darmstädter at Gurs, spoke of her "extraordinary nature," adding: "I am certain that Germany, Europe and the world today has urgent need of a great number of people of her kind."[28] Given this irrefutable fact, the present volume, which continues the work of Walter Schmitthenner, seeks to document Maria Krehbiel-Darmstädter's inner path. For this purpose I studied anew the texts of all available original letters and postcards preserved at Mannheim City Archive, along with many additional documents that relate to her life. I have not tried to write a biography but to gain as precise a picture as possible of the inner path that Maria Krehbiel-Darmstädter actually followed in the years of persecution and deportation, which such terms as "thought construct" and "superstructure" are entirely inadequate to describe. I have quoted from many of her letters—both published and unpublished—in the main body of the book.[29] Part 2 of the book contains longer passages from the letters, which speak for themselves and can stand alone. The selection of letters, with commentaries by Walter Schmitthenner, which the latter published with Verlag Lambert Schneider, Heidelberg, in 1970 after decades of research, has been out of print for a long time now.

The present volume celebrates a human life and is thus partly a commemoration. It also shows what Anthroposophy meant to this person—indeed, what it can become in a particular individual. It would (or does) accord with Maria Krehbiel-Darmstädter's own views if this account not only reveals aspects of her own individual nature but also intimates the quality of things that were of such spiritual importance to her, and whose significance has so far made little headway in our culture: Rudolf Steiner, the Spiritual Science he founded, and the sacraments of The Christian Community.[30]

I am particularly grateful to Gertrud Herrmann (Manheim), who accompanied Maria Krehbiel-Darmstädter as a young girl (together with her sister) to the deportation place in Mannheim and shared her detailed memories with me, as well as Petra Castellaneta and Dr. Anja Gillen from Mannheim City Archive, who offered their unstinting help in accessing posthumous documents, and granted permission for publication.

Peter Selg, Ita Wegman Institute
Arlesheim, Switzerland
St. John's, 2010

Part I

"Living in Dignity to the End"

E. Tillmann-Matter, Hofphotogr.

"*Deus tantum cognoscitur, quantum diligitur!*"

Mannheim i/io. 14.   J.Klein

Figure 2: Christ Church in Mannheim
Postcard from Father Klein to Rudolf Steiner, 10.1.1914.
"Deus tantum cognoscitur, quantum diligitur!"
[God can be perceived only insofar as he is loved]
Bernard of Clairveaux

I.

Mannheim

"Our childhood home had a sober, serious feeling because of my mother's early illness. My father worked hard—I can say that we lived in great prosperity, with loving nannies; and that an evangelical school laid or formed the foundations, too, for my later life: love of Christ and trust in the workings of destiny."

—MARIA KREHBIEL-DARMSTÄDTER: Biographical notes
Gurs, December 1940[31]

Maria Krehbiel-Darmstädter was forty-eight at the time of the deportation of Mannheim's Jewish population on October 22, 1940. For the past few months she had been living in very reduced circumstances in the Old Town barrack in Mannheim 7, 17,[32] the area assigned for the "remaining Jewish populace." On the morning of October 22, Gestapo officers sought her out there and ordered her to pack her things quickly. She was to report to the assembly point at Mannheim Castle in less than two hours.

Maria (Elisabeth Friederike) Darmstädter was born in Mannheim on June 22, 1892, as eldest child of prosperous parents. From the age of eleven she lived with her younger siblings Luise and Franz at 48 Werdestrasse, in an impressive mansion in the city's eastern district—a villa built in 1903 by the architect Rudolf Tilessen for Maria's father Rudolf Darmstädter, a grain merchant, and cofounder and chairman of Mannheim Stock Exchange, as well as a commercial judge at Mannheim district court.[33] Maria's parents were assimilated

Jews with no connection to the Jewish community, and belonged to Mannheim's upper classes. While their three children did attend lessons in the Jewish religion, the parents "gave us free rein as far as our inmost soul life was concerned"—as Maria wrote in brief biographical notes at the time of her incarceration.[34]

Maria Darmstädter's father was forty when she was born, thus no longer young. He had gone to the United States in 1871 at the age of eighteen and had worked there for nearly twenty years, acquiring American citizenship before returning to Mannheim in 1890 to take over his father's business. He married Berta May, who also came from a grain merchant's family. His extensive professional duties, including numerous honorary posts in the city, meant that Rudolf Darmstädter was often not at home while Maria was growing up. Nannies took care of the three children—their mother, the lady of the house was often ill. "Our childhood home had a sober, serious feeling because of my mother's early illness. My father worked hard—I can say that we lived in great prosperity, with loving nannies," she writes in the biographical notes from Gurs.[35] Maria was a sensitive, gifted child with a rich inner life, who lived in her own world and did not immediately reveal herself. In a letter about her early schooling she wrote:

> I had a mass of thick, long hair and sat in the front row because I was shortsighted. Sometimes I would lay my head on the desk and cover myself in the whole forest of hair. Because: too much. Too much there, in my heart or body. No way through. I was seeking protection from myself. Covered over like a natural creature exposed to the gaze; hiding itself.[36]

Nelly Sachs, similarly, wrote thus of her childhood: "I always experienced things acutely. Anxious at school that I would reveal I was different. Always hiding."[37] Maria had friends at her girls' high school, yet went her own way, largely alone. "Loneliness has always been my preferred companion."[38] "Alone, preferring loneliness, was something intrinsic in me from earliest childhood, with almost

Figure 3: Maria Darmstädter, around 1910

painful insistence."[39] In senior classes she developed a close connection with Christianity.

In 1911, at the age of twenty, after graduating from high school, Maria went to Lausanne for a year of finishing school, and there she engaged with French language and literature intensely. This became a kind of second home for her, in which she moved with ease. In a letter she writes that, during the period in Lausanne, she even began dreaming in French; these language skills came in very useful to her when she was deported to France.[40] Her time at Lake Geneva was one of inner upheavals and experiences, with deep impressions of the natural world and intense human relationships. It was in Lausanne that Maria formed what she herself called the most intense friendship of her life with a woman of the same age: Elisabeth, the daughter of the property owner.

After returning to Germany, Maria Darmstädter attended university, but soon gave up her studies because she felt they had no real connection with her. Two years younger than she was, her sister also decided against pursuing the path her father intended for her; she did study economics as he wished, but then went to art school in Munich and became a painter. She liked most to paint portraits of her older sister Maria, whose sensitive spirituality was alien to her, but for whom she nevertheless held in high regard. Luise ("Lulu") lived a different and more worldly life than did Maria. She married three times and exhibited her paintings at Mannheim's Art Society, where she formed a close connection with the important art historian and director of Mannheim Castle's library, Professor Wilhelm Fraenger.[41]

During World War I, from 1914, Maria moved back to her parents' home on Werderstrasse. Little is known of that time in her life, which she felt to be one of historical upheaval, a deep and unhealed wound in the body of Europe, "an era went under."[42] Maria was twenty-two when the war broke out. Rainer Maria Rilke, whose poems she dearly loved, wrote in a letter in September 2, 1914: "All of us have been born violently into a shocking world that has nothing

Figure 4: Maria Darmstädter, 1912

in common with the one we knew before—except that it is incomprehensible; but is so in a new, appalling, fatal way."[43]

Soon after this he wrote in a poem:

> Like the birds who live beside the ringing
> bells in belfries, suddenly sent whirling
> into morning air by clangorous feelings
> so that their ousted flutterings write
> around the towers inscriptions of their fright—
>
> so we, on hearing these tumultuous tones
> cannot remain at home inside our hearts.[44]

Rilke gave hypersensitive expression (and in other writings[45]) to his experiences of this period, and Maria Darmstädter, who had a great inner affinity with him, shared his sense of a mighty caesura in historical evolution, whose consequences could not yet be calculated. During these years at 48 Werderstrasse, she withdrew into literature, but was not entirely alone or lonely, becoming engaged during the war to her friend Willy Altschul, possibly while he was on brief leave from the front. We know little about him. He was six years older than Maria, and he, too, came from a Jewish family in Mannheim.

Maria Darmstädter never forgot the air bombardments that the city suffered at the end of World War I. On Easter Sunday 1942, in considering the figure of Christ Resurrected in Grünewald's Isenheim Altar, she recalled:

> During the last war and nightly air raids, the image of this victorious, hovering, shining, healing, blessing, assured Christ was what I was able to "think." For I had such tremulous fear. Which hurt right into my fingertips.[46]

Shortly after the end of the war, on October 30, 1918, Maria's fiancé Willy Altschul died unexpectedly in the severe flu epidemic. He was thirty-two. Exactly two years later, in October 1920, Maria also lost Elisabeth Keel de Schnueringer, her friend from Lausanne, who took her own life without warning or farewell, leaving behind two daughters and a husband. Maria was twenty-eight at the time, completing the fourth seven-year phase of her life; she went through a dark night of the soul. She fell ill and for a while was unable to conquer her inner tumult. During this period, Her sister Luise painted her on her sickbed, haggard and beleaguered.[47]

Eventually she found new courage and determination, transforming all her sufferings into a therapeutic impetus. After working on farms for a while, she attached herself to the evangelical nursing and welfare service for the Königsfeld and Kayserwerth districts and worked there with great dedication. At the age of 30, she returned temporarily to her parental home to take over from her severely sick mother to run the house. After a lengthy process of inner searching, on February 17, 1921, she was baptized in Mannheim's Christ Church by Father Wilhelm Schmitthenner, with whose wife Karoline Schmitthenner (née Merk) she had been close friends since their school days.

Maria did not join Schmitthenner's congregation (at Luther Church), but instead that of Paul Klein at Christ Church, very near her home. Her closer acquaintance with Rudolf Steiner's Spiritual Science dates from that time if not earlier; this would later become her core spiritual orientation.[48] Given the circumstances in Mannheim and Maria Darmstädter's cultural awareness, it is very likely that she had previously heard of Anthroposophy and may have been studying it in the years of crisis after the World War I, during her troubled inner state and outer difficulties. If this is true, then the content and views offered by this science of the spirit may have helped Maria to regain psychological equilibrium and the courage to continue. In 1910, in his first mystery drama, *The Portal of Initiation*, Rudolf Steiner created the character of "the other Maria," who, after grave biographical experiences ("the heavy hand of fate"), including the death of her husband and complete collapse, found her way to Anthroposophy and thus to herself, whereupon she embarked on welfare work. In the first scene of that play, Steiner gives "the other Maria" these words:

An inner prompting guided me
To dedicate the life
That still remains to me
To those whose destiny
Is full of affliction and adversity.
More often it was the pain
In minds and souls I soothed than any
Bodily suffering.
Often I felt my will was weak
Or powerless to help;
I had to keep on seeking
New strength from the wealth
That flows here from the spirit's springs.
The warm power of the words
That I hear in this place
Pours out into my hands
And flows like balm:
When my hand touches those
Downcast by woe
It changes on my lips into a true
Speech of solace for pain-fraught hearts.
I do not question the origin of these words.
Their truth is visible when they spring
To life in me. And every day I see
That my own will's weak strength is not
What gives them power, but that they daily
Give me back myself anew.[49]

Maria Darmstädter was not "the other Maria," and as some-one highly cultured and educated in literature and philosophy she certainly did ask about the epistemological foundations of Steiner's "words." But, as with "the other Maria," Anthroposophy did give her the strength to go on living, working, and helping others, and this was something that would become lastingly evident in forthcoming years of adversity and deportation.

~

Rudolf Steiner gave his first lectures on Spiritual Science in Mannheim in 1908, when Maria was sixteen and attending high school.[50] At that time Steiner gave both public and private lectures (for members of the newly founded Mannheim branch of the Theosophical Society). The talks were given on the premises of the "August Lamey Lodge"[51] at C4, 12, Zeughausplatz, where services were held at Jewish festivals, and lectures were sometimes given—by Martin Buber and Leo Baeck among others. In subsequent years, Steiner returned to Mannheim and attracted the interest of Father Paul Klein, who came from Alsace and was priest at Luther Church in the city at the time. By 1910, Fr. Klein had become one of Rudolf Steiner's esoteric pupils and the branch leader of the Theosophical Society. On his visits to Mannheim, Steiner often stayed overnight at Fr. Klein's parsonage in Dammstrasse, and after 1912 also at the Christ Church parish premises (15 Werderplatz), where Klein was appointed priest. There the Protestant priest set aside a "branch" room for studying anthroposophic Spiritual Science.[52]

Maria Darmstädter probably heard of Klein's extraordinary sermons early on, since they were given very near her in the imposing building of Christ Church, consecrated in 1911. They attracted a large number of people and played a part in the cultural discourse of the city. She probably also heard about Klein's connection with Steiner and anthroposophic Spiritual Science, which the courageous and headstrong priest did not conceal but referred to in his sermons. Maria was also personally acquainted with another prominent anthroposophist in Mannheim, privy councilor Helene Röchling. The latter (who belonged to her mother's generation) was the daughter of industrialist Heinrich Lanz and his wife Julia, a well-known patron and founder of social institutions in the city. "Röchling Castle," a monumental villa at 52 Werderstrasse, built by Rudolf Tillessen, directly adjoined the Darmstädter family's property. At the instigation of the Lanz-Röchling family, the "Heinrich Lanz Hospital" opened in 1907 as a modern clinic staffed by evangelical nurses from Freiburg, personally supported by Helene Röchling. With her mother Helene Röchling regularly attended sermons by Father Klein—who also held

Figure 5: Rudolf Steiner, Dr. phil. (1861–1925)

services at the hospital's chapel—gave pastoral care to patients and held anthroposophic study evenings with the nurses. Like Klein, she joined Rudolf Steiner's esoteric school in 1910.

Heinrich Lanz Hospital was transformed temporarily into a military hospital during World War I, and Helene Röchling worked there as a nurse. In September 1914, Röchling, too, probably attended Steiner's first aid, or "Samaritan's," course in Dornach, whose key meditation Maria Darmstädter often later mentioned (see pages 193–194). We do not know whether Maria, in her charitable work at Kayserwerth and Königsfeld at the beginning of the 1920s, intended to prepare herself for subsequent work at the Heinrich-Lanz Hospital, but this seems likely. She may also have known the three anthroposophic physicians in Mannheim, who had attended Rudolf Steiner's first medical course in March 1920. They included Hilma Walter, who had met Anthroposophy through Father Klein and, beginning in the summer of 1921, worked alongside Ita Wegman at the "Clinical Therapeutic Institute" at Arlesheim, Switzerland.

Maria Darmstädter attended Rudolf Steiner's last public lecture in Mannheim in May 1922, "Anthroposophy and Spiritual Enquiry." She may also have attended courses and lectures that he gave in other cities until he fell ill at the end of September 1924. Steiner's last visit to Mannheim was already overshadowed by struggles and dangers that would increase in the future; he needed bodyguards to protect him against attacks by right-wing nationalists. We do not know when Maria heard about the founding of The Christian Community,[53] which Steiner helped facilitate as a "movement for religious renewal," or if she was present at the first Act of Consecration of Man in Mannheim on February 18, 1923, in the chapel of Heinrich Lanz Hospital. She remained in the Protestant Church with Father Klein, yet felt a part of The Christian Community and joined it as a member. She also joined the Anthroposophical Society led by Steiner,[54] who died in Dornach on March 30, 1925. At Pentecost 1941, from the detention camp at Gurs, Maria wrote to the former Christian Community priest Gertrud Spörri, who had been present at the last blessing and the funeral for

Figure 6: Heinrich-Lanz Hospital with chapel

Rudolf Steiner in Dornach and had given an account of this to other priests: "Never will I forget that you were present at the Doctor's cremation and funeral. You were "our" representative. A whole wealth of content."[55]

Maria greatly appreciated Albert Steffen's poem on the death of Rudolf Steiner:

> Stretching winter furrows, bare
> Soil moist with grave-like gloom
> Transforms into a shining, fair
> Flower of incandescent bloom.
>
> And now take wing its crown and chalice:
> Christ lifts you from the vale of tears
> Into the brightening countenance
> Of the holiest heavenly spheres.
>
> How the choir of stars resounds
> How all sons of Heaven rejoice
> To see your beauty burst earthly bonds
> And from death gently free its voice.
>
> Yes, in earthly raiment clad
> You come, yet untouched by decay:
> Henceforth angels will be glad
> To see men enter spirit's day.
>
> In love, the angels gaze below
> To earthly colors you purified:
> By your gracious gesture now
> God and humanity are allied.[56]

~

Three-and-a-half years after Rudolf Steiner's death, at Michaelmas 1928, the second Goetheanum opened with a big inaugural conference. Maria Darmstädter attended this event, and heard Albert Steffen's powerful lecture on "The Goetheaum as spiritual home"[57] along with many other very memorable talks. Steiner had conceived the Goetheanum as a modern Christian mystery center, and "School of Spiritual Science." A few months before her death, at a time of culminating atrocities, Maria wrote of the Dornach Goetheanum as "our building":

> And how in every other way, too, all that is essential to life contracts around this island. As one continually senses meaning and blessing emanating from *here*. A home in the spirit! How wonderful that it is embodied somewhere upon the Earth.[58]

Rudolf Steiner's writings, lectures and meditations were of the very greatest importance to Maria, and she saw him as her "spiritual teacher." Steiner taught a methodology of inner schooling—a path belonging to Western Christianity and to its philosophical and spiritual history and evolution. In practicing it, she found what she had long sought—a new image of the human being and the world and a Christology uniting the profound, esoteric nature of true Christianity with a deeply humane outlook. In Dornach in 1928, she first saw Rudolf Steiner's monumental sculpture in wood, the *Representative of Humanity,* depicting the figure of Christ between the adversarial powers. Steiner had envisioned this work as the artistic core of the first Goetheanum building.[59] The first Goetheanum, built of wood (for which Helene Röchling and many others had donated large sums), no longer existed in 1928, since it had been completely destroyed in an arson attack by fanatic opponents of Anthroposophy at the New Year, 1922–'23. The wooden sculpture had survived the inferno, however—a fact that acquired symbolic significance in the dark abysses of destruction that would follow. During the twentieth century and beyond, the "figure of Christ" was to remain visible and, as Rudolf Steiner remarked in numerous writings and lectures, would gain even deeper meaning: "From the twentieth century onward, people will feel the life of Christ increasingly in their souls as a direct, personal experience" (Rudolf Steiner, 1914[60]).

~

Figure 7: Christ and the adversarial powers;
(woodcarving by Rudolf Steiner. Dornach, Switzerland)

Development of The Christian Community and its sacramental rituals was of key importance for Maria Darmstädter. Rudolf Frieling, who was a leading individual in the new movement together with Friedrich Rittelmeyer and Emil Bock, worked in Mannheim until the summer of 1926. During these years, Maria formed a personal connection with Emil Krehbiel, a coworker at The Christian Community, and eventually agreed to marry him. Krehbiel, who adored her, was seven years younger than she was and worked at The Christian Community's Stuttgart office. They married on August 23, 1928, at the Stuttgart registry office when Maria was thirty-seven; between this and their Christian Community wedding in November of that year in Mannheim, they took a honeymoon trip together to attend the inauguration of the second Goetheanum.

Emil Franz Krehbiel had grown up in Mannheim, and met Anthroposophy through Maria Darmstädter. After working as an administrator at the Waldorf Astoria cigarette factory, he transferred to The Christian Community's Stuttgart office. He had a study and workroom at the "Urachhaus" in Stuttgart, the scene of much lively activity. As well as providing accommodation for the Rittelmeyer and Bock families, students attending the priests' seminar also lived there. The Christian Community monthly periodical and the priests' newsletter were dispatched from there, as well as a remarkable new series of paperbacks, "Christ of All the Earth," initiated by Friedrich Doldinger from Freiburg. All correspondence of the priests and parish leaders with The Christian Community coordinators passed through the Urachhaus. There was religious instruction for children and adolescents in the Stuttgart congregation, a regular Act of Consecration of Man for the seminar students and a great deal more.[61]

Emil Krehbiel (according to Kurt von Wistinghausen) had a responsible post at the office as the priests' "liaison man." He typed out the internal priests' newsletter, as well as transcripts of the courses that Steiner gave for theologians; he was committed and devoted to the work. At his suggestion, Emil Bock's reflections on the Gospels were distributed in typescript from 1927, and the proceeds of this

CHRISTUS ALLER ERDE

Eine Schriftenreihe ♦ Band 22

DIE
SIEBEN SAKRAMENTE

✳

Von

Dr. Rudolf Frieling

✳

1 ✳ 9 ✳ 2 ✳ 6

Verlag der Christengemeinschaft ♦ Stuttgart

Figure 8: The Seven Sacraments, *by Rudolf Frieling, Stuttgart 1926*

were placed at the disposal of a new church building project planned in Stuttgart. The 2,000 copies printed sold out in less than a week.

Various paths of destiny were woven at the Urachhaus. It was here that a Mannheim acquaintance of Maria Darmstädter—Maria Neumann, who came to work in the office through Emil Krehbiel— met the priest Franz Gnädinger and later married him. Together they later went to Bern, where Maria Gnädinger was able give great support to Maria Darmstädter at the internment camp in Gurs. At the time of deportation, she became a significant friend to her, writing to her and helping in whatever way she could.

At the end of 1928 or 1929, Maria Darmstädter went to join Emil Krehbiel in Stuttgart, later moving with him to Ulm, where he likewise worked for The Christian Community. "My marriage—ah, everything of importance is connected with it," she would later write in a letter from Gurs.[62] She took part in the large Christian Community summer conference in Stuttgart in 1929, held at the music conservatory premises where, since the movement was founded, its service, the Act of Consecration of Man, took place. There she listened to Emil Bock's reflections on St. Paul, along with Rudolf Frieling's significant evening lectures. Her marriage with Emil Krehbiel lasted only a few years, however. At a time when Maria once again succumbed to illness, he fell in love with a younger woman and soon afterward asked Maria for a divorce.[63] He wanted to start a family with his new partner, which he later did. Maria wished him well and tried to include his new wife and child in her loving thoughts despite the hardship of her personal destiny. When Walter Schmitthenner wrote to her in 1942 about the death of a friend in battle and his continuing connection with the fallen comrade, she wrote back to affirm this:

> I can fully agree that there is no *true* separation, because I have experienced it myself. Death does not sunder us. There are, though, "untrue" separations in life, which are very, very painful because they violate a law of life. Here people treat sacred things willfully and wantonly, and one day I will tell you how I behaved

instinctively in response to one lasting separation (in a way, in fact, intended to render it unreal!)

It is a very precious prerogative that we may gain pure insight into a lofty experience of "things made eternal." And naturally this cannot be free of pain! Yet pain itself is also, in fact, "eternal"—that is, removed from a transience that would otherwise consume and wear this pain away if it succumbed to it.[64]

A few months before this, in June 1942, she wrote to her brother to say she had no idea how things were going for Emil Krehbiel, and added: "But I dreamed last night a long, long and so loving dream about him."[65]

After the separation and divorce from Emil Krehbiel in 1933—the year the Nazis took power—Maria once again returned to her parents' home in Mannheim, now facing a very uncertain future—once again single and a Jew in the eyes of the law and, as such, at risk. Three years earlier, in 1930, Adolf Hitler had said in an address, "We must seek to awaken anti-Jewish instincts in our people, to stir and whip up these sentiments until they resolve to join the movement that is willing to draw the resulting conclusions."[66] In 1931, two years before Maria returned to her native city, the Nazi party periodical *Hakenkreuzbanner* [swastika banner] was founded in Mannheim as official party organ; it launched an aggressive propaganda war against the city's 6,400 Jews. In later years, the well-regarded, Jewish-owned *Neue Badische Landeszeitung* newspaper was successfully marginalized and eventually forced out of business.

Once the Nazis seized power in March 1933, the life of Jews in Mannheim changed rapidly and radically. Jewish officials, including professors and teachers, were dismissed, and Jewish artists working at the National Theatre were "granted leave of absence." Within a short time, all mass media were participating in a targeted hate and defamation campaign. Political dissenters soon started being arrested and maltreated. As early as March 13, 1933, the first interim measures were introduced to boycott Jewish businesses prior to the official boycott on April 1. Members of the SA (paramilitary wing of

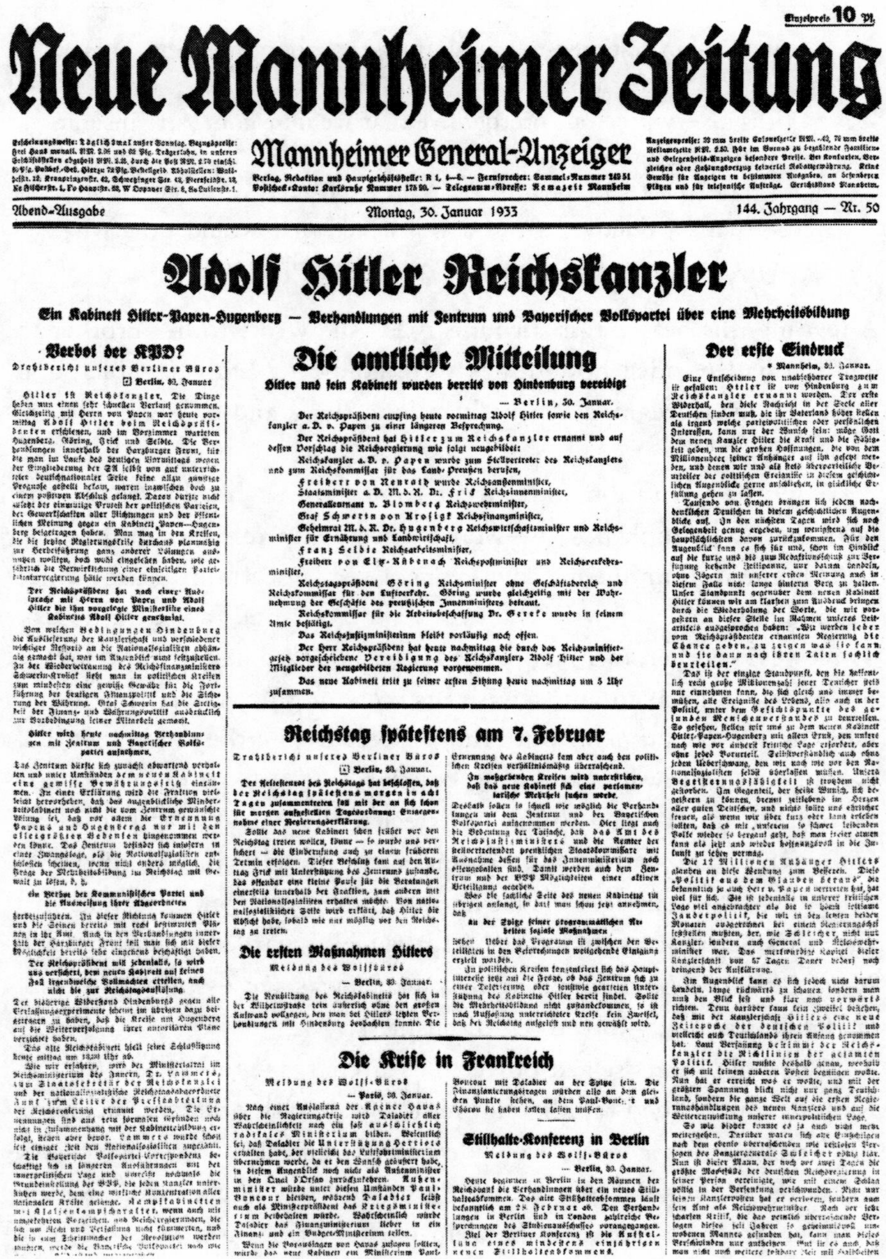

Einzelpreis 10 Pf.

Neue Mannheimer Zeitung

Mannheimer General-Anzeiger

Abend-Ausgabe — Montag, 30. Januar 1933 — 144. Jahrgang — Nr. 50

Adolf Hitler Reichskanzler

Ein Kabinett Hitler-Papen-Hugenberg — Verhandlungen mit Zentrum und Bayerischer Volkspartei über eine Mehrheitsbildung

Die amtliche Mitteilung

Hitler und sein Kabinett wurden bereits von Hindenburg vereidigt

— Berlin, 30. Januar.

Der Reichspräsident empfing heute vormittag Adolf Hitler sowie den Reichskanzler a. D. v. Papen zu einer längeren Besprechung.

Der Reichspräsident hat Hitler zum Reichskanzler ernannt und auf dessen Vorschlag die Reichsregierung wie folgt neugebildet:

Reichskanzler a. D. v. Papen wurde zum Stellvertreter des Reichskanzlers und zum Reichskommissar für das Land Preußen berufen,

Freiherr von Neurath wurde Reichsaußenminister,

Staatsminister a. D. M. d. R. Dr. Frick Reichsinnenminister,

Generalleutnant v. Blomberg Reichswehrminister,

Graf Schwerin von Krosigk Reichsfinanzminister,

Geheimrat M. d. R. Dr. Hugenberg Reichswirtschaftsminister und Reichsminister für Ernährung und Landwirtschaft,

Franz Seldte Reichsarbeitsminister,

Freiherr von Eltz-Rübenach Reichspostminister und Reichsverkehrsminister,

Reichstagspräsident Göring Reichsminister ohne Geschäftsbereich und Reichskommissar für den Luftverkehr. Göring wurde gleichzeitig mit der Wahrnehmung der Geschäfte des preußischen Innenministers betraut.

Reichskommissar für die Arbeitsbeschaffung Dr. Gereke wurde in seinem Amte bestätigt.

Das Reichsjustizministerium bleibt vorläufig noch offen.

Der Herr Reichspräsident hat heute nachmittag die durch das Reichsministergesetz vorgeschriebene Vereidigung des Reichskanzlers Adolf Hitler und der Mitglieder der neugebildeten Regierung vorgenommen.

Das neue Kabinett tritt zu seiner ersten Sitzung heute nachmittag um 5 Uhr zusammen.

Verbot der KPD?

Der erste Eindruck

Reichstag spätestens am 7. Februar

Die ersten Maßnahmen Hitlers

Die Krise in Frankreich

Stillhalte-Konferenz in Berlin

Figure 9: Neue Mannheimer Zeitung, *January 30, 1933; a headline in Mannheim's local newspaper announcing Adolf Hitler's chancellorship*

the Nazi Party, or Brown Shirts) positioned themselves outside shops and businesses they had marked with a yellow star and prevented customers from entering. Targeted exclusion of Jews from business, culture, legal redress, and intellectual debate had begun with arbitrary interventions and brutal measures. Maria's sister Luise, who in 1930 had married her third husband Stefan Kayser, editor of the *Neue Mannheimer Zeitung,* left the country the year that Hitler seized power and fled to Czechoslovakia. Maria did not follow suit.

Maria's return to her parental home in 1933 at the age of forty-two was a loving sacrifice; there were other things she might have done and other opportunities. Maria Krehbiel-Darmstädter, as she called herself after the "untrue" separation, had many friends and acquaintances in the city, as well as in nearby Heidelberg; they would have welcomed her gladly. But her mother's severe illness and the ruin of her father's business, badly damaged by the world financial crisis and further affected by the current boycott measures, conspired to create a situation that their eldest daughter could not and would not ignore—"times when my parents were in great affliction, poor and sick."[67] Despite their former high standing in society, and Rudolf Darmstädter's many public services, Maria's father and mother were now largely isolated and ignored. Old friends and acquaintances, business partners and employees had withdrawn, and few visitors came to 48 Werderstrasse. Anti-Jewish propaganda was taking hold, and the situation in the house offered no prospect of improvement for either the parents or their daughter. Nine years later Maria recalled:

> When things got so bad for my parents, due to their illness and poverty (and also their isolation) I felt for years that I might not properly put my feet down anywhere on the Earth. You see, there *was* no Earth. The ground beneath me felt like cold steel. A knife edge. I'm not speaking metaphorically. At the time I experienced the fact that there is such a thing as a knife edge on which feet must stand; and must walk with endless caution so as not to fall off or bleed to death.[68]

In mid-September 1935, the "Nuremberg Laws" were passed, including the "Reich Citizenship Law," depriving Maria—like her Jewish friends and relations—of all their civil rights. She was now no longer a "citizen of the Reich." Two months later, in mid-November, the Anthroposophical Society was prohibited throughout Germany, having already been proscribed in Baden. The *Frankfurter Zeitung* of November 16, 1935 stated:

> Due to conflicts between the views of the Anthroposophical Society and ideas of national identity propounded by the National Socialists, there was a risk that the continuing activities of the Anthroposophical Society might have harmed the interests of the National Socialist government. The organization was therefore disbanded due to its anti-government and state-endangering character.

Rudolf and Berta Darmstädter both died at the beginning of 1936, the former on January 11 and the latter on March 10, and were laid to rest in the family burial ground at the "New Israelite Cemetery," under a birch tree beside the Neckar river—a peaceful place that Maria often thought of during the deportation years. Fewer than ten people attended the funerals of these formerly highly-regarded and well-known individuals, who had lost almost everything except their family. The death of Maria's parents was a further blow in her much-tried life: "When parents die, you suddenly become a generation older."[69] But at the same time it seemed to her that their destiny had been fulfilled and resolved in close union, in their almost simultaneous departure before the real period of persecution commenced. At Gurs, in her biographical notes, Maria Krehbiel-Darmstädter reflected on the special nature of the final days she spent intensively nursing her parents, and the lasting blessing of that time: "And yet, from this most grave and also physically strenuous time, the greatest strength and faithfulness toward life still flowed."[70]

~

At New Year 1936–'37, nine months after her mother's death and now alone at 48 Werderstrasse, Maria suffered a collapse and required many weeks of hospital treatment. Shortly after this, the lovely house and home was compulsorily auctioned, and now nothing remained of the old life of the family. Her sister Luise urged her repeatedly to leave Germany and emigrate to Czechoslovakia while this was still possible. But Maria refused categorically and stayed in Mannheim, attending The Christian Community, which unlike the Anthroposophical Society had not yet been banned. "I will stay here as long as the services are still held at The Christian Community in Mannheim," she replied to friends' questions, through into October 1940, despite knowing the dangers. On Michaelmas Day 1922, just two weeks after The Christian Community was founded, and the first Act of Consecration of Man celebrated, Rudolf Steiner had given a lecture in Dornach in which he referred to the future importance of esoteric ritual and worship. It was a matter, he said, of introducing into civilization the "power" emanating from the Mystery of Golgotha. Connected with this, he continued, were spiritual beings who need the Earth and the human being for the future of evolution—"the spiritual, elemental beings who are invoked whenever a rite or act of worship is enacted and who need such services, for they draw their sustenance from them, their powers of growth."[71] Rudolf Steiner regarded the liturgy as a contribution to the world's resurrection from its "destruction."[72] It was in this sense—and not for her own soul—that Maria Krehbiel-Darmstädter wished to participate in the spiritual work of The Christian Community as long as this remained possible. The Act of Consecration of Man depends upon conscious participation and enactment by human beings; and here she saw a real task in the face of the destructive powers whose aggression grew daily.

Nevertheless, she consented to visit her sister in Brno (Czechoslovakia) for a while, to recuperate—but then encountered problems, or threats, from the authorities. On May 11, 1937, she wrote as follows in relation to her "notice of removal," to the Chief of Police of the City of Mannheim:

Figure 10: The Darmstädter's villa (left) at 48 Werderstrasse

I hereby submit the following request to the Chief of Police:

I am the divorced wife of Emil Krehbiel, and since my divorce have been living in the house at 48 Werderstrasse, which belonged to my deceased father, Rudolf Darmstädter. The house was recently auctioned by compulsory order. I was previously staying temporarily in the house, and my furniture is still there.

In view of the agitation surrounding the compulsory auction and my severely compromised health—I was recently hospitalized here for 6 weeks—my sister Luise Kaiser in Brno, Czechoslovakia, has invited me to stay with her for a period of convalescence, since I have no means whatever and am unable to fund a period of convalescence myself. I envisage staying with my sister for the whole duration of the leave of foreign absence granted me, that is, until August 12 of this year.

I therefore submitted my vacation papers to the general registry office on May 10, 1937, noting in writing that I was going to visit my sister in Brno for three months. Only upon my return do I intend taking a room and equipping it with my own furniture.

The desk official at Counter K told me, however, that no importance whatever is attached to my subsequent return to Germany. He further stated something that, in my agitation, I did not precisely understand, and therefore cannot reproduce. I believe he said that from now on I would be under observation.

Figure 11: Maria Krehbiel-Darmstädter, 1937

Since I definitely do not wish to emigrate and thus lose my right to live in Mannheim where—except for brief exceptions—I have spent all my life, I ask if you would kindly inform me whether I may experience difficulties in returning after I have visited my sister. In this case, naturally, I would not visit my sister. I would be very grateful if you could inform me of your decision soon. I would also be willing to come in person to receive it.[73]

No reply was received from the Chief of Police. We do not know whether Maria went to Brno or not.

~

In 1937, she left 48 Werderstrasse, and moved into a small basement room in nearby Bassermannstrasse, number 27, not far from the Jewish old people's home and hospital, and the cemetery where her parents were buried. In 1938 and '39, she cared for many old, sick and helpless people who were too ill, impoverished and depressed to emigrate, or whose age meant they could no longer get a residence permit in other countries (not even Israel). In her biographical notes from Gurs, Maria Krehbiel-Darmstädter wrote about her last employment in Mannheim: "I cared for old people and tried to keep their spirits up. The Jews were the ones in greatest need."[74] In a letter sent from the camp she sketched her stance and outlook during these years of affliction, crisis and growing persecution in Mannheim:

What this hour of the eons asks of us is to serve. In places where we can expect great need of it—in former times, when I wished to withdraw from things that were unpleasant, embarrassing or difficult (withdrawal *is* the first instinctive action of our nature) I was brought up short by reflecting that I therefore loved my neighbor less than myself! For another had to suffer in my place, and all "places" after all are occupied by living beings! Then it might as well be me as another, surely? This made many things much easier, and gave my weakness an aid for overcoming itself; and so it stopped in its *place,* so as: to go on existing. However this strikes you, you must completely quieten your anxieties about me; this has protected me wonderfully so far, and will continue to do so, I feel, if I know how to take my destined place without refusal.[75]

In Mannheim and Heidelberg Maria continued to have true friends—both Jews and "Aryans." As long as this was still possible, she went on visiting the family of Karoline Schmitthenner in Heidelberg and was a friend of philosopher Karl Jaspers' wife, who came from a Jewish family and likewise lived in danger. Owing to his "mixed marriage" and philosophical discourses, Jaspers himself, with whom Maria Krehbiel-Darmstädter discussed a great many humanistic themes, was considered an enemy of the state. In 1937, at the age of fifty-four, he was forced into early retirement, and publication of his works was forbidden soon after. He had procured cyanide in case his wife Gertrud—who was repeatedly concealed in the early forties—was deported. Maria's welfare work in Mannheim brought her into touch with new people, too, who became her friends and companions, including Hermann Maas, priest at the Church of the Holy Spirit in Heidelberg, who (as Christian Zionist) resisted the government in exemplary fashion and was a focus of efforts to help Jews emigrate, especially to England. She also grew close to a member of Maas's staff, sociopolitical advocate Dr. Marie Baum, who, until the "cleansing" of Heidelberg university, had occupied a post in the faculty of social sciences and political economics, and who had previously worked successfully in Karlsruhe in the welfare field as a public welfare consultant.

Like Maria Krehbiel-Darmstädter, Marie Baum stood out as a highly educated, insightful and courageous Christian. She was a friend of Ricarda Huch, and had gained early insight into Hitler after reading his manifesto *Mein Kampf*. Baum knew and followed the examples and resistance initiatives of religious figures such as Martin Niemoeller, Friedrich Bodelschwingh, Theophilus Wurm, Michael von Faulhaber and Clemens August van Galen—and was herself being watched by the Nazis. In her memoirs (published after

World War II) she wrote as follows of her encounter with Maria Krehbiel-Darmstädter:

> Originally from a very prosperous background, she lived in poverty, in complete inner independence and with utter humility, embodying the value of a life of religious contemplation (she belonged to The Christian Community) and practicing unceasing loving kindness within a large circle of friends. In a most wonderful way she united in herself qualities of psychological centeredness with profound empathy for others. Every hour one spent with her was filled with warmth, spirit and love.[76]

There is no doubt that after all her difficult experiences, Maria Krehbiel-Darmstadter had found her strong "I" within her. Her health fluctuated, and she struck people as somewhat fragile; but at the same time impressed them as a self-reliant individual, someone of profound meditative religiosity, who practiced a fully grounded devotion in her attention to others. Many years previously Rudolf Steiner had spoken of a culture of selflessness that would be necessary in future, a "perceiving selflessness" that acts in full, "I"-centered awareness of and empathy with the situation of another.[77] Steiner himself had embodied this practice in his life, even if his public critics had never understood this.[78] In her own way Maria pursued this same path, with a strongly religious accent. She was a Christian in the original sense—extraordinarily tolerant toward all who thought differently from her or held different beliefs, but demanding the highest standards of herself in the sense of *Imitatio Jesu*. All her friends and acquaintances were aware of her deep connection with Anthroposophy and The Christian Community; she never concealed the fact that the Spiritual Science founded by Rudolf Steiner was the core of her life. People accepted her avowal of Anthroposophy because she was such a highly educated woman and so evidently spiritual.

～

She continued to attend The Christian Community's large conferences, which were still permitted by the authorities. Since 1933,

*Figure 12: Mannheim's Kaiserring square with a poster:
"Give the Führer your Yes," on the national referendum
on the "annexation" of Austria, April 10, 1938*

Figure 13: Maria Krehbiel-Darmstädter in Heidelberg, 1938

these conferences had focused increasingly on the world mission of Christianity in apocalyptic times—something that required courage and spiritual alertness in relation to the anti-Christian Nazi regime. On New Year's Eve 1937, Maria Krehbiel-Darmstädter once again heard an address by Friedrich Rittelmeyer, chief coordinator of The Christian Community, just a few months before his death: "Unforgettable, the huge, candle-lit hall. The text: Christ walking on the water. 'Fear not. I *am*.'"[79] In the summer of 1938 she attended two weeks of Christian Community conferences in Hannover and the Harz (Bellenstedt),[80] on what may have been her last trip before deportation. Not long before this she had visited the island of Reichenau with a Sister she knew.[81] Reichenau was the former center of a distinctive Christian spirituality, to which both felt deeply connected. In May 1942, writing to an art historian friend, she said of Reichenau ("my Reichenau"):

> It is an island of greater inspiration than people mostly are aware of today. A pure essence remains and rises from it. Still today this essence attaches to its former shrine as a site of—promise. Have you ever visited it, this island? I scarcely dared breathe for joy and—ineffable bliss.[82]

In November 1938, three months after Maria returned from The Christian Community conferences at Hannover and Bellenstedt, the organized excesses of *"Kristallnacht"* occurred, in Mannheim as everywhere. Throughout the country, Jewish synagogues were destroyed, Jewish homes were demolished and plundered, and countless people were maltreated and deported—to places such as Dachau concentration camp. In Mannheim, SA activists blew up the big synagogue in F2 on the morning of November 10, and later proudly showed local citizens and children round the smoking ruins, charging ten pennies admission. For Jews still living in the city, conditions worsened after these acts of violence. "Aryanization," the dissolution of all Jewish enterprises, artisan businesses and shops, was implemented, and from then on Jews were prohibited access to loans

Figure 14: Mannheim; the ruins of the main synagogue after "Kristallnacht"

from the city's savings bank. It was now illegal for Jews to go to theaters or cinemas, drivers' licenses had to be returned, and use of trams was forbidden to them, as was leaving the city precincts. Jews could no longer go to Bassermann Park, very close to where Maria lived, or visit cafés and public baths. Identity cards were introduced for Jews, stamped with a large "J" and with an additional Jewish name added ("Maria *Sarah* Krehbiel-Darmstädter"), while the doors of Jews' homes were likewise marked with a "J" to better identify and segregate them. Jews were allowed to perform only unskilled labor; physicians and lawyers had already been banned from practicing their professions in the fall of 1938. Since Jews had now been driven out of all professions, but were not eligible for social welfare, establishment of labor camps for them in and around Mannheim was discussed ("ensuring that in undertaking such work they do not come into contact with non-Jewish workers"[83]).

Maria's brother Franz, who until then had been running a bank, and was sitting tight in Mannheim, left the country with his family in November 1938—after *Kristallnacht*—and emigrated to Switzerland, intending to travel further to the United States. Franz Darmstädter was fortunate to secure an exit and entry visa, for the latter was no longer easy to obtain, not even for travel to Switzerland. Formerly a free and open land, Switzerland had recently drastically tightened its immigration laws, in fear of being "flooded" by emigrants of Jewish origin. In March 1938 it had introduced compulsory visas for Austrian nationals, following the flight of many Jews from Vienna. A compulsory visa was also being considered for German passport-holders, though this had not yet been introduced. However, the passports of German Jews, which bore a large red "J," invalidated their attempts to seek asylum. A Swiss decree of October 4, 1938, four weeks before *Kristallnacht*, stated additionally:

> German nationals who are not Aryan under German law will only be allowed entry to Switzerland if their passport bears assurance of a residence permit issued by a Swiss consulate, or a permit to transit across Switzerland.[84]

In 1939 Switzerland tightened up its laws still further, and usually only granted entry where "further travel beyond Switzerland" was assured. Increasingly stringent border checks were put in place, and refugees were systematically sent back to Germany. Later enquiries found that over 24,000 people had been turned back from the border, and inevitably ended up in concentration camps.[85] "Sometimes Switzerland seemed—and I think, almost, never more than *now*—to have a special mission and place, so that it might be the heart of Europe," wrote Maria Krehbiel-Darmstädter in the summer of 1942,[86] when deportations from France to Auschwitz began, and the Swiss borders still remained closed.

Franz Darmstadter got out in the nick of time, in 1938; and Maria's sister Luise Kayser likewise continued her wanderings that year, leaving Czechoslovakia—which was no longer safe—with her husband and child, and escaping to the United States. Maria was troubled by the greater geographical distance between them. In 1942 she wrote:

> When m[y] sister traveled to the US, it was unbearable for me to think of her "over the oceans." But I gained some tranquility from reflecting that all our connections with people should become increasingly *spiritualized* (even while we're still alive). Our bonds (that lighten us) loosen and cease to be visible; and "now the high realm of the beyond begins to be populous."[87]

Resistant to leaving, and only bowing to pressure from her siblings, who utterly failed to understand her refusal to emigrate, Maria Krehbiel-Darmstädter lodged an initial application for a visa with the American consulate in Stuttgart in 1938, but then immediately returned to Mannheim and continued her welfare work there. As the child of a father with United States citizenship, Maria would have had the right to become a naturalized US citizen on attaining her majority, but at the time—like her siblings—she had decided to remain German. Unlike Luise and Franz who eventually both emigrated to the United States and spent the second half of their lives there, Maria never sundered her ties with "Germany."

~

The last big conference of The Christian Community, with more than 2,000 participants, took place in Stuttgart at the end of July 1939, and was entitled "Working to serve the spirit." Five weeks later, World War II began with the Wehrmacht invasion of Poland.

The evening curfew for Jews in Mannheim, imposed after the war started, further restricted Maria's mobility without changing things much otherwise. Her work increased—more Jews, including many old and needy people, had come to Mannheim in recent times because they found the situation in the city more bearable than in the surrounding villages. But the food situation worsened rapidly: food rations for people bearing a "J" on their ID card were further restricted, and life was made difficult in many other ways too.

In September 1939, Maria saw her beloved cousin Margot Junod again as the latter was passing through Mannheim on her way from Berlin to Lausanne, and also her six-month-old godson Jean-Christophe Junod. Again, she witnessed a successful emigration to Switzerland that she herself did not wish to take advantage of. She was aware of the danger in which she lived. She gave away many of her—remaining—personal possessions and was prepared for all eventualities. "The unique thing we experienced with her was her gradual detachment from all earthly possessions. She sensed what was coming and went forward to meet it, so that by the time of her departure there was no more ballast to discard," a friend recalled.[88] In the summer of 1940 Maria moved out of Bassermannstrasse to precinct M 7,17, close to Mannheim railway station. From there she could easily get to The Christian Community at L 2,11, where services continued to be held.

Maria Krehbiel-Darmstädter was not oblivious to the fact that a deportation of all Mannheim's Jews was possible, or even already being planned. Back in 1938, Jews from Poland had been expelled from the city, at the same time that Vienna's Jewish population was driven out. These events were reported in newspapers. Nor was it any secret that in the winter of 1939 to '40, Jews had been deported from Bohemia, Moravia, western Prussia and Pommerania to the "General Government" of Poland, sometimes under appalling, terribly cold conditions in cattle trucks. At the time Maria moved to M 7, 17, similar things were occurring in neighboring France: all Jews in Alsace had to leave their homes in July 1940, in trucks, and were transported to the unoccupied part of France. On October 20, 1940, "Gauleiter" [Nazi district leader] Robert Wagner declared at the first National Socialist rally in Strasbourg: "We have begun to liberate Alsace from all those elements that have plagued the people of Alsace for centuries." [89] More than 2,000 Jews were deported from Alsace at that time. Maria often visited the Herrmann family, her friends since 1938, as well as members of The Christian Community who lived at 12 Tullastrasse to discuss current alarming developments. Despite this, she did not live in fear and anxiety.

From mid-October 1940, rumors about imminent deportation were circulating among Mannheim's Jewish community, as their leader Dr. Eugen Neter later recalled. The secret decree by Baden's Ministry of the Interior, to "arrest and deport all full Jews" is actually dated October 15. A leaflet for Mannheim officials entrusted with this task, who had one week to prepare for it, outlined the following precise procedure that should be adhered to on October 22, the day planned for arrest and deportation:

> After receiving the names and addresses of Jews, the officials involved are to attend the homes of the latter. They are then to inform them that they are under arrest for the purpose of deportation, and that they must be ready to decamp within two hours. Each of the arrested parties is to take the following with him, where possible: a) for each Jew one suitcase or parcel containing appurtenances; the permitted load to be fifty kilos for adults and up to thirty kilos for children, b) a complete outfit of clothes, c) a woolen blanket for each Jew, d) food for several days, e) plates and cups, f) up to 100 Reichsmarks in cash for each person.... It is essential that Jews should be treated correctly at arrest. Excessive measures must definitely be avoided.[90]

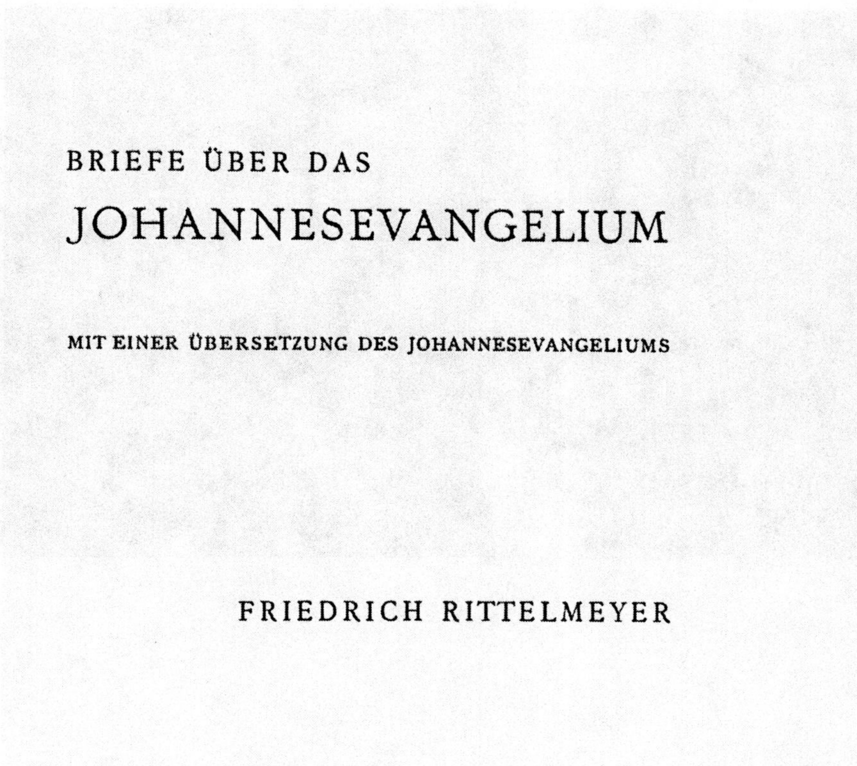

BRIEFE ÜBER DAS

JOHANNESEVANGELIUM

MIT EINER ÜBERSETZUNG DES JOHANNESEVANGELIUMS

FRIEDRICH RITTELMEYER

1938

VERLAG URACHHAUS STUTTGART

Figure 15: Friedrich Rittelmeyer,
Letters on the Gospel of St. John, *Stuttgart, 1938*

Figure 16: Salomon Oppenheimer (1865–1942); the last Torah scribe in Mannheim, deported to Gurs at the age of seventy-five

The only exceptions were Jews living in "existing mixed marriages"—that is, in a situation that no longer applied to Maria since Emil Krehbiel had left her seven years before.

October 22, 1940, the day of arrest and deportation, was intentionally arranged for the important Jewish festival of *Sukkot,* the cheerful and serene festival of leaf-adorned tabernacles. On the morning of this day, Maria—like the other 1,992 Jews living in Mannheim—was visited by police officers and informed of what would now happen, and that she must be ready to "decamp" at very short notice. Maria was listed as number 883. She had been informed of the deportation in advance, during the night, but had turned down a last opportunity for flight. She reacted to the news with shock, very serious but fully composed,[91] and gave her last possessions to her friends. They included a—to her very precious—framed reproduction (wrapped in a blue cloth) of the image of Christ by Vincenzo Foppa, *Il Redentore* (The Resurrected One)—the altar picture of The Christian Community. With a rucksack, a bag and her mother's old cushion, she made her way to the castle, her official "collection point." Many people were already waiting there in desolate mood. The oldest Jew deported from Mannheim was ninety-eight, and the youngest a baby aged three-and-a-half months. The deportation order for Baden, Saarland, and Pfalz applied even to Jewish patients from old people's homes and psychiatric clinics, to children in the "Israelite Orphanage" (which most recently had been housed in the synagogue at R 7, 24), and to women in childbed and sanctuaries. "Women and men unable to walk were transported to the trains on stretchers, as ordered" an official report recorded one week later. Eight of the 1993 Jews arrested in Mannheim escaped deportation by suicide, most of them by taking poison that they had with them or in their homes.

Berta Altschul, née Seligmann, the seventy-six-year-old mother of Maria's deceased fiancé, was also among those at the collection point, where a wait of several hours ensued before deportation. The castle was only a little way from The Christian Community chapel at House

L2, 11, and Maria Krehbiel-Darmstädter caught sight of it for the last time as she passed by. Eventually Wehrmacht trucks arrived and took the Jews to Waldhof train station. From there special trains conveyed them to an unknown destination.

Der Chef der Sicherheitspolizei und des SD

IV D 4   *2602* /40

Berlin SW 11, den ~~29~~. Oktober 194 0.
Prinz-Albrecht-Straße 8
Fernsprecher: 12 00 40

Bei in der Rückgabe vorstehendes Geschäftszeichen u. Datum anzugeben

An das
Auswärtige Amt,
z.Hdn. SA-Standartenführer Gesandter L u t h e r ,
B e r l i n .

Der Führer ordnete die Abschiebung
der Juden aus Baden über das Elsaß und der
Juden aus der Pfalz über Lothringen an. Nach
Durchführung der Aktion kann ich Ihnen mit-
teilen, daß aus Baden am 22. und 23.10.1940
mit 7 Transportzügen und aus der Pfalz am
22.10.1940 mit 2 Transportzügen

<u>6.504 Juden</u>

im Einvernehmen mit den örtlichen Dienststel-
len der Wehrmacht, ohne vorherige Kenntnisga-
be an die französischen Behörden, in den un-
besetzten Teil Frankreichs über Chalon-sur-
Saône gefahren wurden.

Die Abschiebung der Juden ist in
allen Orten Badens und der Pfalz reibungs-
los und ohne Zwischenfälle abgewickelt worden.

Der Vorgang der Aktion selbst
wurde von der Bevölkerung kaum wahrgenommen.

Die Erfassung der jüdischen
Vermögenswerte sowie ihre treuhänderische
Verwaltung und Verwertung erfolgt durch
die zuständigen Regierungspräsidenten.

In Mischehe lebende Juden
wurden von den Transporten ausgenommen.

*Figure 17: Letter from Reinhard Heydrich to SA-Standartenführer [colonel]
Luther, October 29, 1940, reporting on the transportation of 6,504 Jews
to unoccupied France, October 22 and 23, 1940; he states that
the operation "went smoothly and according to plan."*

43

2.

Gurs Internment Camp

*"Egoism grows ever less; the joy of humbling oneself to help others
kindles the heart and broadens one's mind to infinity. Even the
simple life, the landscape—the routine—the isolation, even the
severity: these are useful. I, at least, attempt to take everything
that happens as a tool for learning.*
    —And the time spent here: I see it on a grand scale.
    A most earnest consecration."

        Maria Krehbiel-Darmstädter: Gurs, March 24, 1941[92]

Seven days after the deportation, Reinhard Heydrich, chief of the
"Reich Security Head Office"—who in 1941 was commissioned
to devise the "final solution to the Jewish question" and subsequently chaired the Wannsee Conference—wrote the following to SA
Standartenführer [colonel] Luther at the ministry of foreign affairs:
"Deportation of the Jews took place smoothly and without incident
in all locations of the Baden and Pfalz districts."[93] Decades later, a
historian confirmed:

> The testimony of eye witnesses reveals that the population looked
> on without any apparent sympathy when its fellow citizens were
> sent away. People remained silent, showing no apparent emo-
> tion, let alone any solicitousness, even though the deportees were
> acquaintances and neighbors they may have known all their lives.[94]

For a long time the deported Jews were not sure where the special trains were taking them. Crossing the Rhine signaled that they were travelling west, rather than toward the "General Government" of Poland, and this fact was greeted with great relief. But the harassment continued:

In Muehlhausen German money was changed into French Francs. Before the train stopped, SS men ran through the corridors. "Anyone who has more than a hundred Marks must hand it over now. We will search all your belongings. Anyone who has more than this will be shot." Matches were lit and flames consumed the notes; or, torn into tiny shreds, they flew out of compartment windows or were flushed down the toilet. Hundreds of thousands of Marks were destroyed in just a few minutes. No search was ever carried out, but apart from a few who risked death and held onto their money, the aim was accomplished: the Jews were now poor as beggars.[95]

Just one day after deportation, Robert Wagner, Nazi district leader, ordered the confiscation of all property and assets left behind by the Jews. Maria Krehbiel-Darmstädter, however, no longer had anything left in Mannheim.

Groups of Gestapo and SS guards accompanied the train to the border of occupied France. The French railway officials did not know the nature of this transportation, mistakenly imagining that the carriages contained French citizens expelled from Germany. Via Belfort the special trains finally reached the demarcation line at Chalon-sur-Saône, and thus the unoccupied zone of the country that the Wehrmacht had invaded in May 1940. The accompanying guards left the train, leaving the rest to the French authorities, who, on German instructions, were to establish a suitable internment camp in the South of the country. The carriages were shunted back and forth for hours at stations, until a track became available along with a further destination. During the journey more of the passengers took their own lives, in despair at their situation and in dread of what was coming, as reported later by Eugen Neter. Despite living in a "mixed marriage," he had traveled in the transport voluntarily, refusing to leave his parishioners in the lurch, and determined to share their fate.

~

French government officials repeatedly conferred with the ruling powers in Berlin, asking for information about the intended destination of the transport, which—as they were told—was to mark the beginning of deportation of Jews from Germany. Protests were lodged by the French. On October 29, 1940, an official letter from Karlsruhe stated:

> Since the intention is to deport to France the remaining Jews, too, from the old German Empire, the Ostmark [Austria] and the Protectorate of Bohemia and Moravia—a total of 270,000 persons, largely of advanced age—the Vichy government has expressed its concerns regarding these measures. In consequence, the envisaged expulsion of Jews from Hessen has been postponed for the time being.[96]

France resisted to a certain extent, despite having been conquered, and over the next few weeks demanded that German Jews deported from Baden, Pfalz, and the Saar region should be sent back:

> The French government can no longer grant these foreigners asylum. We therefore urgently request that the German government takes appropriate measures to return the persons in question to Germany, and to reimburse the costs that have arisen during their stay in France.[97]

However, the German government made it clear that it would not contemplate taking these people back again. "France must deport them as it sees fit, either overseas or anywhere else. Germany has no further interest in the fate of the Jews."[98] Already prior to the outbreak of World War II, plans had been drawn up in Berlin for a "territorial final solution" of the Jewish question, including expatriation of all European Jews to Madagascar, the new "settlement region for the Jews of Europe." Adolf Eichmann had stated, "On concluding peace, France should be compelled to relinquish Madagascar and turn it into a 'Jewish colony.'"[99] A transit camp in southern France, not far from the Mediterranean and thus on the route to Madagascar, certainly fitted in with the German government's plans.

At the Catholic pilgrimage destination of Lourdes, where the chartered trains were stationed for the whole of one night, some Jews learned from French gendarmes and station officials that they would be traveling on via Pau to a place named Gurs close to the Pyrenees, the site of a "family camp." On the evening of October 24, the passengers briefly caught sight of the shimmering Mediterranean near Sète. Soon after this, they reached the station of Oloron-Sainte-Marie, the capital of Béarn Province at the border with the Spanish Basque Country, where the train journey ended.

The station manager was baffled as to what he should do when he heard cries from the sealed carriages. After much thought, and consultation with the president of the Red Cross in Oloron, he decided to have the carriage doors opened after a nearly five-day journey. More than 6,500 people had been cooped up in these chartered trains from Germany, and now stood in complete chaos on the platform in this town in southern France, whose population was scarcely any larger than this influx. Finally, the gravely ill were taken to hospital on stretchers, while all other occupants of the trains were taken by lorries to the "family camp" close to the village of Gurs, about 18 kilometers away. It was pouring with rain when Maria Krehbiel-Darmstädter arrived there in a crowd of thousands. The peaks of the Spanish Pyrenees could be seen in the far distance.

～

The camp was situated on a broad plain and consisted of monotonous rows of flimsy, ramshackle wooden huts, some of whose black chipboard roofs had been torn off in storms. The sea of huts, surrounded by thick barriers of barbed wire, stretched away for nearly two kilometers. The huts were closely packed on either side of a single asphalt road running through the middle. Thirteen barrack units (*ilots*), each consisting of around twenty-five huts, stood in the flat and

Figure 18: The camp at Gurs

almost treeless landscape. They had mud or wood floors, no windows, no water, just skylights in the roof with wooden shutters, a feeble stove and little fuel. Straw lay on the floor and there were straw mattresses—but not in sufficient quantity. Each *ilot,* as camp subdivision, was again surrounded by much barbed wire, and its entrance to the camp road guarded by a French policeman with a rifle. Prisoners hung their laundry on the barbed wire to dry, and it was torn and sometimes blown away by the wind.

Gurs camp had been built a year and a half before, in April 1939, in a damp valley bottom on clay soil, previously a marshy wasteland. The distant Pyrenees were the old visible landscape feature. Internees themselves had been compelled to build it—people who had fled to France from the cruelties of the Spanish Civil War. They had come largely from the Basque Country, and fought for the Republican army against the fascist Franco. In France, they enjoyed asylum as political refugees, as did refugee soldiers of the "International Brigades" from fifty-two countries who had signed up voluntarily to fight in Spain against the Franco regime. But then, after their crushing defeat and flight across the Pyrenees, all these people fell victim to the increasingly right-wing, anti-foreigner mood in their "host country," France. Due to existing laws that protected political refugees, the French regime had been unable to expel them, but made their stay as problematic as possible, and recognized the fascist government in Spain. In Gurs the refugees first had to sleep on the ground in ditches and tents before they could move in to the self-built, provisional barrack.

In mid-April 1939, around 20,000 internee soldiers were living there. But when the transportation of Jews arrived in October 1940, only about 2,000 still remained. After war broke out in September 1939, the majority of original internees had joined the auxiliary forces, in some cases against their will. Others had joined the Foreign Legion or, having no other alternative, returned to Spain. But since then many others had been newly interned at Gurs. In May 1940, five months before the deportations from the Baden, Saar and Pfalz regions, over 2,300 women and children had been delivered by buses from Paris and its surrounding areas. These were largely Jews and political émigrés from Germany, who as "enemy foreigners" lost their right to freedom in France, where they had fled to escape Hitler. Further internees were sent from other regions of France. In the first half of October, thousands of Jews arrived there from Pyrenean regions following anti-Semitic laws passed by the Vichy government. This meant Gurs was now the largest of around a hundred internment camps that had been opened in France since war broke out. It was already considered to be full before the arrival of the German transportation—whose arrival the camp authorities knew nothing about until a few hours before. There was scarcely any room or food for the 6,500 new arrivals and they had to be packed into the barrack with a width of only seventy-five centimeters allocated for each sleeping place. After the new admissions, as winter approached, nearly 16,000 people were living behind the barbed wire barriers.

~

Like the other deportees, Maria Krehbiel-Darmstädter descended from the lorry at the southern end of the camp, at the entrance beside the road to Oloron where the administration and guards' barrack stood. In a seemingly endless line, one by one the new arrivals entered a service building where they had to give their name, place of birth and last place of residence, and were then assigned to particular barrack. Maria was sent to Barrack 11 in *ilot* "L," lying furthest northwest of the whole camp. She saw a great deal of misery all around her—families being separated and hearing nothing of each other for many weeks since men and women were allocated to different *ilots*, and at first could not visit each other because a pass was required to do so. "This uncertainty about the fate of loved ones and the impossibility of finding anything out, was worse than anything else."[100] As they were led into the barrack many of the old people were completely exhausted and devoid of will, hopelessly weakened after the long journey. The luggage of the new internees was only delivered four days later, and lay soaked through, and plundered beyond recognition, in a pile on the camp road. Hanna Schramm, a German émigré, who had arrived in Gurs from Paris back in May, wrote:

> The luggage carts were emptied of their contents, the luggage was piled high beside the camp road and there got soaked and soggy, its contents often stolen. Pieces of clothing changed hands on the camp black market for crazy prices. When the arrivals from Baden finally received permission to look for their luggage, much had either vanished or been spoiled by the rain. Anything left over, which may have belonged to the sick or lame, was swept up and disposed of as rubbish.[101]

Despite relief that the train journey was over, and, in the first few hours, the helpful welcome of numerous Gurs internees, arriving in the camp was an almost unendurable shock for many of the deportees. In Mannheim and elsewhere, living conditions by the end had been far from easy; but the German Jews largely came from a middle-class milieu and had led a well-ordered life. Now, without any preparation, they found themselves in primitive barrack at the edge of the Pyrenees, camping under the open sky and in utter neediness. Many of the trucks from Oloron did not arrive until the evening, after darkness had fallen, and in pouring rain. There were no beds, not even for the eldest, and not even enough straw mattresses. There was hardly any food. It stretched the camp administration's resources to the limit even to offer the 6,500 new arrivals some watery coffee the next morning, and some soup for lunch and supper with a little bread. Farmers in the surrounding region were poor and largely lived on turnip, pumpkin and cabbage. There was little or no meat or dairy produce.

Maria Krehbiel-Darmstädter was given a place by the outside wall of the hut, which was cold but not entirely hemmed in by surrounding people. It was dark in the wooden shelter, and, to begin with, the name *Gurs* reminded her of the term *le gouffre* (the abyss). The clothes of the camp inhabitants were hung up on cords to protect them from rats that, hungry themselves, lived under the floorboards and came out at night to eat whatever they could find. There were fleas, lice,

Figure 19: In Gurs camp

cockroaches and mice. The primitive latrines were a long way from the huts, and were difficult to get to in the night, especially for the elderly. An atmosphere of desolation reigned. The internees froze at night and had to learn to live alongside each other, packed together in the closest proximity in bad air. In the quandary between fresh air and cold, quarrels soon broke out about whether the "window" lights should be open or shut. There was a lot of noise, but it was often dark, too, even during the daytime. The weak bulbs of the barrack lamps were only turned on for two hours in the evening, and gave so little light that even then it was hard to write or read. The most necessary things were lacking—blankets, crockery and cups, medicines and everything else. Plates for meals only arrived after six months, in May 1941, and until then the soup, and whatever other small provisions were provided, was just spooned out of old tins. Washing facilities were located on the camp road where eight taps were allocated for more than a thousand women in the *ilot*, functioning for certain periods in the morning, afternoon, and evening.

Yet Gurs was not an SS labor camp, let alone an extermination camp. There were no German officers, no morning roll call, no compulsory work, no selections and gas chambers. The French soldiers assigned to guard the internees did not torment them. The barrack and *ilots* were run by the refugees themselves. Cooks, physicians, and nurses were also exclusively recruited from the ranks of the prisoners, and sought to do everything they could to improve things and ease suffering.

～

The new arrivals from Baden, Pfalz, and Saar began to settle into these unfamiliar circumstances. Some of the younger women tried to keep the huts and the ditches between the huts clean. They organized monitoring of the latrines and provided night care for the elderly. Most of the internees, however, sat on their straw mattresses in gloom and boredom, waiting for the next meal or some change to their circumstances that never came. Conversations were monosyllabic and kept

Figure 20: A prisoner in the mud at Gurs

circling round the same subjects. "People were no longer living but just vegetating, growing angry or impatient or sinking into lethargy," wrote one prisoner in a memoir.[102]

For the first two weeks the weather was almost summery, which made life easier both inside the barrack and in the small areas surrounding them. But winter was approaching and at night the temperatures dropped very low. In the mornings there was frost on the grass, and far away new snow could be seen on the peaks of the Pyrenees. At the end of October, on the thirtieth and thirty-first, another 4,000 prisoners arrived, largely German and Austrian men who had been detained until then at the Saint Cyprien internment camp near Perpignan. Almost all of them were Jews who had emigrated to Belgium before Hitler came to power and had been arrested and deported after the German occupation. They included the rabbi Leo Ansbacher who became the camp's spiritual leader, and did a great deal for his fellow prisoners, offering both social and religious support. In mid-November the winter began in earnest, with endless rain and cold.

> A sun shorn of its beams stood in the grey sky, the nights were damp and icy. And then it started raining. Rain in Gurs. It drummed on the barrack roofs, rattled against the thin boards of the walls, streamed, muttered and gurgled in the ditches. The smell of the urine-soaked clay—the typical smell of Gurs—grew stronger.[103]

In no time, the huts were surrounded by a sea of mud and knee-deep mire, which set the tone for life in Gurs for many months to come. The nightly walk to the latrines became still more arduous, and people carrying the big cauldrons of soup often slipped and fell, spilling the food in the mud.

At this time, in November 1940, first reports of the catastrophic conditions in the camp appeared in the German-Jewish exiles journal *Aufbau*, that was published and distributed in New York. The journal was edited by Manfred George, a cousin of Nelly Sachs, who had emigrated to Czechoslovakia in 1933 and from there went to the United States. Appeals for help and letters from prisoners in Gurs to relatives in the US were published in *Aufbau*, such as this one:

> We had to leave all our belongings behind and quit the house in half an hour. And now we look like cave-women. We hope America will help and if possible receive us as soon as possible. We got here without passports, so perhaps we can reach you without them, too.[104]

The Jewish emigration organization HICEM set efforts in motion to secure entry permits to America, but this was highly complex. The US authorities not only demanded a visa and "support affidavit" but also imposed special restrictions on people of German origin, which amounted to an immigration ban.

~

On November 6, 1940, Maria Krehbiel-Darmstädter wrote her first letter from Gurs. Writing in French to her relation and friend Margot Junod in Lausanne—who had visited her a year before in Mannheim on her way to Switzerland ("For you see: related *and* friends, that surely is the perfect earthly relationship"[105])—Maria briefly described life in the camp: "We've been here two weeks, as guests of France. Naturally poorly equipped and now under harsh and difficult conditions." She also wrote about requirements for possible emigration to the United States, for which most of the prisoners in Gurs were hoping. She requested the help of the Red Cross in providing food parcels, if possible, and beverages ("tea and something to quench thirst, since the water is undrinkable"), writing utensils, rubber boots and warmer clothing. Of her own personal state she said:

> You know that I am fortunate to be alone in all this, my neighbor for my relative. And one has an opportunity to help in so many circumstances—the poor people, the poor, old people. One has to keep one's courage up and stay healthy. Having learned humility previously means drawing now on a wonderful source of strength.

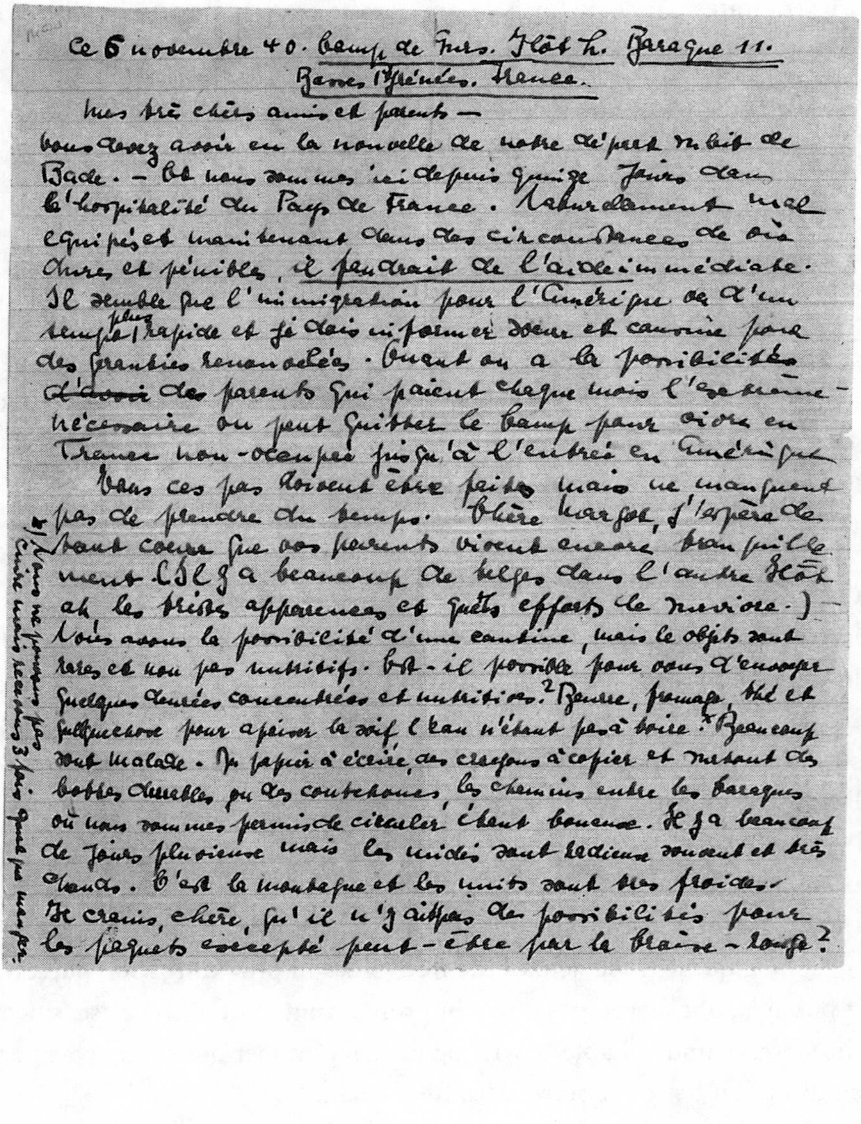

Ce 6 novembre 40. Camp de Gurs. Ilôt K. Baraque 11.
Basses Pyrénées. France.

Mes très chers amis et parents —
Vous devez avoir eu la nouvelle de notre départ subit de Bade. — Et nous sommes ici depuis quinze jours dans l'hospitalité du Pays de France. Naturellement mal équipés et maintenant dans des circonstances de vie dures et pénibles, il faudrait de l'aide immédiate. Il semble que l'immigration pour l'Amérique va d'un temps plus rapide et je dois informer soeur et cousine pour des garanties renouvelées. Quant on a la possibilité ~~d'avoir~~ des parents qui paient chaque mois l'argent(?) nécessaire on peut quitter le camp pour vivre en France non-occupée jusqu'à l'entrée en Amérique.

Tous ces pas doivent être faits mais ne manquent pas de prendre du temps. Chère Margot, j'espère de tout coeur que vos parents vivent encore tranquillement. (Il y a beaucoup de belges dans l'autre Ilôt ah les tristes apparences et quels efforts de survivre.) Nous avons la possibilité d'une cantine, mais les objets sont rares et non pas nutritifs. Est-il possible pour vous d'envoyer quelques denrées concentrées et nutritives.² Beurre, fromage, thé et sucre(?) pour apaiser la soif l'eau n'étant pas à boire.* Beaucoup sont malade. Du papier à écrire, des crayons à copier et surtout des bottes durables ou des caoutchoucs, les chemins entre les baraques où nous sommes permis de circuler étant boueux. Il y a beaucoup de jours pluvieux mais les [illegible] sont tièdes(?) souvent et très chauds. C'est la montagne et les nuits sont très froides. Je crains, chère, qu'il n'y ait pas de possibilités pour les paquets excepté peut-être par la Suisse - Lisbonne?

*) Nous ne pouvons pas cuire mais recevons 3 fois [illegible]

Figure 21: Maria Krehbiel-Darmstädter's letter in French from Gurs, dated November 6, 1940 (first page)

It is certainly true that Maria Krehbiel-Darmstädter was inwardly prepared like few others ("You can say that my house was in good order when I left. For a long time I had only the absolute essentials—which then one thought of as "the absolute essentials," but was of course luxury compared to here. But I was always ready for this kind of upheaval.") She now continued, as though uninterrupted, the welfare work she had done in Mannheim in her last years there. The elderly in particular needed much support, both of an outer and inner kind. There were far too few places in the infirmary hut belonging to each *ilot*. Most of the weak, sick and despairing old people were nursed in their huts, and Maria helped do this, largely ignoring her own situation ("Each of us has our role in the bar[racks]. Mine is primarily to care for the old and support them."[106]) She also thought about those who had remained in Germany, and her friends in Mannheim, to whom she asked her respondent to write since no letters could be sent directly to Germany. "Send them my very warmest thoughts. And say that my heart is at peace about everything." *"I stand in peace with the world. This peace with the world can also be with you, for I give it unto you,"* were the words she had often absorbed in The Christian Community's Act of Consecration in Mannheim and elsewhere.[107] With this outlook Maria began her life in Gurs. She did not complain or bemoan her fate but tried to use all her powers to serve the good, and to live out of the conscious ground of her being, her "I," to live "peacefully" in Christ: "Leaving everything—that is, leaving all behind, one journeys with him and toward him; toward what is imperishable in the 'I.'"[108]

~

She received a reply from Margot Junod in Lausanne that same November. Margot had been deeply anxious about Maria's welfare before the letter from Gurs arrived, and had asked her brother Franz for news of her whereabouts.[109] Franz also subsequently wrote from Basel to Maria at the camp, as did many other friends. These letters were bridges for her with the wider world, and extremely important,

henceforth becoming a vital part of her life behind barbed wire—
"One hopes for letters, which are like gentle blessings."[110] Later she
wrote as follows about the frame of mind of Gurs internees: "We
survive on small signs of love, on tenderness. This keeps us human,
so that we do not become merely "names and numbers" or forgotten
symbols of the age."[111]

Although survival in the camp took all her strength, Maria
Krehbiel-Darmstädter continued to give great attention to the lives of
her far-away friends and relatives, asking about everyone and everything. ("During the nights one fetches them all here to the camp and
tells them one's wishes."[112]) Her spiritual devotion to the "you"—conscious accompaniment of the other—was something she expressed in
every letter, and was intrinsic to her life and her views of it. She wrote
to individuals and sometimes also to small groups of people, always
on *one* sheet only, since no more was permitted: "I have so much to
reply to each of you, and each ought to have their own letter. But reason dictates that I must simplify. Yet to each I turn a particular gaze,
which seeks to rest upon him in love."[113] Likewise her friends' thoughts
and their soul-spiritual presence, meant a great deal to her. She had
many warm connections with people who loved her; and she knew
that members of The Christian Community in Mannheim also sent
her their thoughts during the acts of worship there. On December 7,
she sent Margot Junod a recollection of her early days in Gurs:

> In the very first days here—which knocked me sideways—I had a
> clear sense that my friends' care and prayers surrounded me like
> a circle of light. It was really vital at that time. One still "existed,"
> yet no longer by one's own powers, but suspended. And I gave
> myself up to the loyalty of my friends, which never lapsed or let
> me down.

Three months later she wrote to a female friend:

> A stream of love flows around us and testifies to great faithfulness.[114]

~

In subsequent letters she asked for medicines for the barrack and other essential things:

> Dressings, ointment for bedridden patients, peppermint or similar (because we shouldn't drink the water here and so are often thirsty). Cocoa-oats would be a wonderful food, and all would like it. (Dysentery is our great enemy.)[115]

A first parcel arrived from her brother, at last, on December 21 1940, three days before Christmas Eve and two months after the deportees arrived in Gurs. Though rich, prosperous and secure, Switzerland had become restrictive regarding dispatch of even modest aid: export of (even used) clothing was prohibited, and the upper limit on food parcels was two kilos per month. Only food that was not rationed in Switzerland could be sent. Margot Junod, living on small means, and Franz Darmstädter's family, tried to send frequent parcels despite the arduous, time-consuming formalities involved in this.

Maria kept almost nothing for herself of what arrived in these parcels. Her friends and relatives may have suspected this, but probably not to the radical degree that Maria actually practiced it. The Gurs winter, starting in November, marked the last days of many of the new arrivals. Soon up to twenty-five people were dying each day, including the first children, and over the coming months over 1,100 deaths were recorded in the camp. The prisoners suffered from flu and diarrhea, infectious meningitis, and tuberculosis, and many of the elderly were weakened beyond recovery, especially the old men who looked after themselves less well than the women did, letting themselves go and giving up hope. Several times a day a truck carrying coffins drove up the camp road and was soon just part of daily life. It took the corpses to the North end of the camp, not far from Maria's *ilot* "L," where the cemetery was situated, and where the number of graves increased continually. The Spanish prisoners, responsible for labor in the camp, dug grave after grave. The dead were buried the day they died—often before the priest could arrive from Oloron. There were far too many burials for him to attend each one. Special permission was required to go to a funeral, and events at the cemetery were often shocking: "It was terrible. The dug graves were half-filled with ground water that could not be emptied, and the dead were placed in it."[116] On December 12, 1940, however, Maria wrote as follows to her brother:

> For me the most incisive experience here was: the area set aside for the ever-increasing rows of graves in the cemetery. There are many of my acquaintances there already. I saw it once (you can only go there when people close to you are buried) in its magnificent position and so also perceived the whole nature of this situation here. The camp is surrounded by the most interesting ring of mountains, also a far view of eternal snows; but from the camp itself you can witness only what is very close at hand—and terribly earthly.
>
> You have to look *up* to gain more than anguish and fear...all life is purchased at such a cost, every need such a problem. Where all is lacking and one lives "under the open heavens."
>
> But—where difficulty is *so* weighty, suddenly the burden is lifted and the clouds part.

In various letters Maria mentioned how pleased she was that her parents lay in their graves in peace and freedom, and that the Jewish cemetery in Mannheim was left undisturbed. She did not view their death with alarm but as the earthly sign that they had attained a new, spiritual existence and a different safety beyond earthly bounds. "How well my parents lie. How glad I am that these beloved ones have found safety both above and beneath the earth" she wrote to Margot Junod on December 8, 1940. Four days later, likewise, she wrote to Franz Darmstädter, "How peaceful, dear brother, it is to think of the grave where our parents lie under the little birch tree in quiet seclusion."

~

By November, already, Maria's health was suffering. She requested medicines and clothing for the others but was herself only just managing to survive, hinting at this seldom and usually in impersonal terms ("there are grave demands on one's physical and mental

Figure 22: Coffin lorry at Gurs camp (above);
Graves in the mud in Gurs cemetery, 1941

strength"[117]). On November 19, she wrote to her brother, "Thank God I have been able to overcome some health problems, and there is huge opportunity for giving loving service to others." She battled through every day in order to be able to help her weaker fellow inmates, yet was herself suffering from the cold and wet. She had few physical reserves, and found life in the barrack very hard. As someone who had lived alone until then, with an esoteric orientation, Maria missed the complete absence of any chance to withdraw to reflect, meditate and pray. She almost never wrote about this either, but accepted her circumstances as part of her destiny. To Anneliese Herweck, her brother's thirty-year-old sister-in-law, who lived in Basel with her family, she did however admit the following on November 27:

> It is bitterly cold at night. I think how good it would be to have mother's plaid here with me, a sleeping bag, a fleece. One starts wishing for things, knowing them to be beyond reach, and then tries to summon *from within* the warmth one lacks, the absence of protection.
>
> Deep feelings—and simple ones—pass through you here. Things to do with life and death. What one wrestles with is not to lose one's love for one's neighbor....
>
> "Naked" egoism initially wants nothing but to live. The unaccustomed fact of living so closely together with others in noisy misfortune is *not yet* something that is taken for granted.

~

In her second letter from Gurs to Margot Junod, dated November 12, Maria urged the latter to tell her friends in Bern—the Gnädingers—about her situation, and if possible to send spiritual-scientific and Christian Community literature to her at the camp, or the monthly journal of The Christian Community: "I knew these people well, and they will be very interested to know how I am, and might be able to send some of the group's literature and even my beloved *monthly journal* (at printed paper rates)."

Despite her dire circumstances, Maria Krehbiel-Darmstädter inwardly prepared herself for Advent and Christmas. For many years previously she had lived with Rudolf Steiner's *Calendar of the Soul* and the esoteric reality of his verses for the Christian year in the Act of Consecration and its epistles ("festival prayers"). Much of this was her inward possession, in its precise wording, even without any external act of worship. She knew that all this must now prove its worth—not in terms of its reality but in her own capacity to keep it fully alive in herself through times of dire extremity.

Even in the overfilled barrack she succeeded in creating a personal space in the narrowest quarters, the tiniest refuge for her to withdraw into. She managed to procure a piece of chipboard to place beside her straw mattress, upon which she placed a picture of her spiritual teacher, Rudolf Steiner, which she had brought with her to Gurs; also an image of the Madonna and a photograph of her young godson Jean-Christophe Junod that Margot Junod has sent her with her first letter. On November 27, she described this in a letter to Anneliese Herweck in Basel:

> Sunday is the first of Advent. I have two candles with me. Also a picture of the Madonna. My little corner is the outermost one in the hut, the coldest—but also the most secluded and quietest, and this is a great help to me in bearing up. A beautiful angel, faithfully included in my thoughts, hovers over this spot. I have a picture of my teacher R. St. and of Margot's little Jean-Christoph, which I was so glad to receive a few days ago as a loving greeting.

Martha Besag, who had been deported from Baden-Baden with her three daughters and her mother, wrote many decades later about Maria's little shrine in the barrack, and how she set up her simple wooden board amidst the dark and gloomy atmosphere:

> Her "place" had a different and special appearance. On a wooden board that one of the helpful Spanish men had probably nailed to the joist beside her straw mattress, lay a clean, white cloth on which were some lovely or interestingly shaped stones. A couple of flowers—which she found on her walks through the *ilot*—always

Figure 23: Interior of a hut at Gurs barrack, 1941, by Kuno Schiemann

stood in tin cans. She took such pleasure in every least flower. And there were always pictures, too, usually art postcards that friends had sent her.[118]

Maria Krehbiel-Darmstädter's shrine drew many of her fellow inmates although it was the coldest spot. "Friends and guests pass by and stop each day there, saying that they draw joy and a moment's reflection from it."[119]

Outside, storms sometimes raged, bringing icy cold and tearing the roofing felt from its beams. Wet penetrated every crack, and swamps and vast puddles of water formed between the huts. It was sometimes impossible to get outside. In a letter to Margot Junod on December 8 Maria wrote, "Bare creaturely survival sometimes pushes one's true inner nature aside when these equinoctial storms pour their thunder and lightning over us." The waves of disease did not ebb but took stronger, more lasting hold on the prisoners amidst all the anxieties and battles around daily survival:

> The tragic situation often degenerates, of course, into primitive bickering, dirt and loss of human worth. One is robbed of greater dimensions.
>
> The inconceivable dirt (caused by unusual downpours of rain that soak the ground already softened and exposed by all the dearth) seems almost to gloat at one, and to mock efforts to battle with it. It is our great enemy (and seeks to bring every other ill in its train). For that reason *water* is our best friend, however limited to certain times it is, however cold and hard to get hold of.... One keeps having to find new meaning in all this.[120]

Maria Krehbiel-Darmstädter was capable of finding this *new meaning*. It was not just to comfort Margot Junod that we she wrote the following to Lausanne:

> I want you to know that I am *not* unhappy. I am grateful for having so far survived in good health—and always having had enough to eat.
>
> I have a strangely intensified feeling of being given entirely into a higher hand, of sleeping at night close to and cradled by the

ground....When the time comes, then: I will let myself fall—and this will be to sink into God's lap—deep into safety. Especially at the beginning I sensed this: in the midst of unimagined chaos being still protected by the greatest power.[121]

~

At the beginning of December 1940, Father Pierre Toureille, director of a welfare service for Protestant refugees run by the World Council of Churches visited the camp at Gurs. Maria was deeply impressed by the moral caliber of this forty-year-old priest, and his profoundly religious outlook. He stayed for a week, and visited all Protestants in the camp, helped with emigration applications, celebrated services and gave sermons. He showed great dedication to every one of the Protestant inmates of the largely Jewish internment camp: "He once told us that he was able to call to mind each of his many "children" at any moment...because he prays for every single one."[122] Maria later wrote as follows about her encounter with Toureille at the beginning of December 1940:

> He is an outstanding, brave human being whose presence brought us courage and gave me an *impetus* to endure at the beginning of our time here. His sermons were powerful, and the blessing when he gave communion was one that remained with us for a long time.[123]

Pierre Toureille came as the representative of a small group of ecumenical priests who recognized the signs of the times and were doing their utmost to offer spiritual, psychological and social support to refugees and the destitute. Three years previously, in 1937, the Oxford Conference on "Christianity in practice" had discussed the grave dangers of nationalism and racism in Europe, and expressed its solidarity with the *Bekennende Kirche** in Germany.

---

* *Bekennende Kirche* (Confessional Church) was a resistance movement against the Hitler regime within the German protestant church. Some of its members—such as the priest Dietrich Bonhoeffer—died in Nazi prisons and concentration camps.—ED.

The Ecumenical Council established in consequence made the setting up of a department for refugee problems its primary task. This was instigated by George Bell, Lord Bishop of Chichester, who had been actively combating Jewish persecution since 1933, collaborating with the "Confessional Church," and later issuing a stark warning in the House of Lords about the "final solution." Father Adolf Freudenberg was appointed as first secretary of the new refugee service; he was an able man, influenced by Niemoeller and Bonhoeffer, who had worked in Germany's foreign ministry, but had left it because of political circumstances to study theology. Freudenberg was married to a Jew and worked as a priest in London in 1939, then moved his work to Geneva and from there coordinated an emergency service for "non-Aryan" Christians, focusing especially on the dire conditions in camps in southern France. Father Toureille worked on his behalf, and Maria Krehbiel-Darmstädter later corresponded with both men, whom she greatly esteemed. She experienced them as embodying active Christian service in times of hardship, people of moral power and decisiveness in the sense of Solomon's saying:

> Free those who are dragged to their death
> And those who slump to the killing floor—still save them!
> If you were to say: "But we knew nothing of this"—
> Will he, who tries all hearts, not see through you?
> He who attends to your soul, he knows
> And to each gives just desserts according to how he acts.[124]

Besides Toureille, other outstanding helpers arrived in Gurs in December 1940, to work and live there by their own free initiative. French women Madeleine Barot and Jeanne Merle d'Aubigné, working for a Protestant aid organization, succeeded in gaining entry to the camp, and taking over a hut of their own where they set up an *"Assistance Protestante."* From here they did good work throughout the camp, which had a beneficial effect on many areas of life there.[125] The young Swiss nurse Elsbeth Kasser behaved in a similarly courageous and resolute way, gaining access to the camp in December 1940 as a member of the *"Cartel Suisse de secours aux enfants victimes de la guerre."** She wrote, "At last I was given an iron bedstead and a blanket in the corner of a hut near the camp graveyard. The first night was cold and hard. But I knew I was in the right place."[126] Elsbeth Kasser lived very close to Maria's *ilot* "L," and near to Madeleine Barot and Jeanne Merle d'Aubigné, too. She took over a hut from the camp police that had previously served as a brothel, and provided food and help for children in the camp. Every morning children and teenagers got extra food provided by Swiss donations, and soon also regular lessons in a school started by Elsbeth Kasser and run by volunteer inmates, with many artistic and musical activities and a regular rhythm to the day. In the spring of 1941 she secured more help in setting up gardens and primitive workshops, eventually even establishing an orchestra ("skilled hands made amusing plucked instruments out of milk powder tubs."[127]). Maria Krehbiel-Darmstädter described Kasser as an "extraordinary individual... full of the purest devotion"[128] and requested her friends and relatives to send donations for the "Swiss barrack" to provide books and other things needed there. Finally, Charles Cadier, the priest of Oloron, became a bright figure of unexpected succor too. He had worked previously in the African Congo, and knew Albert Schweitzer. He held services for the various *ilots* and concerned himself with the welfare of many internees, whose uncensored letters he smuggled out of the camp until he was denounced and prohibited from entering the camp.

On December 5, 1940, Maria wrote to Margot Junod, "The...services still take place a long way away, in a really icy hut. Yet one experiences what inner strength can accomplish, feeling oneself especially connected with all those who are present." Two days later, referring to Paul (2 Cor. 12:10) she wrote again to Margot: "'When I am weak, I am strong.' This mysterious saying fills me with deep emotion, and suffering, and gratitude and longing." Maria spoke of Psalm 23, which she had lived with intensely already before her deportation, as

---

* Swiss aid organization for child war victims

Figure 24: Sister Elsbeth Kasser and a child at Gurs

her "inmost daily prayer" in the camp. "And still I feel the comfort of being in accord with goodness and mercy, and hope to keep connected with the love that guides us."[129]

> Who speaks the "I" within me is my shepherd;
> I shall not want.
> He gives me repose on green pastures,
> He guides me to the waters of life.
> He restores my soul.
> He leads me upon the path of truthfulness
> Within his "I"-being's prevailing power.
>
> Though I pass through the abyss of the dark shadows of death
> I shall fear no danger of evil, for you are with me,
> Your rod and your staff are my support and comfort.
> You lay for me a table in the presence of my enemies.
> You anoint my head with oil,
> You fill my cup to overflowing.
> Yes, goodness and mercy shall bear me through
>   all the days of my life,
> And in the house of the Lord, who speaks the "I" in me,
>   I will repose for ever.

~

It was in this way that Maria prepared for the Christmas festival amidst the cold and rain of Gurs, in its wet, dark huts and in the swamp around them—which kept the gaze of inmates fixed on the ground.

> Christmas here—is really an experience of the utmost impoverishment. Wooden joists and straw and night and the sense of being forlorn—how strong the certainty of conquering light has to become. And how happy he who has the gift of memories of celebration and altar and annunciation.[130]

She continued to feel sustained by her spiritual friends in Mannheim and elsewhere, in the "celebratory warmth of memory that they uphold."[131] In Gurs she found that a special feeling for the Christmas festival was evoked in internees by an existential sense "that adversity draws from their depths as the longing for redemption and love."[132] In 1940, the festival of Christmas coincided with the Jewish festival of Chanukah, so that both Advent and Chanukah lights burned in peaceful accord next to each other in the barrack. A group of prisoners prepared a Christmas festival and organized small gifts and even a simple, candle-lit tree. An unforgettable atmosphere was created that moved many of the inmates profoundly, and was later described as the "Christmas miracle of Gurs." There was a profound sense of community beyond all differences of religious denomination, and an ultimate honoring of purely human qualities. In his formulation of the Credo for The Christian Community, Rudolf Steiner had stated: "Communities whose members feel the Christ within them, may feel themselves united in a Church to which all belong who experience the healing power of the Christ."[133] In a Christmas letter addressed to her brother's family, Maria Krehbiel-Darmstädter wrote on December 28:

> These celebrations were of utter simplicity and grandeur. The tree, with just 10 candles, yet so richly alive, was something so beautiful, so full of reconciliation. The old songs, the sacred story, and its interpretation by the priest—felt like the gift of nourishment. Only now did I really understand the grace by Angelus Silesius: "It is not bread that feeds us. What feeds us in the bread is God's eternal Word, is spirit and is life."

All this took place in a threshold realm between life and death. At Gurs, in the bitterly cold Christmas night, thirty inmates died in the huge camp.

~

At the beginning of January, the first snow of the winter fell on the black roofs and muddy tracks.[134] The monthly journal of The Christian Community, which Maria had hoped for, arrived, as did news of relatives and friends who were making efforts to secure her possible emigration to the United States. A few months' vacation from the camp on grounds of illness was also being considered—subject to testimony

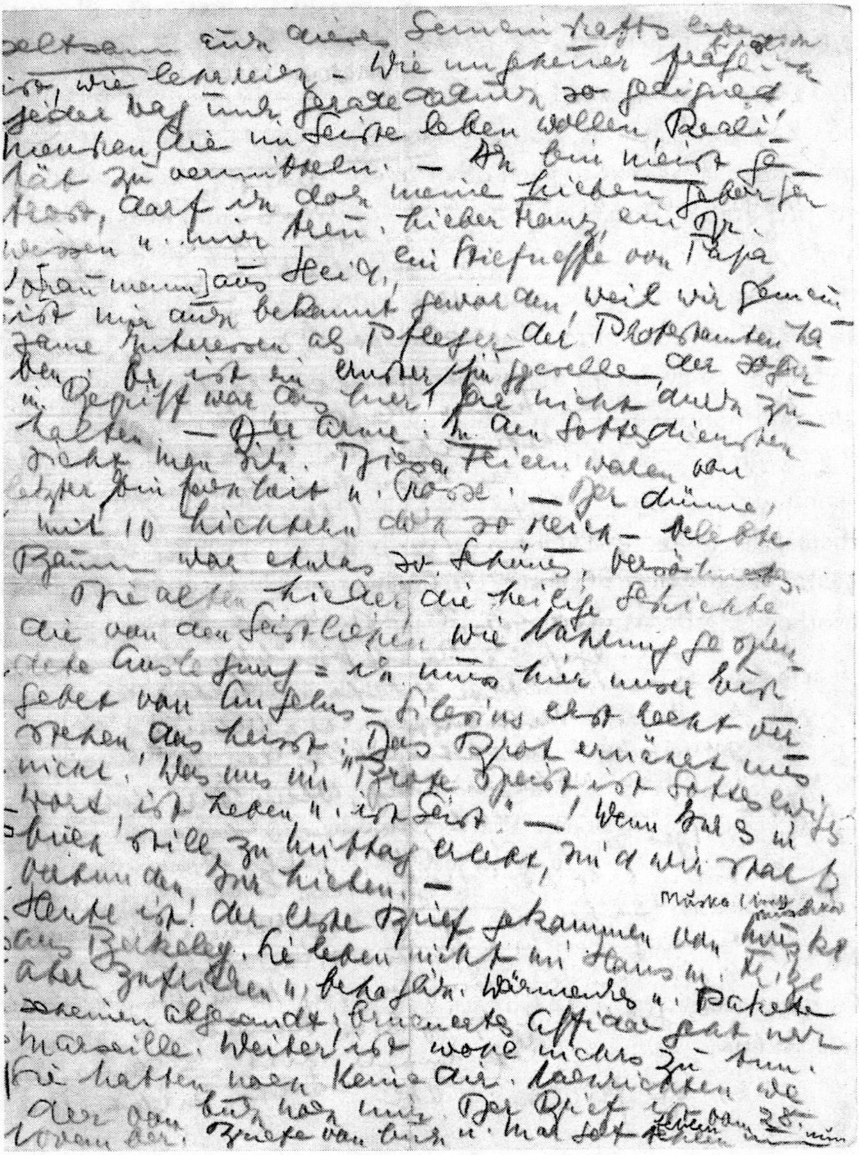

*Figure 25: Maria Krehbiel-Darmstaeder's letter to Franz Darmstädter,
December 28, 1940 (second page)*

from a camp doctor, financial support and accommodation under the monitoring and surveillance of the French authorities. Maria was weak and unwell; yet she was ambivalent about efforts by her friends and relatives to rescue her. When, before Christmas, Margot Junod in Lausanne offered the prospect of getting her temporary leave on grounds of illness to stay with friends in Lyon, she wrote back:

> Of course, that's like a glimpse of dawn. And yet: On the sinking ship when a life raft appears: to disembark while the others carry on to their doom! You see, that is really very difficult. Please forgive me, Margot. I can say this to you because it is the absolute truth. No one should reject an opportunity to do what one can. Especially not when it has any objective benefit.... (Or even if I might believe—subjectively—that the whole context would lack me if I were absent.) Whether, when "free," one can be more solicitous to those who live in fear and limbo?[135]

It is certainly true that Maria Krehbiel-Darmstädter was needed in the Gurs community, and would have been missed if she had left. From the very outset she supported many people, and had the capacity to give them something important through her personal, spiritual qualities and her maturity. Countless fellow inmates were in despair, and needed inner light and courage to persevere. There were frequent suicides in the camp; and even the patients suffering from psychiatric disorders, who had been collected from clinics at the time of deportation and were later treated temporarily at a hospital in Pau, were subsequently sent back to Gurs. The daily death rate continued unabated in January, and even rose higher ("The gravity of those densely-packed rows of the dead: old—and young."[136]) In view of this situation Maria wanted to stay in Gurs and help as far as her capacities allowed. On January 27, she wrote to her brother, "O what a strange place in the world this is! A place where you are equally worn down and lifted up. Outside of the "earthly order" you can say, and therefore a very important place of the greatest advancement and epiphanies beyond time."

565 c

COMITÉ INTERNATIONAL DE LA CROIX-ROUGE

AGENCE CENTRALE
DES PRISONNIERS DE GUERRE

Rappeler dans la réponse :

SCC. O.1381/AC

GENÈVE, le **16 janvier 1941**
Palais du Conseil-Général

Herrn Franz DARMSTAEDTER
Hasenrainstrasse 85
BINNINGEN (Basseland)
Schweiz

      In Beantwortung Ihres Schreibens vom **10. Januar 1941**
bedauern wir sehr Ihnen folgenden Beschluss der Handelsabteilung
des Eidgenössischen Volkswirtschaftsdepartementes in Bern bekannt-
geben zu müssen.

      Dem Internationalen Komitee vom Roten Kreuz wurde
mitgeteilt, dass von Beginn dieses Jahres an alle Einzelsendungen
von der Schweiz aus an fremde Staatsangehörige (Kriegsgefangene,
Zivilinternierte und nicht internierte Zivilpersonen) untersagt sind.

      Wir bedauern ausserordentlich Ihnen keine günstigere
Antwort geben zu können und zeichnen.

Hochachtungsvoll

F. Bordier

(Frl.) R. BORDIER
Mitglied des Internationalen
Komitees vom Roten Kreuz

P.S. : Die Sektion für Ein- und Ausfuhr in Bern hat Ihnen
den blauen Zettel zugestellt und wir bitten Sie,
die Marken von dort zurück zu verlangen.

*Figure 26: Letter from the Red Cross to Franz Darmstädter,
January 16, 1941, informing him with much regret that the Swiss
authorities would no longer permit the delivery of individual parcels*

Back in December, Father Toureille had asked Maria to take on official pastoral care of the Protestants in her *ilot*, and she gladly agreed to do so. She corresponded with Toureille and Freudenberg, and kept in direct touch in the camp with Madeleine Barot and Jeanne Merle d'Aubigné. By agreement with them she visited Protestants in their various barrack and brought them small necessaries, also helping them to compose letters and giving them pastoral care:

> She reported and discussed any special troubles of those in her care, for whom she received additional food or warm clothing from the Assistance. Then she went from hut to hut to offer her help. But however urgently needed was material help, the support she provided in conversations with the women...was still more valuable, giving them new courage and the strength to endure.[137]

With a birch staff—or two—she struggled through the deep mud to different barrack. On January 24, 1941, she wrote to her sister in the United States:

> A birch stick is my walking stick: making progress over the terrain here is more like rowing. I couldn't do without my faithful staff, which is faintly reminiscent of another—a slender, crowned birch trunk that stands upon a grave, and will soon be putting forth new leaves.

In a letter of January 1941 to Margot Junod (who had made contact with Adolf Freudenberg at Maria's suggestion), Freudenberg wrote of Maria's commitment and the intensity of her spiritual and moral resistance in Gurs: "In this 'bare wasteland,' God has allowed a spiritual life and a stance of love to blossom in a way that can scarcely be found in places of warm security."[138] This "spiritual life," however, had to be wrestled for anew each day in complex circumstances: "You have no idea," wrote Maria, "how *strange* this communal life is, how instructive—how enormously problematic every day is, and thus so suited to conveying reality to those who wish to live in the spirit."[139]

~

By the beginning of 1941, her strength was critically weakened. She reflected on her forthcoming death ("perhaps we will soon be reunited with our loved ones"[140]) but still struggled on, trying to make the best of the "strangeness and yet also the great scope of this situation":

> The bread and soup I receive tastes good; for after all, in this whole context of life together there lies an important social element. And dependency is something I become aware of only as that of man upon God. Should I not therefore be grateful?[141]

She continued to write her letters in the dim light of the hut and thanked her correspondents effusively for the post and parcels she received. ("To receive this: you have no idea how good it is. There is such strange, powerful happiness in the colors of the heavens."[142]) Now and then she started to speak of her longings for friends and home, for people and landscapes, but then paused and tried to gaze in a different direction: "And yet I am so comforted in my whole being. I *only* live *each day* at a time, each hour, each need that comes toward me."[143] On January 10, 1941, she told Margot Junod that she "had always been a grateful person, since I found my way to insight."

In January, despite her inner ambivalence, the prospect of several months' sick leave became more likely due to her health problems and the successful efforts of Margot Junod's friends in Lyon, along with her brother's financial support. On January 15, 1941, Margot Junod wrote to Franz Darmstädter in Basel, "I am pleased to be able to tell you that your sister will be released in 8 days, as long as no other unexpected eventuality intervenes. She has been assigned residence in Lyon, and I am pleased that my loyal friends will be able to welcome and look after her there, although she is not allowed to live with them."[144] As so often in Gurs, though, things did not work out after all: exit and vacation permits thought to be almost "certain" were turned down at the last moment, leaving people in despair at the fading of a tangible prospect. Maria Krehbiel-Darmstadter did not allow herself to succumb to a hope-despair dynamic of this kind ("for we are no doubt fated to remain here a long time. There is no point

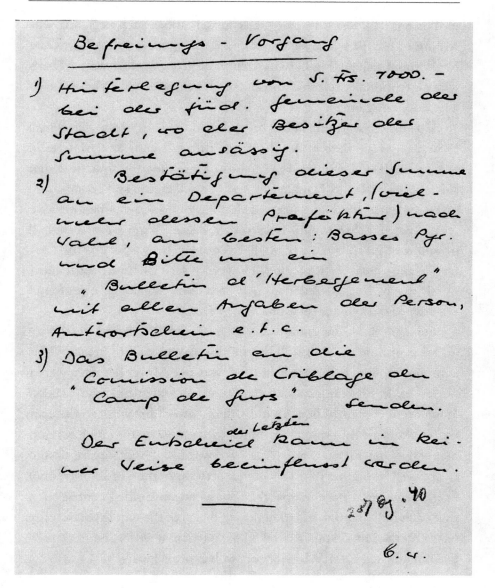

*Figure 27: Maria Krehbiel-Darmstädter outlining
steps needed to secure "leave" (first page)*

in illusions"[145]). She wanted to raise herself above such tugs, and was willing to accept whatever might come, continuing to work in Gurs but without exhausting her strength in an irresponsible way. "That's why I intentionally refrain from convulsive exertions, which have such a demoralizing effect."[146]

However, the people in her barrack and the staff of the *Assistance Protestante* took care of her. In letters to her friends and relatives in the first half of February 1941, Maria hinted for the first time that she had been ill, was being nursed by her colleagues and friends, and receiving extra food. She stressed that her outlook remained positive, even if her life path should turn toward death: "I am pleased that all of you, my loved ones, are well! Keep up your spirits *and be comforted and inwardly protected.* How very seriously and consciously this is meant by someone who lives here, and is granted a profound experience of divine revelation."[147]

For her, the Gurs community represented the shared destiny of a group of human beings. "Give us this day our daily bread." This community, now helping her in turn, was one Maria felt deeply committed to. In his comments on the "fundamental social law," Rudolf Steiner had explained how an individual "owes" his work to the community, and in this way contributes to its preservation and development—beyond all material wage or reward.[148] "And forgive us our trespasses"*—Steiner interpreted this petition in the Lord's Prayer not in the sense of a moral culpability but as an unfulfilled contribution that each individual needs to make, or owes, to the whole community, based on the individual "assets" of his particular skills and powers.[149] On January 24, 1941, Maria wrote to her sister Luise:

> It is the same, great sense of the enormous certainty of protection that I live and breathe in now, doing with joy what is needed here, as the member of a community. Inexpressible opportunities here for good will, for help and deed. And there are many here who are lonelier than I, and who, though "alone," are reached by others

---

* In German, the word *Schuld* also means "debt."—Tr.

who sustain them to such a powerful degree with loving friendship and the deeds of friendship.

Four days later she wrote in another letter: "What bears us up is the love that streams toward us, a much needed, *living* commitment whose inwardness sustains us." This—broad—sense of community and living fraternity also extended to her family, her spiritual connections within The Christian Community and her sustaining bonds of friendship with many individuals. "To live here [in Gurs]," she wrote, "is service—and: we are served."[150]

~

Nevertheless Maria missed the visible community of esoteric Christians in Gurs, along with the realm of sacramental worship at the heart of The Christian Community, and also spiritual-scientific literature. She was overjoyed to get a first letter in January from Maria Gnädinger, in Bern, and pleased to know that there was a member of the Freiburg Christian Community in the camp, fifty-five-year-old Toni Schwarz, although she was in a different *ilot*. Occasionally she admitted in her letters to a deep loneliness in this respect. In February 1941, Maria Gnädinger not only sent her the next monthly issue of The Christian Community journal but a new reproduction of "Christ Resurrected" by Vincenzo Foppa. Letters from Rudolf Meyer and Gertrud Spörri, who had been part of the founding group of Christian Community priests, also arrived in Gurs from Switzerland. She was delighted and started a correspondence with them. It is possible that Spörri, now working for the Red Cross,[151] succeeded in visiting the camp. Subsequently recalling this, Maria Krehbiel-Darmstädter wrote at Pentecost 1942: "Her visit—so unexpected—connected me so strongly to the best, most precious realities—with which one kept faith—this visit was among the most memorable of things."[152]

Maria survived her grave health crisis at the beginning of 1941, but was greatly weakened by it. Initially she had exerted all her strength to cope with the dire circumstances in the camp, and to help others.

Figure 28: Women at Camp Gurs, 1941

But as Christmas ended and January began, her own inner state grew more problematic despite the pastoral care that she continued to give: "As time goes on the impulse triggered by all the suffering here slowly wears away. Then you have to try not to let yourself become prey to dull routine—or fade out altogether."[153] In her letters during February and March she spoke of settling into routines "that are like being worn down spiritually,"[154] and also of occasional exhaustion. But she repeatedly summoned her powers again, and then expressed her satisfaction with the life in Gurs. There was no need for sick leave she said:

> Strangely, I live here without wishes—prepared to give each day its due and wring from it what is required, feeling this destined community as something entirely natural. We will go ever onward, and each of us—many—will finally "come home." I am at home everywhere, really. Can you understand this? I simply carry the little house of my being with me. And the love that points me on my way is not limited to any one country or situation.[155]

On March 7, 1941, she wrote as follows to friends in Heidelberg and Mannheim:

> It is strange what happens to everyone in these times: a great forgetfulness occurs. An emptiness that often lurks in wait—with what can it be filled?—that can grow ever emptier because our perceptions are dulled; often all that arises is a greed to be satiated. Nothing but that. But occasionally, Sun-like powers break in. Then the emptiness is filled so strongly and utterly that there *is* nothing but this Sun, fullness, life, love. The grief is extinguished; in fact, all that is ours altogether.

As previously, Father Toureille's sporadic visits, her meetings with him and the services he held, were of vital importance. In her letter of March 7 to her Christian Community friends at home, Maria wrote about the last service she had attended in Gurs, which Toureille celebrated:

> It was a powerful communion. You should have been there. The reformed (Calvinist) Church is quite different from our own dear

Church and accords with the situation we have here: its utter simplicity—not severity.... But such simplicity. Do you know? Like the way our life continues altogether, without altar—the barest table, the plain, empty cross, which even the Earth that plagues us here stuck to: a grey clump. Metal cups, that we use for drinking here. Simple plates we eat from for the holy bread. Wine bottles to pour the communion drink, with a napkin under them. And presiding, a magnificent human being. A person mighty in word, and in spirit and soul: young and fiery. Full of the power of belief in others, and of support and aid. And the unity among the very many! And the coming and going, and the receiving of holy provisions. As in our own conferences. Also a great freedom allowed here in the sacrament, allowing admission to all as is familiar to us. Of course *we* miss the ritual aspect, the *color* above all. Here you can say there is only grey (earth—i.e., mud), blue—sky—and the transitions one can read morning and evening in the dialog between Heaven and Earth.

Maria missed the Act of Consecration of Man as the mystery fulfillment of a true "divine service" ("I miss our rites very much however. The language."[156]). Yet she also wrote that the whole life in Gurs might be "meant as rite."[157] Four weeks previously, at the beginning of February, she had written to tell Gertrud Spörri that "It is inexpressibly hard and inexpressibly sacred and serious to live like this. Really given up to the divine—to what is human—to things of primary importance. Yes, what a stance toward the One, and what an opportunity."[158]

~

Even in the extremely harsh conditions of Gurs, Maria watched the changing seasons and the natural world with the greatest attentiveness: the light and the colors of the sky, the weather, the world of plants, and everything connected with it. On January 10, 1941, she wrote to Maria Gnädinger:

The grace that speaks of the "bread that does not feed us" is continually true. We eat and drink spirit, and cannot live otherwise.

The most wonderful signs in the heavens and the clouds just a little way above the darkest atmosphere of Earth are experiences that offer continual healing.

A little later she reported that birds were singing, and a "new shoot of grass" was sprouting beside her sleeping place. Spring arrived slowly at the beginning of March:

Outside green shoots are appearing, and birds are singing happily, but strangely quietly on the verges. Very tame. They have grown used to us. But many people have not yet seen them. Sometimes I hear them very early in the morning. I get up very early for a lonely, often rather strenuous walk in the grey of dawn. But I keep rhythm alive in me, and it is always fresh and invigorating to breathe with the sunrise.[159]

She "kept rhythm alive in her" with the verses and meditations of her inner practice, starting and ending the day very consciously, and observing many other moments of pause, reflection and awareness. Few lived in Gurs as she did, and conditions remained as harsh as ever. In February and March there were not only birds and sprouting vegetation but also hurricanes, lakes of water, torrents and the mud-swamps.

In March 1941, many of the inmates were allowed to leave Gurs— old people and families with children were transferred to other, more pleasant camps; a sense of restlessness pervaded the place: new opportunities for liberation seemed possible. Martha Liefmann, who had arrived in Gurs from Freiburg with her brother and sister, wrote in a letter:

There is no end of vague or more detailed rumors, all running through the camp like wildfire. One day you are registered or written down for a particular option, but the next day everything has been turned upside down again. So you never know what you should do, and still less what is the best or the right course of action.[160]

Maria Krehbiel-Darmstädter remained calm in the midst of this, and told her sister: "Nothing and nowhere is assured or certain as far as the eye can see here. But the mountains stand strong and exquisite on the horizon, and comfort and strength live also in the heart."[161] She continued to pursue her social and therapeutic task, which she loved, and felt to belong intrinsically to her:

> If you have a responsible role you have to counsel many who ask you things. I am often fairly weary in consequence, but also often content—so much so that I don't even wish to leave but am learning to regard this place as the most fitting for me. You might say that my whole former life seems to have equipped me to serve here and stand the test. Even in purely physical terms. The limitations and constrictions here become *rich* in renunciation—and also offer a freedom that cheers and strengthens you. It is as though a juice were pressed out of you that in turn has a regenerating effect, like a refreshing drink.[162]

Less in terms of physical strength than spiritually and morally, the whole of Maria's "former life" had "equipped" her for her work in Gurs, imbuing her with what she could now say and give to people there. In previous years she had suffered a great deal, but overcome and transformed this suffering. She had encountered anthroposophic Spiritual Science and The Christian Community, in which she found a source of new life, meaningful values and inner support for her personal development: a tangible path of soul-spiritual schooling. All this now flowed out of her, informed by inner certainty and love, and the gift of working creatively for others by affirming each person's own existential reality. She wrote to Gertud Spörri: "Things one experienced at an earlier time have such resonance and influence as gifts that are passed on and take effect. One *has* something to give."[163]

When her brother Franz Darmstädter was temporarily employed on fatigue duty in a camp for émigrés in Switzerland's Aargau region, working in the kitchen there, Maria—unlike him—did not view this as negative in the least. She once again affirmed the value of her own life in Gurs, accentuating its moral dimension:

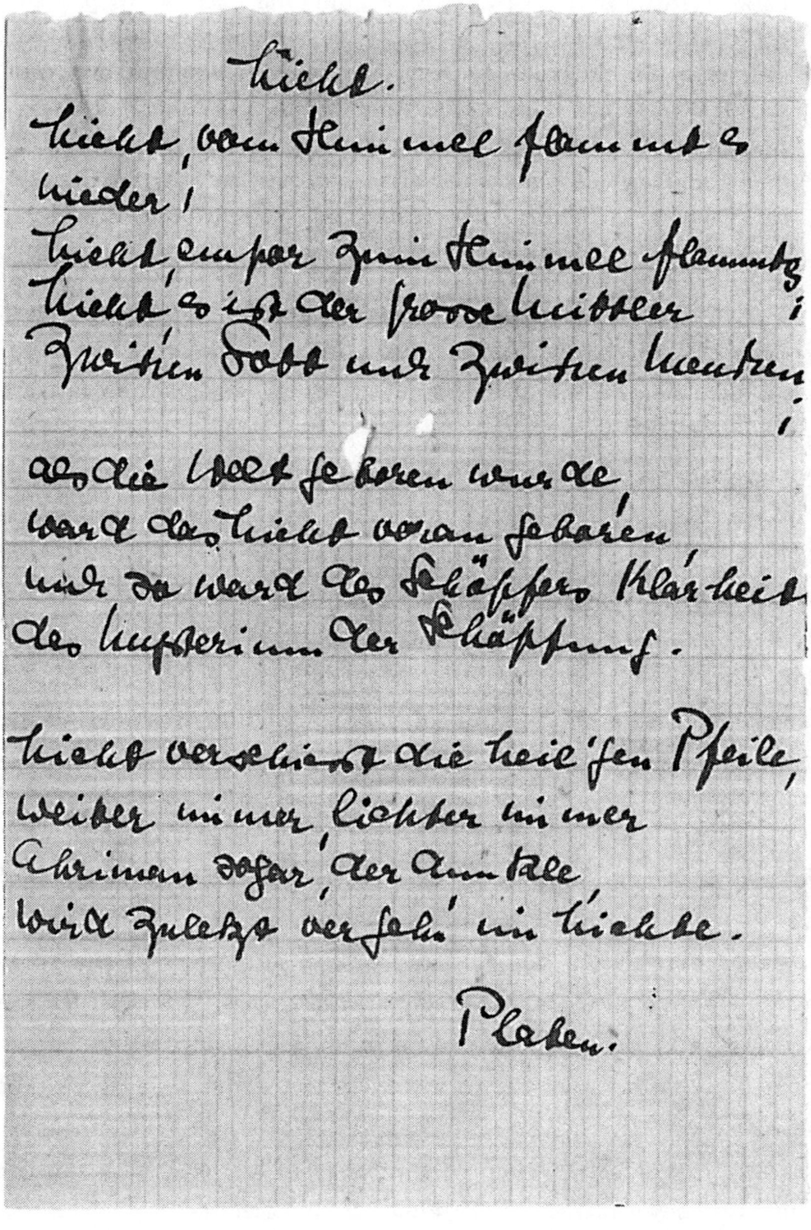

Licht.
Licht, vom Himmel flammt es
nieder;
Licht empor zum Himmel flammt's
Licht, es ist der grosse Mittler ;
Zwischen Gott und zwischen Menschen ;
Als die Welt geboren wurde,
ward das Licht voran geboren
und so ward des Schöpfers Klarheit
des Mysteriums der Schöpfung.

Licht verschiesst die heil'gen Pfeile,
weiter immer, lichter immer
Ahriman sogar, der dunkle
wird zuletzt vergeh'n im Lichte.

Platen.

Figure 29: "Light" by August von Platen; text enclosed in a letter from Maria Krehbiel-Darmstädter

Egoism grows ever less; the joy of humbling oneself to help others kindles the heart and broadens one's mind to infinity. Even the simple life, the landscape—the routine—the isolation, even the severity: these are useful. I, at least, attempt to take everything that happens as a tool for learning. And the time spent here: I see it on a grand scale. A most earnest consecration: my heartfelt thanks for surviving the winter; the birdsong, even if heard only fleetingly outside; flowers brought in when children come back from walks in the fields.[164]

Franz Darmstädter and his family, including Maria's sister Luise, found such comments strange and worrying. Initial reports on the Gurs camp had appeared in various international newspapers—in Switzerland, too—in February and March 1941, describing the dire conditions there, the lack of human dignity, the pervasive illness and the high death rate. Maria's family could not see how she could accept these terrible conditions, and even find in them positive aspects for her own inner life, at the same time delaying or even refusing possible release. Even before Gurs, Maria's siblings had regarded her way of life as a major conundrum. Her spirituality was alien to them, although they appreciated her personality and felt her love for them.

∼

Meanwhile Maria had—with the help of a Spanish internee—managed to get hold of a bed in the form of a simple wood frame, and also a colored blanket. In the grey and brown monotony of the ground and the barrack at Gurs, she sorely missed colors: "I hunger for them so much, and the sky elevates me with an inconceivable range of unearthly colors. I paint with my eyes, and drink them in thirstily," she wrote on March 24, 1941, in a letter to Basel.[165] The words of Pasalm 23, which had become the focus of her prayer in imprisonment, were never far from her thoughts: "He gives me repose on *green* pastures." When green started to push forth more vigorously in April around the barrack, she was joyous: "The green beside the huts we live in, is greener than any green I have ever seen before. It may be

DAS ELEND IN FRANZÖSISCHEN KONZENTRATIONSLAGERN

14.000 Menschen in einer atembeklemmenden Atmosphäre in Gurs – 500 Kinder und 1200 Personen über 70 Jahre – Täglich 15 bis 25 Todesfälle – Menschen, die seit drei Jahren von einem Konzentrationslager nach dem anderen geschleppt werden

"ATEMBEKLEMMENDE ATMOSPHAERE MENSCHLICHER HOFFNUNGSLOSIGKEIT"

Philadelphia, 25. Januar — Das "American Friends Service Committee" hat eben jetzt Berichte ihrer Untersuchungskommissionen im Ausland erhalten; "in einer gewissen Anzahl von Todesfällen" in den französischen Konzentrationslagern wird direkt Hunger als Todesursache verantwortlich aufgeführt.

Aus einigen der Lager, insbesondere aus dem Lager von Gurs, in der Nähe der Pyrenäen, in dem 14.000 Menschen verschiedenster Herkunft untergebracht sind, wird von einer "atembeklemmenden Atmosphäre menschlicher Hoffnungslosigkeit" berichtet, von "ausgesprochener Todessehnsucht" bei den meisten der älteren Lagerinsassen.

"Sie werden nicht mehr kämpfen: apathisch liegen sie auf ihren Strohsäcken, weisen oftmals Nahrung zurück und warten auf das Ende", wird aus Gurs berichtet. "Viele der Frauen und auch der jungen Leute zeigen eine ähnliche Haltung."

Der Bericht gibt ein lebendiges Bild über die Verhältnisse in diesem Durchgangslager; 50 Aerzte kämpfen "unter den primitivsten Verhältnissen gegen unglaubliche Schwierigkeiten, um die ohnedies sehr hohe und täglich noch steigende Sterblichkeitsziffer herabzudrücken, deren Ursache in dem Mangel an Nahrungsmitteln und Medikamenten und den unhygienischen Lebensbedingungen zu suchen ist, wobei man in Betracht ziehen muss, dass die physische Widerstandskraft der meisten Flüchtlinge schon durch langes Leiden geschwächt ist."

Im Lager von Gurs befindet sich die gesamte frühere jüdische Bevölkerung Badens, etwa 7500 Personen, ausserdem 3000 Mann aus St. Cyprien, die zwar schon an das Lagerleben gewöhnt, aber durch lange Entbehrungen geschwächt sind", ausserdem eine Gruppe erst kürzlich internierter Ausländer, die in Frankreich gewohnt hatten, und 500 Frauen, die seit Mai in Gurs interniert sind.

Unter den Lagerinsassen sind etwa 500 Kinder und 1200 Personen über 70 Jahre – der Aelteste ist 106 Jahre alt. Geistesgestörte und Schwachsinnige, Krankenhauspatienten und frühere Insassen von Altersheimen befinden sich unter der Gruppe der Badenser.

Die Zahl der Todesfälle in Gurs wird mit 15 bis 25 täglich angegeben, die Schätzung für November nennt mehr als 300. In dem medizinischen Teil des Berichts wird ausgeführt:

"Eine grosse Anzahl der Insassen des Lagers Gurs befindet sich im Stadium gefährlicher Unterernährung, wohlgenährte Körper sind völlig verschwunden. Gleichzeitig sind oftmals die Merkmale von Vitaminmangel festzustellen, aufgeschwemmte Gesichter, blutendes Zahnfleisch mit lockeren und ausfallenden Zähnen.

Herzbeschwerden sind sehr häufig Viele der Herzleidenden sind chronisch kranke Personen. unter ihnen Rekonvaleszenten nach schweren Erkrankungen; es gibt immer noch eine gewisse Anzahl von Typhus-Rekonvaleszenten, die aus St. Cyprien gekommen sind, die nicht geheilt werden können, und das nicht etwa wegen Mangels an Pflege — denn die Bemühungen der Aerzte sind rührend —, sondern wegen des Mangels an notwendigen Medikamenten.

Zwei weitere Gefahren erregen die Besorgnis der Aerzte. Sie drohen von den Läusen, die sich mit umso grösserer Schnelligkeit und Leichtigkeit verbreiten, als es wenig Instrumente zur Entlausung gibt. Die Rolle, die die Läuse in der Verbreitung von Typhus spielen, ist ja allgemein bekannt.

Eine weitere Quelle gefährlicher Infektionen sind die Ratten, die sich in grosser Anzahl vorfinden."

Das Leben in Gurs spielt sich in "Blocks" ab, zu denen jeweils ein paar Dutzend Baracken zusammengefasst sind und die mit einem Stacheldrahtzaun umgeben sind. In einem der Raum zwischen den Baracken "wegen der völligen Ungepflegtheit und des Schmutzes" unbetretbar ist. sind die Gefangenen, die die Blocks nur mit besonderem Erlaubnisschein verlassen dürfen, "praktisch zu völliger Bewegungslosigkeit verurteilt", wie in dem Quaker-Bericht ausgeführt wird

Es gibt keine Glasfenster. nur Dachluken aus Holz, die spärliches Licht einlassen, wenn sie offen sind. und bei Regen geschlossen werden müssen", heisst es weiter. "Auch wenn alle Dachluken geöffnet sind, ist es unmöglich, im Innern der Baracken zu lesen.

60 Menschen, deren Anwesenheit man mehr errät, als dass man sie sieht, liegen auf ihren Strohsäcken oder stehen herum, denn es gibt weder Tische, noch Stühle. Die Kinder können nicht spielen und die Frauen können nicht arbeiten. Bei Regenwetter ist dies erbarmungswürdige Bild begleitet von dem unterdrückten Geräusch von Weinen und Seufzen.

Der Luftraum pro Person ist unbedingt unzureichend.

Man hat jetzt damit begonnen, die Kinder in eine Einzelbaracke von Block M zusammenzulegen, und es mag sein, dass hierdurch viele Kinder gerettet werden können. Die Kälte macht sich empfindlich bemerkbar und besonders die älteren Leute können sich nicht warm halten. Es sind kaum ein paar Wärmeflaschen vorhanden. Die meisten der Baracken lassen Wind und Regen durch."

Aus dem Bericht geht weiter hervor, dass nicht nur zu wenig Holz zum Heizen der Baracken und Wärmen der Kindernahrung vorhanden war, sondern es fehlte sogar an Brettern für Särge. So musste man einmal eine leerstehende Baracke niederreissen, um Material zum Begraben der Toten zu bekommen.

Einige der Gefangenen von Gurs waren schon vorher in deutschen und spanischen Konzentrationslagern und im Lager von St. Cyprien (ebenfalls in den Pyrenäen) gewesen, nachdem sie jetzt das zweite Jahr in Gefangenschaft sind. Bei Beginn des Winters waren viele barfuss und ungenügend bekleidet.

Die Untersuchungskommission berichtet, dass trotz der deprimierenden Umstände sogar in Gurs mit Hilfe von Musikinstrumenten, die von einer privaten Organisation zur Verfügung gestellt wurden, ein "bemerkenswertes Orchester" gebildet werden ist. Man schreibt, dass dadurch "gewaltig" zur Hebung der Moral der Gefangenen beigetragen wurde.

"Der hohe Prozentsatz einer intellektuellen Elite, Kristallisationspunkt des moralischen Halts für alle Insassen, hat die Durchführung eines kulturellen Programms ermöglicht, das zu sehen und zu studieren in den grossen Städten Europas sich das ausgewählteste Publikum eingefunden hätte", heisst es dann weiter. Die Pfarrer verschiedener Kirchen spielen eine ausserordentlich wichtige geistige und moralische Rolle. Ausserdem ist die ausserordentliche Selbstlosigkeit der Aerzte zu erwähnen, die getreulich die Tradition ihres Berufes hochhalten.

Der Bericht aus Gurs schliesst mit einem Aufruf zur Stiftung von Mitteln zum Ausbau der Baracken und zur Beschaffung von Medikamenten etc.

Aus dem Lager von Argeles am Mittelmeer, dicht oberhalb der spanischen Grenze, berichtet ein Quaker, dass der Lageradjutant "ein freundlicher Mann", durch die schwierigen Verhältnisse völlig entmutigt und hilflos vor dem Problem der Verdoppelung der Zahl der Lagerinsassen stand, die Folge der Schliessung des Lagers von Bram, einige Meilen weiter im Innern. Argeles wurde im vergangenen Monat, als der Bericht geschrieben wurde, als "eine unglückselige Gemeinschaft von 18.000 Männern, Frauen und Kindern" geschildert.

Zum Teil dank der Anregung von Miss Mary Elmes, einer Vertreterin des "American Friends Service Committee" bei den französischen Offizieren wurde in der Frauenabteilung des Lagers eine Nähstube eingerichtet, und man kann eine neue Baracke nur für die Näherinnen bauen, die Kleidungsstücke aus dem von den Quakern zur Verfügung gestellten Material herstellen. Man plant die Einführung von Unterrichtskursen in Schneidern, Kochen und Hilfspflege für junge Mädchen zwischen 14 und 18 Jahren.

Im Männerlager ist eine Spielzeugwerkstatt eingerichtet worden und die Quaker haben Werkzeug zur Errichtung einer Tischlerwerkstatt zur Verfügung gestellt. Ferner hat man die Einrichtung einer Handelsschule für die älteren Jungen des Lagers ins Auge gefasst, und zwei Baracken sollen hierfür eingerichtet werden.

Figure 30: A page from The Argentinian Daily, *February 9, 1941, describing the misery in French concentration camps*

that all the surrounding grey makes it seem so strong by contrast."[166] At Easter the priest's raiment in The Christian Community changes to red and green, the colors of resurrection and life.

Maria repeatedly asked her friends to send her art postcards for her corner in the hut ("a beautiful card, now and then, would be very welcome, to bring some *color*"[167]). The significance of artworks grew in Gurs, their content and colors perceived and absorbed existentially. Maria wrote to her brother, who was studying art history in Basel and often sent her art reproductions, describing their importance both to her and to the needy and sick fellow inmates she was caring for: "My patients love art with almost fierce devotion, and our great masters appear powerfully here against this backdrop of strange circumstances."[168] Maria also asked her friends to send specific poems, written out by hand and if possible in colored ink. She would place these on the board beside her mattress and lived intensely with their words. As people passed, some stopped to read the poems and look at the pictures.

At last came the Easter festival, so long desired and urgently needed ("where all else comes to an end, the miraculous must enter in"[169]). On Good Friday, Maria wrote as follows to her sister in California:

> The festive days we celebrate here are earnest and rich in impressions in a way that many feel, and in response to which they change. But sadly not all. Most are too accustomed to complaint and haste, and get nowhere with either, and cannot overcome the void![170]

To Christian Community friends in Bern she described Easter itself in positive terms, with the services she attended and the mood there; but again admitted how much she missed the act of worship in The Christian Community—and asked Maria Gnädinger to send her some literature by Friedrich Rittelmeyer and Rudolf Frieling: "Yet I do very much miss our beloved festivals. And if I might have Dr. Ri[ttelmeyer]'s booklet on the A[ct of] Cons[ecration]—and the one also by Friel[ing]. Something—that would be the greatest help here."[171] In the same context she wrote of her own situation:

Christus aller Erde

Eine Schriftenreihe Band 21

Friedrich Rittelmeyer

Die Menschenweihehandlung

1926

Verlag der Christengemeinschaft, Stuttgart

Figure 31: The Act of Consecration of Man,
by Friedrich Rittelmeyer, Stuttgart, 1926

The image [of the Savior] is above my bed. A small board bears a candle and books. It is covered with red paper; and the finest little cloth that I was given here is spread over that. I think you would be pleased to see it. And here I am at home, dear one. Should I not be glad?

Maria knew by heart The Christian Community epistles for Easter. These speak of the shrine of the human heart, of blood and breath that pass from "grief" and hope through the healing power of the process of Easter to "fulfillment" and "spiritual solace" in the presence of Christ, at times of profound distress. "The comforter of your earthly existence/walks in the spirit/before you."[172]

~

The year continued. On April 25, Maria wrote to Anneliese Herweck in Basel:

I am often so tired in the morning—as if bound to my bed. The earliest early morning—dawn—almost *wrenches* me upward.

But then there is always so much to experience. This morning gift of the sky is always different. The dawn. When the distant mountains rise out of the mist—pink snow peaks, flaming and so tender, the flowing colors speaking like winged messengers and—all far away. Close by the same grey-brown huts: our homesteads. And here we live. How long already it has been. How long it may still be. We no longer count. We simply live.[173]

Three days before this she had told Margot Junod:

In our morning sermon today I was struck by a word that aptly describes what we can be and do here: that embodies—in its sound already—a quality of learning, of attending and finding solace—as something that appeared fully accurate to me. It is the word *docile*.* Don't you agree? It is lovely and so simple. I would like to meditate on it.

---

* The word given here in the original, *docile,* is the French word, spelled the same as in English, but with a slightly different, less passive meaning of "hearkening obediently." —Tr.

Figure 32: Butterfly on a barbed wire fence at Gurs (watercolor by Kurt Loew and Carl Bodek); "The chain of mountains, both so solid and so changing, is most beloved of all to us. Feelings of redemption are medicine here, you see, and the sacramental must thrive because we need it so very much." (to Maria Gnädinger, around March 20, 1941)

Maria once again asked for a few necessaries to be sent to her, both for herself and others: toothpaste, darning thread and cotton, a pillowcase and candles, clothes (already for next winter) and books by Novalis and Jakob Böhme. She made these requests reticently— "You know I am a little worried about collecting 'possessions' again. Isn't the real purpose of our condition to no longer own anything— and therefore possess all? Traveling light is a state that—ought not to be endangered." She wrote that she did not think much about either the past or the future, but tried to be fully present in the here and now. "It is enough that I *am* where I am," she wrote in another letter to her brother's family, again asking him not to be too worried about her and not to get too frantic about her possible release. As she described it, her personal situation was just part of the general situation of humanity and the world, and ultimately not a private misfortune or misery. She was preoccupied, she said, with ways of engaging with this reality, and of contributing to the spiritual and moral future of humanity and the Earth. In his lectures in 1911, "Evolution from the Perspective of Truth," Rudolf Steiner had spoken of inner processes at work in angelic beings who bring about the origin and evolution of the Earth, of sacrificial processes and what he called "creative resignation."[174] Steiner had also spoken of the reflection of these processes in the soul of the human being—whose existence and deeds would determine every aspect of the future of Creation. On May 9, 1941, Maria wrote as follows to her concerned and dissatisfied brother[175] and his family in Basel:

> At fainthearted moments, in bad weather, and when lacking much that seems necessary one's soul does sometimes yearn longingly for relief. Seeks healing and peace. But if you seek rightly—without expecting that what is happening here will suddenly stop, like a nightmare—and consider that this is just one little part of the whole world situation—then peace descends. Renunciation, like grace, is something you can acquire. Not resignation. This renunciation is creative because it relinquishes nothing except your own

willfulness. And instead the healing powers spread in you—take up the spaces that stood empty. Are gently inhabited by angels.

A tender gladness. Unnameable. Unknowable *in the outer world*. Believe me, you can be free of anxiety. You can, indeed, draw comfort and hope from our steadfastness.[176]

~

In the last week of May, Maria Krehbiel-Darmstädter asked Maria Gnädinger in Bern to include in her dispatch of The Christian Community journal one of Rudolf Steiner's *Calendar of the Soul* verses. Steiner had first published these fifty-two seasonal meditations in 1912, writing as follows in a foreword:

The human being feels connected with the world and its temporal changes. In his own being he feels the archetypal image of the cosmos reflected. But the image is not some pedantic, metaphorical copy of the archetype. What is revealed in the seasonal changes of the greater world corresponds to a swinging pendulum within us that does not unfold in the element of time. Rather, we can feel that when our being is given up to the senses and their perceptions, this corresponds to summer, with its light- and warmth-pervaded nature. By contrast, being grounded in ourselves, living in our own world of thinking and will, is something we can experience as winter existence. Thus the rhythm within us between living in the outer world and interiority relates to nature's cycle between summer and winter. But by relating our rhythm of perception and thinking, which is not subject to time, to the temporal rhythms of nature, great secrets of existence can dawn on us. The year then becomes an archetypal image of the activity of the human psyche, and thus a fertile source of genuine self-knowledge. In the Soul Calendar presented here the human spirit is conceived as passing through seasonal moods from week to week, so that it *comes to feel and sense* an image of the activity of its own soul arising from impressions of the year's cycle. A *feeling* self-knowledge is invoked here. Drawing on the characteristic verses given for each week, this feeling self-knowledge can experience the cycle of soul life as something timeless within time. I would expressly say that this offers the possibility of pursuing a path of self-knowledge.[177]

In various lectures given in 1912 around the time the *Calendar of the Soul* appeared, Steiner stressed the significance of these seemingly unimposing meditative verses: "They contain what can come to life in the soul and that then truly corresponds to a living relationship between powers of the soul and those of the cosmos."[178] They were, he said, "temporal meditations" for inner soul experience, "which can thereby connect with processes of divine, spiritual experience."[179] It was not easy, he said, to fully internalize what was connected with "the deeper meaning" of these verses. "To do this, the human soul requires many, many years."[180]

In Mannheim Maria had been living with these temporal meditations by her teacher, but did not yet know them all by heart. She now asked Maria Gnädinger to send them to her, and added this reasoning:

This would be the ideal place to contemplate their content, don't you think?

Our existence is both delivered up to the elemental and cosmic and yet—at the same time—we are endowed with all the capacities needed to master it—by "embracing" and hearkening to it. The inexpressible nature of this earthly realm becomes most apparent when it touches our hearts most directly: in the silence of insight. Then one does something with it: one blesses.[181]

In this context she also drew Maria Gnädinger's attention to a poem by Rainer Maria Rilke, writing: "In Rilke's collection, *Late Poems*—which you may know—is one centered on the words '*I praise.*' The tone he finds here, and maintains, and sings, truly expresses what I mean." At the end of May, in a similar vein, she wrote to her sister Luise: "You know that I what I feel here is like—a mountain peak examining its life. The remarkably rarefied air of altitude: a closeness to God."[182]

The Rilke poem that Maria Krehbiel-Darmstädter referred to, and that was one of the trove of literary, religious and philosophical texts

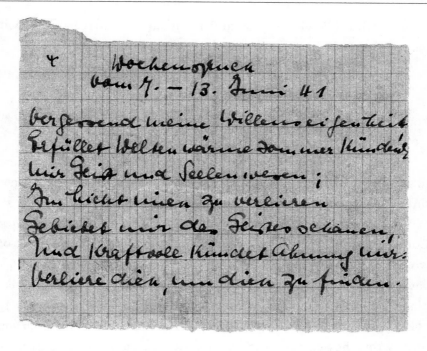

Figure 33: Calendar of the Soul *verse by Rudolf Steiner for the week of June 7–13 (Maria Krehbiel-Darmstädter's handwriting)*

she lived intensely with—and that gave her sustenance at difficult moments in Gurs—runs as follows:

> Oh tell me, poet, what do you do?
> > —I praise.
> But all that's deadly, monstrous, how
> Do you endure it, how accept?
> > —I praise.
> But all that's nameless and anonymous,
> Poet, how can you call it up?
> > —I praise.
> What right have you to be, though, tell me,
> True through every garb and mask?
> > —I praise.
> And how is it that stillness and ferocity
> Like star and storm both know you?
> > —because I praise.[183]

Over the following weeks and months, Maria received Rudolf Steiner's mantric *Calendar of the Soul* verses from Bern:

I cannot describe what it felt like to see once again a sequence of words so well known and, for that very reason, *so new here*. (It is only in such encounters that we suddenly recognize the path we have taken; and do so with a shock.)[184]

Months later she wrote again to Maria Gnädinger: "It is interesting to see, retrospectively, how we experienced these weeks—whether something of what is valid here can also grow in us without guidance."[185]

Maria continued to long for the whole text of the Act of Consecration of Man, which no one could send her: "But our act of worship is still lacking—the texts—only traces of which I can rediscover in myself: that is and remains unavailable."[186] She was largely alone with this longing in Gurs—except for Toni Schwarz whom she could only seldom see (with a "pass") and speak to, but to whom she often wrote, however, via the "camp post." There was no opportunity in Gurs to gather together, as there was at Theresienstadt concentration camp, where each Sunday at ten in the morning the interned Jewish members of The Christian Community could meet and together speak the words of the Act of Consecration.[187] A community like that would have meant so much to Maria.

~

In mid-May 1941, Maria lay on her bed once more, with flu and high fever. She was not admitted to the *infirmière* but received medical attention in her barrack. She was pleased with the doctor who attended her, saying with some astonishment in a letter that he had the "same sort of ideas" as she did: "That was an unexpected gift."[188] Around Ascension time, she wrote to Marie Baum in Heidelberg, sending greetings and asking after the work she had been doing there with Hermann Maas on behalf of refugees and victims of persecution ("I have been thinking of your patients, dear Doctor Baum"). She also sent her some verses of her own composition:

You are,
O Christ.
From your
gentle hand
daily I receive
my earthly raiment.

You are,
O Christ,
from your
cloud feet
dew falls.

I learn—
to atone for trespasses through work.

You are,
O Christ,
your heart of worlds
receives
what affliction and pain
have guided toward peace.[189]

The events of Ascension prefigure and are a precondition for Pentecost, and for empowering of the group of disciples to work outward into the world in a healing way, in the name of Christ and with his support. On Ascension Day, in blessing, Christ had withdrawn from the disciples' sensory vision ("While he was blessing them, he left them and was taken up into Heaven" [Luke 24:51]). He had promised his disciples that the power of the holy spirit would come upon them—and this they experienced ten days later at Pentecost: "And surely I am with you always, to the very end of the age" (Matt. 28:20). This presence of the Christ being informed Maria Krehbiel-Darmstädter's inner experience and path of schooling in Gurs—a path that traversed crises but essentially maintained its integrity. Rudolf Steiner's comments on the increasing human capacity to perceive the Christ during the twentieth century continued to mean a great deal to her[190]—she lived with this idea. And also with the spiritual experiences themselves that Steiner had foretold: "You know that I what I feel here is like—a mountain peak examining its life. The remarkably rarefied air of altitude: a closeness to God."

At Pentecost, friends in the Mannheim Christian Community sent Maria a reproduction of Piero della Francesco's great work, *The Baptism of Christ* (painted around 1450), which she loved very much. She thanked them profoundly, describing it as a "powerful image of great humility"[191] and writing of her inner state of mind and of questions that the Pentecost festival threw up for her. The phrase referring to the "weakness of souls" in The Christian Community's Pentecost epistle was something she dwelt on. The event of Pentecost, and the consciousness associated with it, remained a gift of "spirit revelation" for her, something that must always be achieved anew at each moment and into which even the disciples had only grown through a path of intense suffering.[192] Maria wrote to the Christian friends in Mannheim about the question of inner development and the creation of true community:

> All that comes from "former times" is present here again as though for the first time. Have we made progress? Is our devotion more willing—are our eyes more radiant? There is a *single* absorbing and a *single* outward enacting. The breath is more delicate, counts as nourishment, and this is surely how it was first breathed into us at the dawn of time—so that it may take effect, spiritualizing what touches our mouth and what is sent forth from our mouth. Our inner gentleness grows, no doubt, in the constant practice of never being alone, a state that one cannot imagine in one's dreams. And—that ultimately becomes something like the prerequisite for existence altogether. I and you: are we.[193]

～

On Pentecost Sunday, June 1, 1941, two priests were ordained in the new church of The Christian Community in Stuttgart: the first and also the last ordainment in these premises. Eight days later the priests of The Christian Community were arrested by the Gestapo; and in the coming war years the Stuttgart building, for which Emil Krehbiel had been gathering funds back in 1927, was destroyed in bomb attacks.

Figure 34: The Baptism of Christ, *by Pierro della Francesca*

The arrest of the priests was accompanied by confiscation of all books by Rudolf Steiner and all literature published by The Christian Community's press.

Emil Bock, successor to Friedrich Rittelmeyer in the office of chief minister or coordinator, was also deprived of all his manuscripts and pictures. The Gestapo did not even leave him his Christmas candles. The publishing premises of Urachhaus were sealed off and all further publications prohibited. In May already the Reich press department had forbidden any further issues of The Christian Community's monthly journal, and its June issue never appeared. The Mannheim priest Carl Stegmann was also arrested, along with all his colleagues, though they were detained only for a few weeks—with the exception of Bock who remained in detention at the Gestapo's "protective custody camp" in Welzheim near Stuttgart until February 1942, for much of this time with no idea what his fate might be. An internal "secret" report by the Reich Security Head Office, dated June 1941, which preceded the arrest of the priests and the ban on Christian Community activities, detailed the latter's close connection with Anthroposophy, and in consequence its grave risk to "the unified National Socialist outlook of the German people." ("If one were to accept in its entirety the thinking informing this worldview, and its effects upon the human being's overall outlook and stance, there is no doubt at all that an adherent of Anthroposophy must inevitably come to be an opponent of National Socialism."[194]) The report cited the sacramental core and doctrine of the Movement for Religious Renewal, including these words:

> The seven sacraments...are the means by which the Christ will for redemption integrates its powers of transformation into humanity and the cosmos; these powers then stream forth from Christ-permeated human beings upon all that they come into touch with. The Earth is the body of Christ: *Christ of all the Earth*. The Sun powers penetrate the Earth, *so that it, too, may ultimately become a sun*.

It is not known when news of the arrests and the prohibition of The Christian Community (publicly announced August 6, 1941)

Die Christengemeinschaft

Monatsschrift zur religiösen Erneuerung. Begründet von Friedrich Rittelmeyer
Im Auftrag der Christengemeinschaft herausgegeben von Lic. Emil Bock

18. Jahrgang   Heft 3 / 1941

> Wenn keine Blume mehr
> Auf dieser Erde blühte
> Und in den Nächten
> Traut kein Stern mehr glühte,
> So könnte doch
> Aus deinem Herzen noch
> Ihr Trösten quillen.
> Denn Gott ward Mensch,
> Der Welten Not zu stillen.
>
> Wilhelm Firgau

Pfingsten: Die kosmische Aussendung

Emil Bock

Dem äußeren Bestande nach enthält das Johannes-Evangelium weder einen Bericht von der Himmelfahrt Christi noch von dem Pfingstereignis. Und doch kann man nicht sagen, daß das Johannes-Evangelium zu den Geheimnissen von Himmelfahrt und Pfingsten schweigt. Innerhalb des Reichtums der johanneischen Ostergeschichten tauchen, wie vorausgeworfene Strahlen künftiger Sonnen, in geheimnisvoller Bedeutsamkeit die Motive von Himmelfahrt und Pfingsten bereits auf. Als Maria Magdalena am Ostermorgen in der Gestalt des Gärtners den Christus erkennt und liebend begrüßen will, spricht der Auferstandene zu ihr: „Rühre mich nicht an, denn ich bin noch nicht a u f g e f a h r e n zu meinem Vater. Gehe aber hin zu meinen Brüdern und sage ihnen: ich f a h r e a u f zu meinem Vater und zu eurem Vater, zu meinem Gott und zu eurem Gott" (20, 17). Und als der Auferstandene am Abend des Ostersonntags im verschlossenen Raum des Coenaculums den Jüngern erscheint, spricht er zu ihnen: „Gleich wie mich der Vater gesandt hat, so sende ich euch", und das Evangelium fährt fort: „Als er das gesagt hatte, hauchte er sie an und sprach zu ihnen: nehmet hin den H e i l i g e n G e i s t" (20, 21—22).

Maria Magdalena wird auf die Himmelfahrt als auf etwas Zukünftiges verwiesen; die Ausgießung des Heiligen Geistes scheint dagegen nach der johanneischen Darstellung ein Geschehen zu sein, das bereits zu Ostern beginnt. Der Fortgang des Evangeliums läßt dann aber erahnen, daß auch die Himmelfahrt ein Vorgang ist, der im unmittelbaren Anschluß an Ostern beginnt. Stellt man sich die Himmelfahrt Christi in der üblichen Art vor als eine Entrückung des Christuswesens von der Erde weg in eine jenseitige Sphäre, so muß das strenge „Noli me tangere", das zu Maria Magdalena gesprochen wird, völlig unverständlich bleiben, insofern der Christus es damit begründet, daß er noch nicht gen Himmel gefahren sei. Wenn Maria Magdalena den Auferstandenen jetzt, wo er vor ihr erscheint, nicht anrühren darf, wie soll sie ihn dann anrühren können, wenn er gen Himmel gefahren ist? Wir werden inne, daß uns das Johannes-Evangelium zu einem ganz anderen Verstehen des Himmelfahrts-Geheimnisses anleiten will. Eine Woche nach dem Ostermorgen spricht der Auferstandene zu Thomas das Gegenteil von dem, was er zu Maria Magdalena gesprochen hat: er fordert ihn auf, ihn zu berühren. Wir fragen uns, ob jetzt das Wort schon nicht mehr in Geltung ist: „Ich bin noch nicht aufgefahren zu meinem Vater." Auf geheimnisvolle Weise scheint das Johannes-Evangelium den Himmelfahrtsvorgang aufzufassen als ein Wachstum und eine Intensivierung der hier im Diesseits sich offenbarenden Geistleiblichkeit Christi.

Nicht nur Himmelfahrt und Pfingsten werden bei Johannes in das Ostergeschehen keimhaft einbezogen: für einen Augenblick leuchtet innerhalb der Osterberichte bereits das fern-zukünftige Ge-

33

*Figure 35: The final issue of the monthly journal
for The Christian Community, 1941*

reached Maria Krehbiel-Darmstädter in Gurs. It was not unexpected: Friedrich Rittelmeyer had foreseen this in 1938 when he refused to concede exclusion of Jewish members from services, as demanded by the Nazis in Vienna. Soon after Pentecost Maria Krehbiel-Darmstädter received the last issue of the monthly journal. She regarded this issue as especially well conceived and important, and wrote in a letter to Maria Gnädinger:

> So full and serious; very well matured you might say. We must bend to necessity and—make do with what confronts us. In renunciation we often can become aware, mysteriously, of the real riches one *possesses*—don't you think? The same is true of a sense of home. But let us not forget what Michael Bauer said either, which Dr. Rittelmeyer prized so greatly: "Christ is our most familiar homestead."[195]

When news reached Gurs of the prohibition on The Christian Community—a moon node of eighteen and a half years after it was founded—Maria Krehbiel-Darmstädter wrote as an aside in another letter to Bern:

> That issue—relating to our friends and their work. You know how close this is to my heart—and what this loss must ask of us. I recall that remarkable passage (verse in the "twelve moods"—I believe it belongs to March): "In losing may loss find itself—in gaining gain be lost." It ends here: "Let loss be its own gain." No doubt a reversal worthy of inner contemplation? Could you write it out for me with the precise words?[196]

Further details about the arrest of the priests and Emil Bock's uncertain fate only gradually reached Gurs over subsequent months: "With heartfelt sadness Toni Schwarz and I have received the news about our friends. Dear one, we send our deepest wishes to them. There is a great community spread over the globe. It is called suffering and strength."[197]

Maria Krehbiel-Darmstädter had not wished to leave Mannheim and emigrate as long as it was still possible to hold the services there.

She did not regret her decision, even in Gurs—and she sensed that after being released The Christian Community priests in Germany would continue their esoteric work and worship in secret, as did indeed happen in many places.

~

Three weeks after Pentecost and two days before the St. John's festival, at the summer solstice, Maria Krehbiel-Darmstädter turned forty-nine at Gurs internment camp. Seven seven-year periods of her life were concluded. Her birthday was an event in Barrack 11 of *ilot* "L"; the celebrations started on the eve of June 22 ("as is usual in big festivals"), and Maria wrote to her siblings to describe what happened:

> There was a beautiful sunset (not grandiose but full of flowing peace) and they brought a table from my hut and set it up outside, arranging a poem on it and many little gifts. And since we spend a lot of time outside while the weather is so blazing hot, are out in the early mornings and the evenings—and even stay out under the starry skies at night (though I am too delicate to do that)—there were lots of people around, and a cheerful mood. Full of innocence. We are rich here in an unusual way and can give each other a handful of grass as a gift if need be. But there were lilies this time, and even a painted cross of lilies with a verse ["Behold, I am with you always, even unto the ends of the Earth"] had found its way to me.[198]

From Christian Community friends in Mannheim and Heidelberg, via Switzerland, Maria received the special gift of a—possibly framed or cased—copy of the *Disputa del Sacramento* by Raphael, a fresco in the Vatican palace in Rome, painted in 1509 to 1510. Maria was extremely moved to receive this: her thank-you letter expresses her sense of connection with these friends and with the sacramental content of the painting:

> My dear ones, it is Sunday—and bright thanks to you for what has flowed out to me again from you. The picture of the *Disputa*, concentrated as if into an "essence" by the small form. Also the

intense garnering of what is great—here like nowhere else.... The whole dome of the heavens serves, indeed, as overflowing and Earth blessing. And the altar! The absent or empty center—here given back. It is a deep, deep reassurance to have this copy of it. So that one enlarges it for oneself and renews one's powers through it;—like cleansing oneself, my dear ones, after long days of bitter isolation. Actually, I imagine the altar as standing on the steps that lead down to the old, deserted cemetery where my parents lie. Behind it lies the land of home: the sky of home, the trees and river—the far towers. And you, you dear ones, so precious to me, more so than anyone I have here. Although—and I say this in gratitude—there are people here with whom the same feeling, the same reverence, yes, the same "knowledge" connects me. But who could pass to me the gifts that you can? Today came like—nourishment. And I feel compelled to gaze upon the sacrament, and the benediction of the white figure of Christ who stands there as if—"eternally in my soul."[199]

She also wrote as follows to Margot Junod about the picture she had been given:

Deeply moved by this new possession. For me it is a gateway, despite the small size of the reproduction—yet its significance is lofty and exemplary. A high portal of meaning. That is often the hardest thing: that you feel the meaning of what happens to gradually fade from you because the new, sustaining element has ceased and become habit, whose paralyzing effect pervades everything. From my early youth my prayer was this: not to lose the strength to be renewed—eternal renewal in the life of spirit. As this becomes visible in the rhythms of the cosmos. The best means is this: to experience the dawn. The quietest time, before anything has begun to stir in the huts; when you walk drunken with sleep, and soundless hearing becomes a "humming in the ears of spirit." The passage, that wonderful one in Faust—do you know it? "Rise ever up to higher realms, grow ever unobserved." It's part of the last choruses, the blessed choirs. What would become of us if renewal did not itself raise us as if on—broad, strong wings? For we ourselves alone: we cannot do it, Margot.[200]

Figure 36: Disputa del Sacramento, *by Raffaelo Santi (detail)*

Maria's thank-you letters for the *Disputa* arose from crisis after "long days of bitter isolation." Although the news she sent near her birthday did not mention it, her situation in Gurs had for weeks become almost unbearable to her amid the oppressive heat and dust of the summer, the cramped conditions in the hut, and her increasing need to withdraw and be alone, to find meditative tranquility. Months later she wrote:

> The desire of my soul, its hunger, is directed endlessly to the tiniest room of my own and time to be *alone*. I pass the rest times here almost in "agitation," because of my great need and trembling enjoyment of any trace of stillness, of any moment when one is permitted to hearken to oneself.[201]

She fell ill again, this time with severe dysentery, which weakened her and made it still harder to endure the adverse conditions. Just one week after her birthday she admitted to Margot Junod:

> My heart is crammed full. Things rage strangely around me. And the brightness at the center of my soul is as though obscured. One wishes to be master. Firm. But then your own nature becomes alien to you. One is a poor, distantly living human being. Separated by a gulf from what is most dear. Sundered from peace. The communal life is tough, and at night I stand long by the door, the sleepers behind me, hearkening to the beating of my own heart—until I take fright at it and crawl back in and home. "Grieving expectancy is your mind's due portion"—this phrase from the Passion ritual expresses the feeling that yearns toward Easter—toward resurrection.[202]

In July for the first time Maria spoke to her friends in Mannheim and Heidelberg of a "sharp homesickness," describing her inner state as follows:

> Summer, which shifts our life outdoors more, into nature, withdraws from us a part of our strength of awareness and restraint. It feels like a kind of melting, connected with the fear of loss. A sense of sacrifice could develop strongly in these weeks. We ought to practice voluntarily relinquishing what is involuntarily torn

from us. Then comes pain at the world's suffering, which likewise reaches like destruction deep into your inner being. And insight into the love that is needed becomes so all-embracing that the vision of the Cross, of the grave, of Resurrection, becomes the sole real activity of your being.

Where do we start to be "ourselves," and where do we cease to be this? . . .

St. John's tide: a time of humility and lament. The seriousness and mission of cosmic worlds. It is the crowning transition we pass through. How wondrous that one's soles burn with sensitivity.

This only as a sign of life and love.

Elsbeth Kasser, the compassionate nurse from *Secours suisse* fell gravely ill during these weeks. To the great joy and relief of many inmates she recovered, but had to return to Switzerland to convalesce.

~

But Maria stayed behind. She went on working as well as she could, and fetched fresh flowers for the wooden board by her bed ("She sought and found flowers everywhere—where others saw, at most, only pain and weeds"[203]). She wrote about the flowers she found in her letters: "Just imagine, a little gentian flower from a nearby meadow has, since yesterday, found a place here and—a voice . . . the blue of hope. Loyalty."[204] At the end of August she admitted hesitatingly in several letters that she was no longer feeling strong ("I admit that I am no longer so energetic. Yes"[205]). It took her much effort to get through the day. On August 26, she wrote to Maria Gnädinger:

We had a changeable summer—the heat is now more or less over; already one has—memories soon—of a year that is past. One is no longer very vigorous. By one's own impetus. Yet the world of spirit brings what is lacking where it finds this to be needed; and it will *itself* sustain, surely, what it wishes to sustain, and needs to. One can add less to this than at the beginning. And often the close proximity of many others, who are nevertheless so similar, is oppressive.

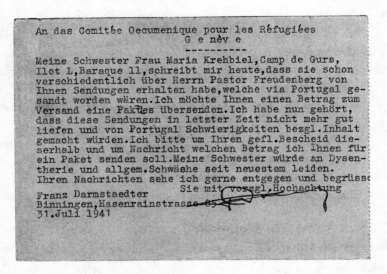

An das Comitée Oecumenique pour les Réfugiées
G e n èv e

Meine Schwester Frau Maria Krehbiel,Camp de Gurs,
Ilot L,Baraque 11,schreibt mir heute,dass sie schon
verschiedentlich über Herrn Pastor Freudenberg von
Ihnen Sendungen erhalten habe,welche via Portugal gesandt worden wären.Ich möchte Ihnen einen Betrag zum
Versand eine Paktes übersenden.Ich habe nun gehört,
dass diese Sendungen in letzter Zeit nicht mehr gut
liefen und von Portugal Schwierigkeiten bezgl.Inhalt
gemacht würden.Ich bitte um Ihren gefl.Bescheid die-
serhalb und um Nachricht welchen Betrag ich Ihnen für
ein Paket senden soll.Meine Schwester würde an Dysen-
therie und allgem.Schwäche seit neuestem leiden.
Ihren Nachrichten sehe ich gerne entgegen und begrüsse
Sie mit vorzgl.Hochachtung
Franz Darmstaedter
Binningen,Hasenrainstrasse 65
31.Juli 1941

*Figure 37: Franz Darmstädter`s letter to the Red Cross,
July 31, 1941, about sending parcels via Portugal*

Harsher or more acerbic phrases now for the first time found their way into her letters—despite her continued efforts to spare her friends and family; words that previously she had always forbidden herself ("everything that is mundane here, deathly, uniform, and never to be accepted in people and existence"[206]). Maria's strength was "largely declining"[207] despite her enormous efforts of will. She was living in a state of huge outer and inner tension: "Weakness and strength: these two opposite aspects of being waylay and besiege us, you can say, because the intermediate stages of 'natural capacity' have been over-stepped," she wrote in a letter at the beginning of September.[208] She told her sister that she had now survived almost a year in Gurs, and interpreted this in positive terms:

It is September now, and soon it will be October. A full year. And in retrospect the grace of this survival seems unfathomable. I have been preserved—here. By powers that are no doubt as tough as diamond, but express cosmic majesty and love as clearly as a mirror.[209]

On the other hand, it was clear both to Maria and her friends that in her present worn-down and exhausted—or self-sacrificed—state she would not have the strength to survive the coming second winter. The "bitter, merciless winter awaits me," she wrote in a letter with no effort at moderation.[210] Elsewhere she wrote baldly:

> The fall is leaving its traces in nature—and in the cosmos. The nights have a different height. Fear creeps up on me. The leaf clings on even when the winds of fall come to release it. We do not yet have the tranquility that the plant can teach us: the new bud grows *after* it, while we tremble in fear.[211]

In this way she left the time of St. John's behind and entered upon Michaelmas.

Her spiritual teacher Rudolf Steiner had given major lecture cycles on the nature of the archangel and time spirit Michael, and, at the very end of his life, written unforgettable essays on this theme that are the most profound and beautiful of his literary works.[212] Steiner had also spoken about Michaelmas in the context of the whole year: about its cosmic significance both for preparation of the Christ event at Christmas, and for each person's journey of soul and body into the season of darkness and cold. The Michael Epistles, whose text he gave to the priests of The Christian Community in September 1923, were among the most important content of the sacramental year—"so that in the light of Earth is not extinguished / the light of Heaven."[213] In the rites of worship, said Steiner, the real presence of the being of Michael could be experienced both in its significance for the sacramental enactment of the consecration *and* for the redemption of the human being.

During the difficult days of September 1941, Maria Krehbiel-Darmstädter would have given anything to have a Michaelmas Act of Consecration celebrated in Gurs. Instead she had to resort to the memories she retained of its rites ("Michaelmas. Going through parts of the Epistles and stirring up mind and soul."[214])—of what she had incorporated and made part of herself, and could bear with her into the future. Referring indirectly to this context she wrote on September 24, 1941, to Margot Junod, who was not close to Anthroposophy and The Christian Community:

> It is remarkable how, amidst a wealth of glorious days and crystalline, sparkling nights, the fall now announces its inexorable approach. And it is good to know that Michael, the regent of our time, is now preparing his festival. In our circle at home this is one of the most important of the whole year's cycle. And the conquering quality, the overcoming and mastering of all that seeks to entangle us from below—bears the greatest power as imaginative content. "He, the messenger of Christ, directs into you the holy will of worlds that upholds human beings."
>
> *Iron* is needed to address bodily weakness; and in the same way it becomes a healing practice in Michael's bold, directing hand. (Power wielded in love.)[215]

~

The barrack physician and the members of the *Assistance Protestante* continued to tend to Maria in her weakened state of health. The physician insisted on a supplement to her rations; and Jeanne Merle d'Aubigné arranged for Maria to eat at the Protestant aid center—to be certain that she did not give her extra food to others. Decades later, in a reflection on this period, Jeanne Merle d'Aubigné wrote:

> I witnessed...how Frau K. distributed among the inmates in her hut all the parcels she received, and I now asked her to eat lunch with us every day. One of us sat beside her and watched what she was doing, for, placing a plate on her knees, she collected what we gave her so as to distribute it later to others.[216]

Maria, who thought very highly of Jeanne Merle d'Aubigné,[217] described the humor of this situation in a letter to Margot Junod in October 1941:

> My health is average. It is terribly kind of the doctor to have again prescribed me Swiss dried milk—a cupful each day; and of the *Assistance Protestante,* in the shape of our manager, the wonderful

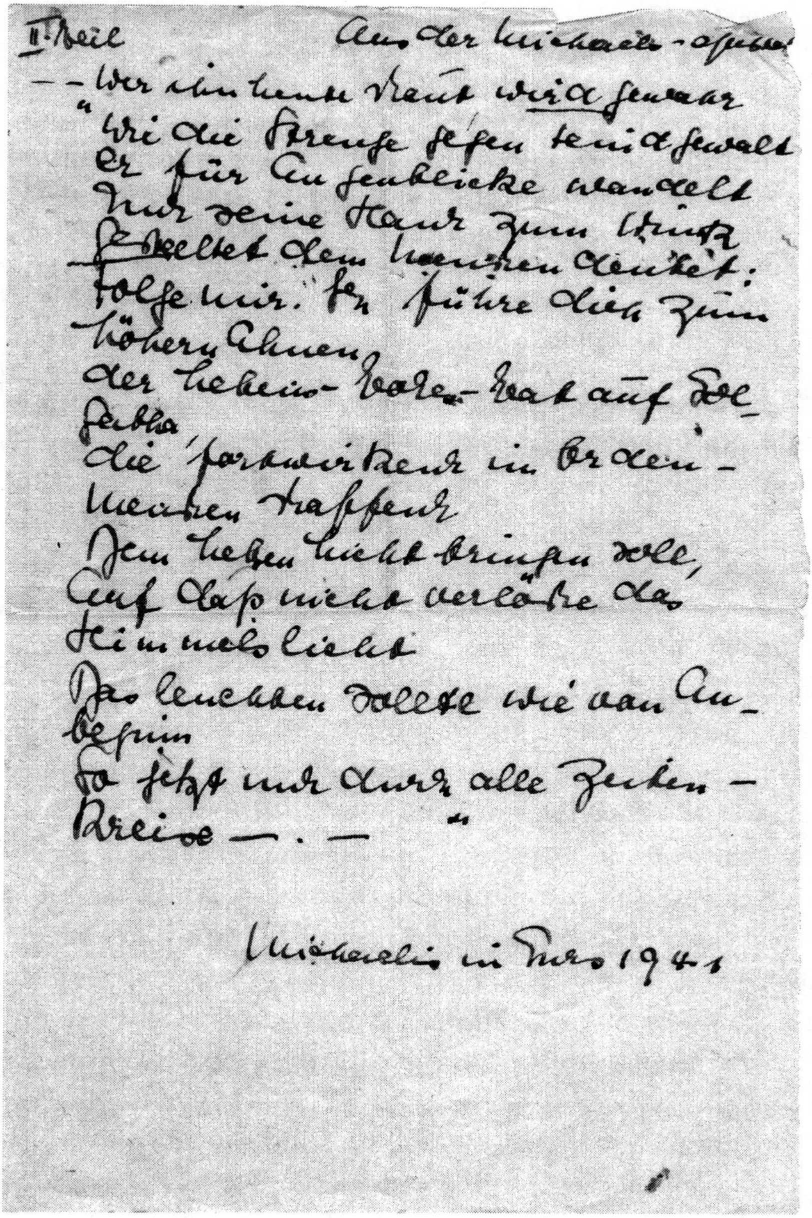
II. Teil Aus der Michaels-Epistel
– – „Wer sich heute Kraft wird gewahr
Wie die Strenge gegen [illegible] Gewalt
Er für Augenblicke wandelt
Nur seine Hand zum Wink
Gestaltet dem Menschen deutet:
Folge mir. Ich führe dich zum
höheren Ahnen
der Lebens-Todes-Tat auf Gol-
gatha
die fortwirkend in Erden-
menschen schaffend
Dem Leben Licht bringen soll,
Auf daß nicht verlösche das
Himmelslicht
Das leuchten sollte wie vom An-
beginn
So jetzt und durch alle Zeiten-
kreise —.— "
Michaelis in Gurs 1941

Figure 38: From the Michael Epistle of The Christian Community; handwritten by Maria Krehbiel-Darmstädter (Gurs, Michaelmas 1941)

Mlle. Merle, to keep a keen eye on my food intake. For a while I was invited to eat with them each evening, where they cook extra food, and where I felt I was feasting in a most select society. Was ashamed to be better treated than my comrades. Yes, but "being away" like this for an hour and a half—to meet other, more cheerful people there than usual—is, despite all my reluctance to allow myself the pleasure, nevertheless a true and delightful boon. When I return home again afterward, I am received almost as a "guest" in my own hut, and am questioned with loving curiosity about the "menu" on which I have dined.[218]

Late summer still prevailed in Gurs, bringing warm October days and nights full of bright stars—as in the first two weeks after their arrival a year before. In mid-October 1941 Maria wrote in a letter to Basel: "We pray that it will remain like this for a while still. Rain is something so bad that one really cannot describe the depth of misery it causes."[219] In view of the unmistakable news that Maria was unwell, her family and Margot Junod, together with the latter's friends in Lyon, Hilda and Jean Lagrange, renewed their efforts to get her temporary sick leave for the forthcoming winter months. In mid-October, Maria was once more confined to her barrack. When she arrived in Gurs a year before, she was already suffering from a persistent kidney complaint with high renal blood pressure and heart problems. The past year had exacerbated this condition ("Health-wise, I have become a bit fragile"). Despite this she still felt ambivalent about the possibility of leaving Gurs, even if only for a short while, and about any return to a "normal" life beyond the confines of the camp ("Will it *still* be possible to live "peacefully" after such an existence?"[220]). She rejected the idea of detaching her individual fate from a common destiny, and followed the events of the world war and all the misery and adversity connected with it with great attention and compassion. Maria Krehbiel-Darmstädter was a highly spiritual, religious individual, a "metaphysician"; and yet, like Simone Weil or Nelly Sachs, she lived in full awareness of historical developments, and incorporated contemporary realities fully and responsibly into her own personal

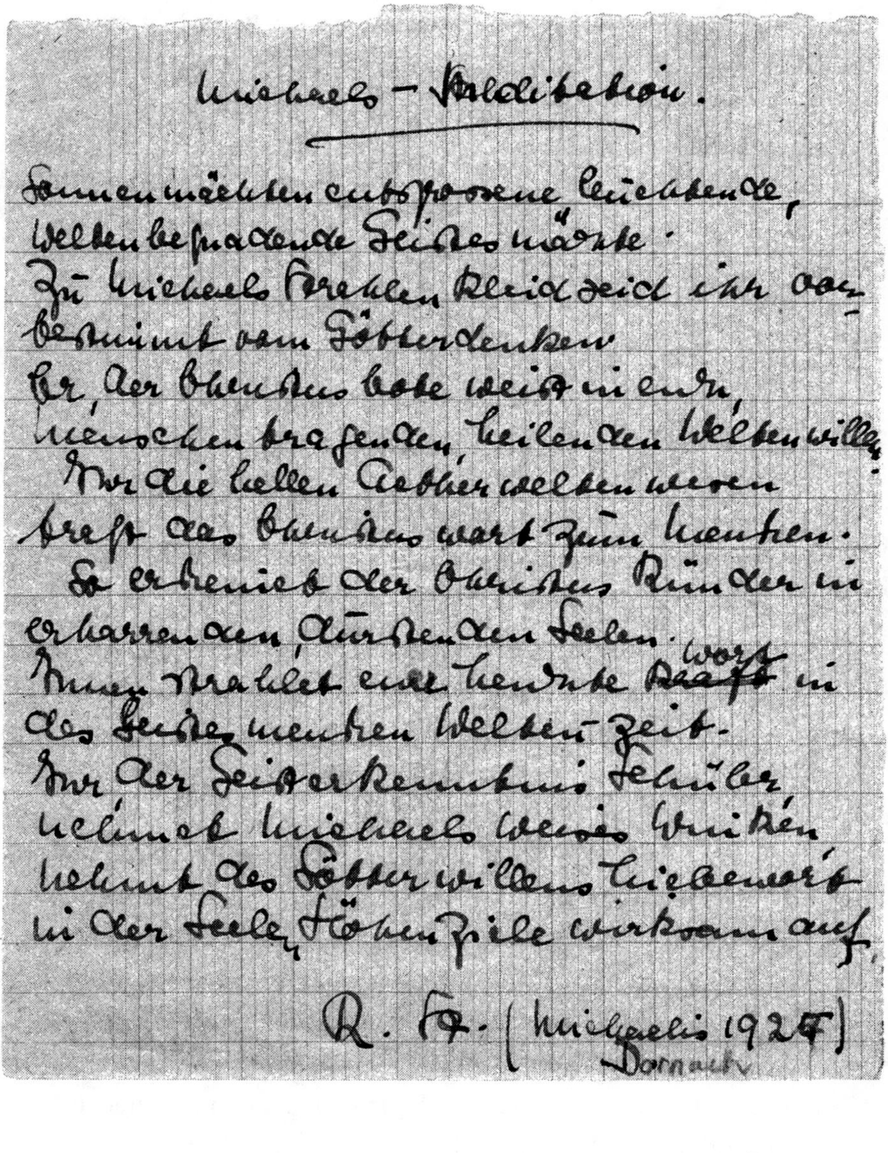

Figure 39: Rudolf Steiner's Michael meditation; handwritten by Maria Krehbiel-Darmstädter (Gurs, Michaelmas 1941)

path. Back in Mannheim she had always kept herself informed of the latest political developments; and likewise did so in Gurs where, via her brother, she received the *Weltwoche* weekly newspaper. She interpreted things in her own way and found her own particular angle on events, but never lost sight of the general situation and the "huge burden of the times." On October 10, 1941, she wrote as follows to Anneliese Herweck:

> Each individual life is so profoundly affected by the current time, its losses and resulting pain.... At night, when I gaze up at the stillness and clarity of the great sky above us, nameless prayers for humanity pass through my heart. How can we wish to lead a "pleasant" life when our brothers are suffering so? We simply belong to all this. To the great suffering.

She believed that there were "worse places of suffering" in the world than at Gurs.[221] This was true: the situation at the Front, and in SS labor, experimentation and death camps was different from Gurs. Many of Maria's fellow inmates, however, would never have agreed with such a comment. They felt that their fate was punishing them most severely: they focused on the scope of their immediate concerns and quarreled with their plight, the injustice they were suffering, the delays in emigration, their own (worse) quarters in the barrack—the fact they were further from the stove than others, and much else besides. Maria refrained from all this, and some in Gurs regarded her almost as a saint, without however understanding the (very different) battles she also had to wage inwardly. In October 1941 she was reading, among other things, Søren Kierkegaard's *At the Foot of the Altar,* which made a great impression on her. It was often impossible for her to read in the barrack, but she deeplyabsorbed Kierkegaard's treatise: "Here indeed one experiences the 'least' as universal," she wrote to Maria Gnädinger, "and here eternal values and inspirations are reality."[222]

~

Figure 40: Søren Kierkegaard, At the Foot of the Altar, *Munich 1923*

Maria's physical condition grew worse. Her heartbeat was weak and irregular ("And then I live entirely from stillness and promise. Listening to my heartbeat that is like a memory of having once lived, of having long endured. And for how long still?"[223]) But she didn't give up, continued to visit the Protestants who were in distress, and gave what she had to give. "Tirelessly she dragged herself around the camp, supporting herself on her "gnome-stick" to offer material and spiritual help to those who no longer had enough strength to endure." (Martha Besag[224]). Heavy downpours of rain had started again, turning the camp into a mud field. Harsh November arrived, with the occasional solace of post from another world. Luise Kayser sent photographs of her new paintings from America, and also of herself, at which Maria wrote to her:

> All my friends praise…your appearance on the photo. There is now a great difference between us, since I am greatly "worn." Have aged irremediably. But—inwardly I feel so much that makes up for this that I do not regret it. You already know how I regard "Gurs."[225]

In the same reply she also wrote: "Certainly we have a strong affinity. Are "sisterly" in an artistic sense, for my pictorial experiences, and their color continually increase in me. They become ever more "imaginative" (in the sense of our terminology)."[226]

It was not often that Maria dropped hints about her inner experiences. But she did, without doubt, perceive "imaginations" in the spiritual-scientific sense of the word.

According to news from Luise Kayser, a permit for immigration to the United States was again with reach at the beginning of November 1941. At the same period Elsbeth Kasser voluntarily returned to the camp, living opposite the *Assistance protestante* and taking up her work again:[227]

> She has returned after a severe illness that she contracted here. Just think: she has returned—in order—to serve. Believe me when I say that no telegram in the world has such power *as this deed*

to convey peace, to ground our hope. Love. It is the profoundest meaning of life and of the way we lead our lives.[228]

Elsbeth Kasser had met Maria Gnädinger in Bern, and brought with her a parcel from her and Christian Community members there, including a hand-dipped Advent candle, honey and a golden star. Deeply moved by this, Maria wrote to her brother in Basel in effusive good spirits:

> Do you know Novalis's words: "He is the star. He is the Sun. Source of eternal life is he. From stone and plant and sea and light, his child's countenance shines bright"? We sang this at our Christmas festival. In the old days. Already Advent's approaching love is shimmering toward me from afar.[229]

If someone like Elsbeth Kasser returned to Gurs voluntarily to bring help and relief, Maria Krehbiel-Darmstädter did not wish to leave either. She was preparing for the forthcoming Advent period, and in a November letter to Maria Gnädinger regretted only that she could not remember all of the Advent Epistles in the Act of Consecration ("I no longer recall them as it would be important for me to do. Yet I also know that you cannot help me here. But please think of me during the service."[230]) She also asked to be sent Emil on Bock's translation of the Gospel of St. Matthew for her work in teaching catechumen pupils at the *Assistance protestante*. After dwelling for a long time on the Old Testament,[231] she had now turned the pupils' attention to the Gospels; "It would be wonderful to have The Sermon on the Mount in our version of it."

It is not known whether—contrary to rules stipulating that the words of the rite and service should only be passed on orally—Maria Gnädinger dared write down the whole text of the Advent Epistles in view of the extreme circumstances, and send them to Maria in Gurs. It is not very likely. She had not done this with the other epistles despite Maria's hints that she would like this. Maria sent no letter thanking her for sending them, and her letter in November made no reference, even a veiled one, to this having been done previously. On

Figure 41: Nursing service at Gurs camp

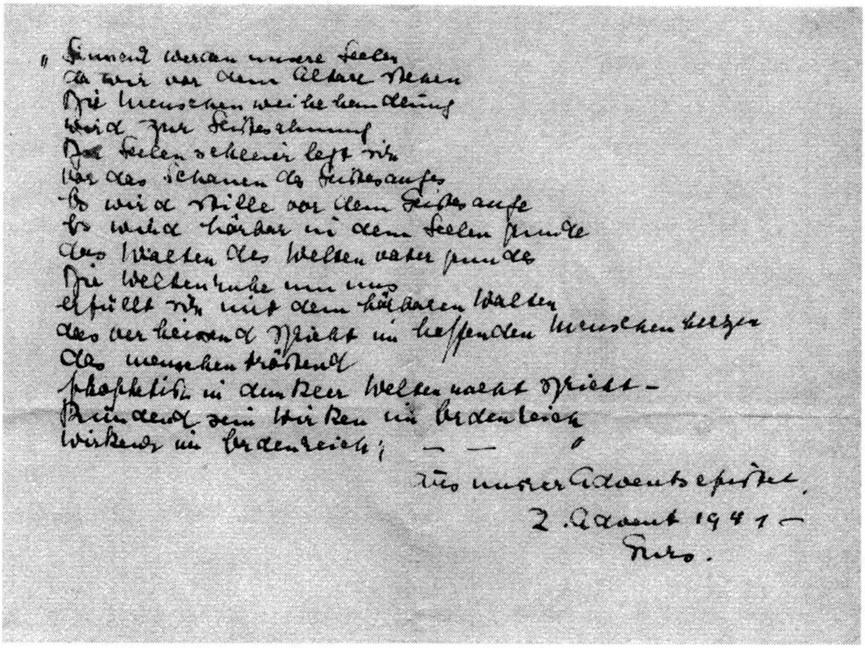

Figure 42: From the Advent Epistle of The Christian Community, handwritten by Maria Krehbiel-Darmstädter (Gurs, December 1941)

the contrary, she wrote: "But I also know that you are unable to help me here." But at Michaelmas, already, Maria had recorded in writing passages of the Epistle that she could recall, sending this to Toni Schwarz. They were preserved as a result (see page 113). She did the same thing again now[232]—in circumstances where she longed for the whole of the Epistle and may possibly have rediscovered it in meditative recall. "You divine power of worlds, / That gleams in the chariot of the Sun / That shines in the bow of colors, / That spans the heavens: / YOU speak within the soul."[233]

For her part Maria also sent stars to Mannheim and Bern, enclosing them in Christmas letters that she wrote well ahead of time (as a precaution?). These letters were full of gratitude for the help and support she had received in previous months. Writing to Maria Gnädinger at the beginning of December, she said:

> Occasionally—in these days, now, that are making their way toward Christmas—one can also sometimes take pleasure in what is good. Can lift one's gaze *only* to the good, just for a moment to something lighter: a stillness, a sense of resting serenity. There is a deep longing in us to bend our knee. To worship. And to be allowed to dwell in this stance in particular. Is this prayer? It is the loving in us that seeks its source. And finds peacefulness. My little star, a little blue butterfly of Advent, brings you greetings, and would be so glad to hang upon your festive tree.[234]

~

But during this time the doctor attending Maria urged her with increasing insistence to take sick leave from the camp. Back in mid-November she had mentioned a possibility of going to stay in Limonest near Lyon with friends of Margot Junod. At the same time however, she again emphasized how problematic she would find this, due to her sense of "betraying" her task in Gurs—the "small yet fitting task" of being the "responsible protestant."[235] She also said it would be difficult to exchange what had become dear and familiar to her for a different and uncertain existence, in which she would "'sacrifice' the accustomed work of an accustomed life."[236] As well as the physician, and her family and friends, Maria's fellow internees also urged her to take this opportunity at any cost. She later recollected:

> And despite all their regret, my friends [in the camp] were ungrudgingly keen to release me. They told me I would better be able to serve them if I regained my strength, and they said many other loving things. All I could see, though, was that I would be leaving them—almost all of them—to their plight. And would be doing so during the winter when—as lies in the very nature of suffering—harsher trials await them. And I had to ask myself: who among them would I still find there on my return?[237]

During the second week of December 1941, she received news that she had been granted a three-month *"permission de santé."* After great inner struggles she decided to accept this, but to delay her leave until the period between Christmas and New Year, after communal Christmas celebrations in the camp. She explained her reasons for this in a letter to Margot Junod:

> Something of greatness lies in what "has been" here—and also in what—after me—must remain here. But turning my gaze back to this asks not sorrow alone—nor just gratitude—
> What *exists* here signifies a portion of the human condition that is full of insight. Thus full of grace and truth. We wish only to remain equal to this, by not forgetting—when released—and by not casting it behind us. Instead by keeping a kind of essential faith with it in our further life.[238]

In another letter, to Maria Gnädinger, she wrote:

> I am very calm, and take things as they come. You see, the general and universal predominates over the personal to such an extent that one thinks "of oneself," my dear ones, as only the "reagent" or facilitator.[239]

Her departure was complicated. She had to leave behind many desperate, weak people who needed help, not knowing if she would see them again and how they would fare in the intervening period. She had meant a great deal to these people, had given them a great deal, and was now withdrawing. All those who liked her and valued her urged her to go. Nevertheless a chasm opened between her and those who would remain in Gurs. Maria made preparations for departure while the others did not. Months later she recollected in a letter:

> My departure...greatly dismayed me, my withdrawal from these friends. (As when an airplane lifts off, or a ship draws out of the harbour.) Spaces open up that are greater than just the distance itself. For the "different" experience one has and—scarcely has the power to communicate—alone gives rise to a sense of unspeakable otherness, where yesterday comradeship still existed and an equal state.[240]

Her friend Martha Besag eventually replaced her in the role of "responsible." Maria Krehbiel-Darmstädter took her farewell from everyone, and also from the camp as such:

> One has nothing more, after all, than this *home of ours, Gurs.* And despite all privation: this ground of Earth and suffering that has become our own. The enormous consecration of this far-flung, harsh island of life. It partakes of the quality Goya painted: hard, shrill and flaming with the fervor of annunciation. As farewell gift I received a wonderful, small color portfolio of the works of this, "our compatriot." The great works of art arose by measuring themselves against life's severity.
>
> We had winter days full of cold and brilliance. Now it is raining again, dripping. So that it is easier to leave.[241]

On December 24 at 5 p.m., the Christmas celebration was held at the Assistance Protestante. Five days later Maria Krehbiel-Darmstädter left Gurs camp for three months' sick leave. She died a year-and-a-quarter later without ever returning.

~

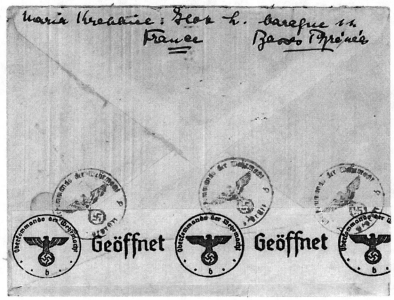

*Figure 43: The envelope of Maria Krehbiel-Darmstädter's letter
to Rudolf Zeitler, sent from Gurs on December 8, 1941;
the official stamp on the back says "Opened."*

Figure 44: Maria Krehbiel-Darmstädter. January 1942

Limonest

*"In sacrifice let the flame of being-creating love arise.
And let the flame kindle timeless existence,
so that good may endure."*

*"Our existence is still greedy for temporality, you can say, although
we are continually trying to cast it off and acquire the habit of
eternity. But this cannot be compelled; in days of danger, our torment is too earthly."* (September 7, 1942)

On December 29, 1941, after fourteen months of imprisonment,
Maria Krehbiel-Darmstädter traveled by bus and train via
Pau and Toulouse to Lyon. On this journey she was already writing
cards to friends in Gurs and those she had been caring for. It was a
long, difficult, unfamiliar journey—her whole situation had suddenly
changed, both inwardly and outwardly: "Traveling across half the
country, my unaccustomed eyes suddenly taking in both magnificent
and dazzling sights."[242]

On December 30, the penultimate day of the old year, she arrived
at Lyon station where she was met by Margot Junod's friend, thirty-
four-year-old Belgian Hilda Lagrange. Maria was wearing a black,
woolen cape. Hilda Lagrange later described their walk home together:
"Although Lyon had its fair share of odd figures, people were staring
out of passing trams, and turning round to look. How skinny she
was—it reminded me of Ghandi or the dying people in Delacroix."[243]
At the Lagrange's flat Maria initially seemed shy, uncertain, fragile

and exhausted—and started to cry when she saw a dish of butter on the table. Hilda Lagrange wrote in her diary:

> What she has told me, little by little, of her life and that of her companions there, is terrible. And my flowers, my books, the soft light of a table lamp, a piece of pastry, moves her to tears. All this loveliness, cleanness, this comfort—modest but incredible to her, convulses her, and me equally. I have noticed her avoiding putting her foot on the carpet as if this seemed frivolous to her. After the packed earth or the mud of Gurs that penetrates everywhere, she cannot accustom herself to a homely atmosphere with its furniture, curtains, chair covers—and above all to a room that may contain no more than two people at a time.[244]

In an earlier letter, Maria had written:

> In our far-flung altitude we are scarcely any longer capable of regarding quite naturally what is entirely natural. It is as if we "come from the country." But then each small detail is experienced with a convulsive impact and—one would like to offer it up on one's knees at the altar.[245]

A day after her arrival, on December 31, she wrote to Toni Schwarz, "At first, in shocked awe, I did not trust myself to pick up a spoon." At the Lagrange's flat Maria ate the paltry bread she had brought with her from Gurs—"my bread" as she called it—and wrote to Toni about the farewell gifts she had received: "I am distressed at all I took away with me, which I experience now as having deprived you of." At the same time she stressed:

> Believe me, everything, but really each and every thing I experience here I give to my people there [in Gurs]—that is, I think "we." And speak to them of it. But not all the time. For this is something people cannot endure.

Despite the kindness and warmth of Hilda and Jean Lagrange, Maria said that she felt entirely alone after arriving in Lyon, and in fact already on her journey there: in a "great, melancholy void"[246] without her companions of destiny, the community of affliction in the

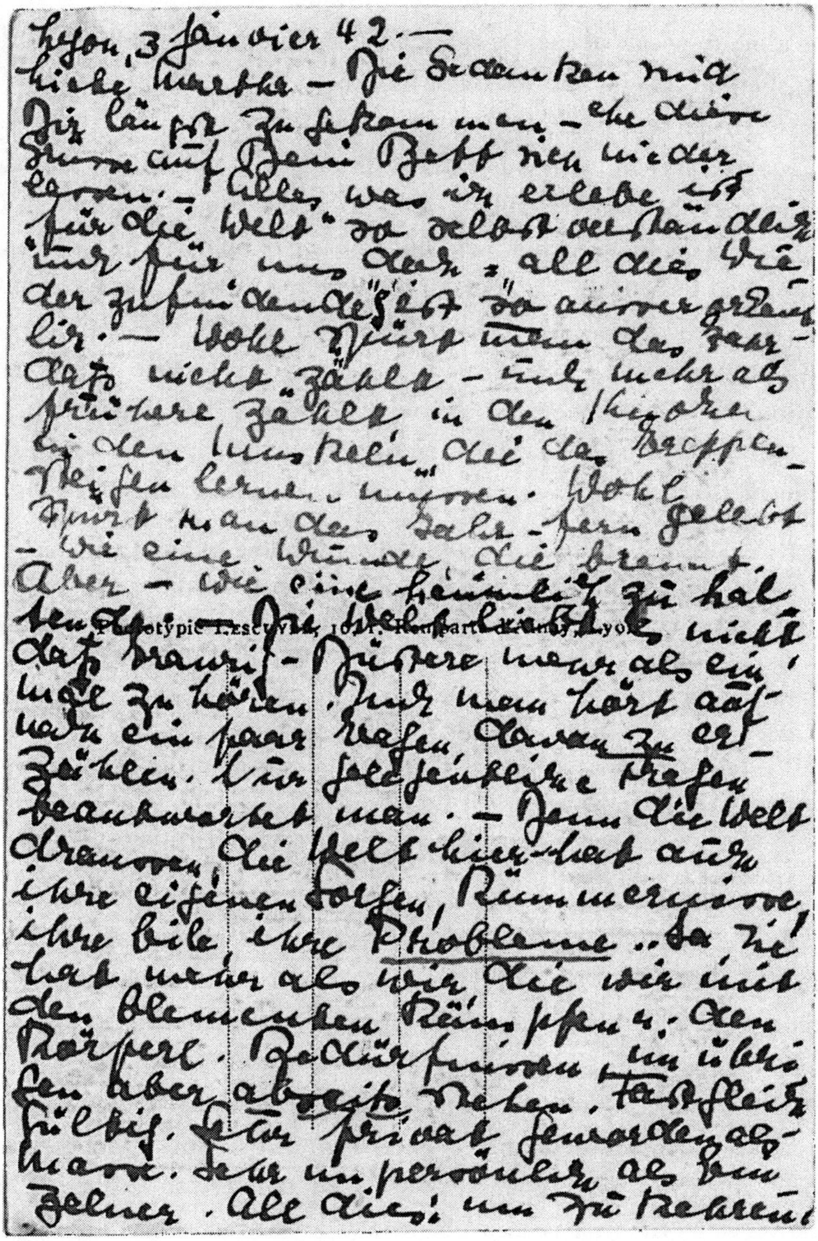

Figure 45: Letter to Martha Besag, January 3, 1941 (first page)

"earned home" of Gurs.[247] Only to a limited extent did she wish, or was able, to speak of the life there,[248] and remained in another world, one she had left behind fourteen months before, and into which no simple return was possible.

Maria's stay in Lyon was extended to eight days until her transfer to Limonest became possible. The Lagranges rented a hotel room so that Maria could be on her own, but saw her regularly. The room was simple and beautiful: "Gentlest of all were the flowers that welcomed me."[249] Nevertheless, Maria slept little and poorly. The nights were difficult, plagued by shame, pain, illness and memories of her companions in Gurs, in their barrack without proper beds or warmth.

Nor was it easy for her to take the necessary trips into town. On January 3, 1942, Maria wrote to Martha Besag and Margot Junod:

> Discharged again into the world! The climbing of steps that one can no longer manage. Getting along on the sidewalk and paying attention in the hum of the big city. Speech in just *one* language, the fact of having left one's friends behind—and being forsaken by them. For this utter difference inevitably means a rapidly increasing separation.
>
> Suddenly you see yourself in the mirror of a big shop window—see yourself as "apparition."
>
> People tell me I am healthy and can live again as others do. But I cannot yet do this.

At the age of forty-nine, she found herself in the city of Lyon "among worldly people and daily life,"[250] and could no longer feel at home in it. Her life in Gurs, under quite different conditions, had alienated her from all this.

In the following weeks and months, in her letters to friends, Maria Krehbiel-Darmstädter reflected on the impact of this sudden transition and her resulting experiences—and on the need to rediscover herself anew. In the first week of February, long after coming to stay in Limonest, she put all this in context in a letter to Margot Junod:

> In Gurs things were simpler inasmuch as one was *compelled* "simply" to go along with the course of the day. And though each

LYON — Panorama sur la Saône

Figure 46: Lyon, view of the Saône; postcard
from Maria Krehbiel-Darmstädter, January 3, 1942

person wore his own soul garment, with its distinctive color and cut, we were still one community. And to become a "separate individual" again, to *exist* responsibly and individually, signifies a *great amount of work*—that has to move forward. Ah no, one cannot reconnect with what used to be. Nothing is more wondrous—and more incomprehensible almost, than holding today up to compare it with a previous time—though only a few years ago. The idea of reincarnation, formed in the context of my worldview, is one that shifts now from the pure, spiritual, spatial realm into a *temporal* one. And so I am astonishing to myself in the new "entelechy" of my existence here.[251]

In another letter, in which she detailed the contents of a letter that had gone missing, which was likewise preoccupied with the move from Gurs to Lyon, she characterized the new phase of her biography as follows:

I wrote to you about the first, difficult period, the extraordinary experience of trying to find my way back into the world, and almost into *life*. You see there [in Gurs] one is already across the threshold...in a very real sense. Almost surrendered to the final sacrifice. And without using one's "feet" since they would cling too strongly to the ground, would grasp the losses too painfully— one "floats" above the things of the world. And then—one departs. Becomes a "civilian" again. Is once again the supposed person on one's ID papers. And individual again. And—has *one's own* destiny. This makes for extraordinarily strange moments of tension and weakness.[252]

~

At the beginning of the second week in January 1942, Hilda and Jean Lagrange brought Maria Krehbiel-Darmstädter to Limonest, a village of a little more than a thousand inhabitants nestling in a beautiful landscape. Hilda Lagrange wrote in her diary of the friendly village "sitting high up on its mountain peak, with all its light and gentleness, where she [Maria] will no doubt find peace and happiness—and will be reborn."[253] In her room in Limonest,

where Maria was to live initially for three months, Hilda Lagrange
had again placed flowers:

> I was given more than the bare essentials. The superfluous. (Surplus
> love, as R.S. [Rudolf Steiner] calls it, and which he says is necessary
> to disempower the adversary forces in the world.) In the middle of
> winter I was given fine, red roses.[254]

The boarding house where the Lagranges had arranged accommodation and meals for Maria Krehbiel-Darmstädter was called *"Le
vieux logis"* and was run by a Swiss couple. Elderly people lived there
mostly, in the simplest circumstances: food was scant and the heat-
ing functioned poorly. To begin with it was very cold. Maria had to
report to the police every three days.

She found the new beginning difficult: "I have only strangers
here," she wrote to Margot Junod on January 13, 1942, just one week
after moving. She dreamed of Rudolf Steiner, Friedrich Rittelmeyer
and Friedrich Doldinger—and spent her first few days writing letters to Gurs (and packing up parcels to send there)—the only help
she now still felt herself capable of giving those she had left behind
("that I can faithfully come visiting many people, go on accompanying them and ask them about their life."[255]) She was pleased at the
"freedom of full correspondence,"[256] since in Gurs only one letter a
day had been allowed. News from Gurs soon arrived copiously at
the *vieux logis* and Maria was kept informed of everything that happened in the camp.

~

The Lagranges often came to visit Maria at the weekend ("we have
formed a great attachment to one another"[257]). Gradually Maria grew
less tense, though her weakness and exhaustion did not improve—"I
had forgotten that one can stay lying down when one is tired. I no longer knew that I was so terribly tired."[258] There was no local physician
available to treat her kidney disease or cardiac insufficiency; Limonest
did not even have a pharmacy.

In her quiet room Maria started reading again, also short stories and novels that—in contrast to her former habits—she had refused to read in Gurs ("Books that were novelistic or dreamlike were scarcely endurable for us").[259] Her desk was in front of the window, next to the flowers. After a few weeks in Limonest she wrote to her brother's family:

> And the gratitude for each day, each *hour* of quiet behind protected walls, for an actual, laid *table*, for sitting *upright*, for a *window*, a bed that does not cause pain every time you turn over in it: ah, do you know what kind of color this gratitude has? How it blossoms—and how one opens one's hands before this delicate gift from God, oh, in the hope that it may last a *little while* longer. And that new harshness will not break it asunder. For who, who knows anything?[260]

Margot Junod made efforts to fetch Maria to Switzerland. There were only very limited opportunities for immigration, but it was, just, possible. Her brother's family was residing in Basel and owned property, and Maria was physically ill and needed help. On January 11, 1942, soon after bringing her to Limonest, Margot Junod wrote to Father Freudenberg in Geneva and asked him for support. She told him that, from Switzerland, Maria might be able to continue her work on behalf of the Gurs inmates, and that she had only reluctantly agreed to sick leave in Limonest, and would probably only consent to this next step on this condition:

> In my view there is only one possibility of saving her, and that is to employ her in working for the people in Gurs.... Frau Krehbiel speaks several languages, and has a special gift for expressing herself. I can imagine that she might achieve a great deal of good for Gurs, having spent 15 months there. To throw herself completely into work on behalf of the Gurs camp would give her life some meaning once more.[261]

Adolf Freudenberg would have greatly valued such help; but he also knew how hard it would be to bring Maria to Switzerland from

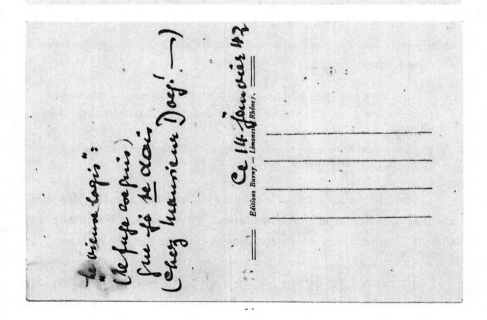

Figure 47: Limonest, vieux logis (old staging post);
postcard from Maria Krehbiel-Darmstädter

her "vacation" imprisonment in France without permission from the German authorities and without a legal entry visa.

~

On January 23, 1942, Maria Krehbiel-Daremstaedter wrote in a letter:

> After three weeks now, life has started to be more ordered again and my backward-turned (unwell?) focus, which revolved around Gurs all the time, has grown calmer. There is no sense of contentment yet, for I have only just embarked on a new experience. But now I am pacified somewhat, as if by a medicine.

She was seeking a new equilibrium appropriate to her situation—but at the same time one appropriate to the state of the world. She simply could not consider withdrawing into the personal and private realm as "an individually rescued" person in dire times. When her brother wrote to her from Basel to say that his house was cold and the family were huddling round a single stove, she answered determinedly and not without severity:

> When I hear how you huddle round your little stove and are united there, I am glad. "Comfort" in the old sense, and in these terrible, world-shattering times, would really be an outrage. No. The capacity for harmony resides only in sacrifice and spirit-borne renunciation.[262]

Maria often pondered on her lonely situation and on the "freedom" she had acquired after much hesitancy. While she was not in any way free in Limonest, her scope for movement was greatly increased. In Lyon quite recently—almost without any transition from Gurs—she had experienced the urban life of a modern, self-aware individual, with its random opportunities. In Limonest she was once more in a position to determine the course of her day, alone and without the direct tasks and obligations of a social context. To Margot Junod she wrote about this situation, and about the way she came to terms with it—as she had to; and, with good reason, cited what the poet Hölderlin had written when his "homeless" period had just begun:

In the camp things were "easy" in a sense since removed from any need for decision; courageous endurance was all that was required of us. I knew immediately that "becoming a responsible individual" again, being "single and isolated" and "detached" from my surroundings, having to structure each day and every hour, was a freedom fraught with anxiety. "To go wherever you like"—this inherently human capacity is also a huge demand.[263]

In a letter to Maria Gnädinger on January 31, she described Gurs as a *"prison de Dieu"* and said of her new freedom: "To stand fully in the here and now we have to experience this freedom as *liberté de Dieu*. As strong and elevated as that. One knows so well that a balance is required. And the first weeks pass between attempts and failures."

As ever, a sense of shame made it difficult for her to accept the pleasant and positive aspects of her new situation without scruples. Something in her resisted any kind of return to normal, middle-class life—which she had already gradually begun to distance herself from before Gurs, but had not entirely forsaken. "Gurs" was a long, involuntary practice of renunciation, but one she herself ultimately embraced and affirmed: not, though as masochism, asceticism and chastisement but as a way of overcoming the world of personal needs, and living out of the essential power of the spirit. She now found it very hard indeed to participate in anything "agreeable"; but at the same time she was sufficiently psychologically aware and self-critical to acknowledge the narrow psychological strictures into which she had—willingly or otherwise—maneuvered herself. On February 16, 1942, she wrote about this to Margot Junod:

> There is such a—well let's call it—perfection—in the situation I find myself in today, which is scarcely "bearable" for my restricted and crushed soul, because there is so much breadth in it...release...because it is so "large"*—and so pure. But I myself am still so cowering, anxious and diffident. "Taking" is something that has to be learned. So that it is not theft. And—I am seri-

---

* She uses the English word here. —Tr.

ous, believe me: freedom of soul is something I lost down there [in Gurs]. Either I hesitate before the good or instead "secretly" clutch it to me, "when no one's looking." Exactly, yes exactly like a small animal, a poor little fox perhaps whose cage has been opened wide. But now, after the shyest, most bashful "sniffing about," it finally allows itself to "take." I'm thinking here very specifically of all beauty, agreeableness, gifts, "nourishment." A definite imbalance has arisen in my soul.

In another passage in the same letter she went on:

You see, there is nothing left for me to wish for: except continuance... eternal human anguish. So new after the other state whose (unacknowledged) hope yearned only for "an end." Perhaps I shouldn't think so much, yet "it" thinks in me—that is, the psyche that anchors itself in the body in accusatory comparisons, whose yearning for enjoyment is a fact and almost reaches the moral domain as—anguish. Can you understand this?

Margot Junod tried to understand—but to grasp and reexperience this all fully from the perspective of her life in Lausanne was not possible. Maria Krehbiel-Darmstädter was a special, unusual and rare human being in her goals and values, her stances, thoughts and sensitivities. Moreover, her profound experiences at Gurs had created a very unusual sensibility in her that was very hard to communicate to others.

Months later, Maria recollected the difficulties she had experienced in settling into life in Limonest:

I neither wished nor was able to give myself up to unconstrained pleasure. Also through fear that I would have to "atone" for my relief. And that losing the habit of strain would leave me unprepared when it was required again, when I returned to it. But ultimately one learns to find peace, and to sleep even in the midst of uncertainty.[264]

~

Figure 48: Interior of a barrack with a man reading,
by Julius C. Turner (Gurs 1941)

Every day Maria sent to Gurs two or three long, carefully conceived letters that were precisely attuned to each recipient—to the
Protestants she had been helping to care for, to her friends and various people whose affliction she received news of. This "letter work"
as concentrated focus on those she kept in her thoughts, filled a
great part of her day in Limonest. But even in this endeavor she
sometimes felt completely helpless: "In the meantime, I have continued with my extensive letter writing, but do not see how *I* can
help anyone since I myself am so plagued by my own inner turbu-
lence."[265] She continued to correspond with Fathers Toureille and
Freudenberg, but was not at ease with herself now—far less so than
at Gurs. Back then she had been ready to sacrifice herself, and it was
far harder to live at one remove, as a contemporary who knew what
was happening and yet had been spared. The prisoners in Gurs were
the people closest to her: "At least we will know forever the meaning of comradeship, loyalty, belonging. It is like a monastic order to
which you belong, whose insignia you must wear; and feel yourself
to be inscribed or incised with it, and *configured* differently than
before" she wrote to Klare Levis-Heinsheimer, who had also been
given leave of absence from Gurs.[266]

Maria did not attend services in the Catholic church in Limonest
village: she felt herself out of place here. But in many letters she mentioned the lamb above the church portal ("Our little church here is
vigorous and unadorned. Less than a hundred years old.... Lacking
any sculptural decorations except for its sole symbol, a lamb: the
whole solid building gathered round this delicate, weak Easter lamb!
So much wisdom in this wordless eloquence. It tells us to hope, tells
us to have faith."[267]) From the friends in Mannheim and Heidelberg
she received further texts by Kierkegaard, including a selection of
his *Journals of Day and Night,* which she read intently and inwardly
affirmed ("enormously serious and for me an appeal to conscience,
one I need so as not to lapse into the extreme of 'tranquility enjoyed'
but instead to reach an active, conscious, oh, *fulfilled* tranquility."[268])
A young nun from a Catholic order, who was caring for a gravely ill

lady staying in the guesthouse, befriended Maria. She often came to talk to her in her room:

> A *mère* of the very remarkable order of the *Soeurs Auxiliatrices du Purgatoire,* who devote their lives to calling to mind, in prayer, souls passing through purgatory, and hold the requiem mass every day and so forth—Their habit is really mourning clothes as worn a hundred years ago, looking strangely beautiful and grave.[269]

Maria felt a strong affinity with the path and goal of spiritual aid offered by these *Soeurs Auxiliatrices du Purgatoire,* something Rudolf Steiner had reformulated in more contemporary form, dispensing with the outward garb of mourning.[270] Maria was very struck by this nun's spirituality and moral bearing. She borrowed books and journals about the order from her, and about "several especially outstanding (and extraordinary) figures who belonged to it."[271]

Her "own" journal, the Dornach weekly *Das Goetheanum—* which, since it was published in Switzerland, was not prohibited by the Nazis—was sent to her at the *vieux logis* direct from Dornach in mid-February 1942. Her brother Franz Darmstädter had responded to her plea to send an issue of this, and ordered her a whole subscription from Paul Bühler, whom Maria also knew personally. "I can't believe that I am to receive this again," she wrote to Maria Gnädinger on February 18 when the package arrived[272] containing all the issues that had appeared since the beginning of January, and a picture of the Goetheanum building. The same day she wrote joyfully to Toni Schwarz:

> Ah, Toni! I should have liked to spread a white cloth on which to lay this treasure. And in the evening it was done like this: a fresh mimosa twig next to the slender wax candle. The doctor's picture, though, on the first one I opened—*his* journal; its paper fine, smooth and shining—I am sure you share with me an inmost sense of this great new joy, exceeding "all that has preceded it."[273]

Two weeks later she sent a second thank-you letter to her brother and his family:

Figure 49: Rudolf Steiner

Das Goetheanum

Wochenschrift für Anthroposophie

mit Beilage

21. Jahrgang, Nr. 7   Redaktion: Albert Steffen in Dornach (Schweiz).   15. Februar 1942

Druck und Expedition: Buchdruckerei Emil Birkhäuser & Cie. A. G., Basel, Elisabethenstrasse 15
Jeder Nachdruck und Uebersetzung ohne Erlaubnis nicht gestattet. — Copyright 1942 by Allgemeine Anthroposophische Gesellschaft, Dornach (Schweiz). — Für unverlangte Manuskripte kann keine Gewähr übernommen werden. Redaktionsschluss Sonntag. — Jeder Autor ist für den Inhalt seines Beitrages selbst verantwortlich.

Administration (Abonnements, Inserate etc.) Dornach (Schweiz), Goetheanum — Telephon 6 2822, Dornach — Postcheck V 5819 Basel.

INHALT:

Rudolf Steiner: Von Jesus zu Christus.
Ernst Uehli: Johann Heinrich Füssli-Ausstellung.
Albert Steffen: Gedicht.
Leopold van der Pals: Otto Fränkl-Lundborg „Reise mit der ewigen Geliebten."
Bilder von der Aufführung „Fahrt ins andere Land".
Literarische Überschau.

Von Jesus zu Christus

Vortrag*) von Dr. *R. Steiner*, gehalten in Hamburg
am 15. November 1913

Es ist ein Thema von tief einschneidender Bedeutung für das Geistesleben der Gegenwart, welches den Gegenstand der heutigen Betrachtung bilden soll, und zwar soll dieses Thema besprochen werden von dem Gesichtspunkte aus, von dem ich über verschiedene Fragen des Geisteslebens auch hier in dieser Stadt schon öfter sprechen durfte. Es ist von unsern Freunden gerade dieses Thema gewünscht worden. Im allgemeinen ist es von dem Gesichtspunkte der Geisteswissenschaft aus nicht leicht, über ein solch spezielles, tief bedeutsames Thema zu sprechen, weil dabei die Voraussetzung gemacht werden muss, dass die verehrten Zuhörer an manches sich erinnern, was in andern Vorträgen gesagt worden ist über die Grundlagen jener Wissenschaft, die hier gemeint ist. Diese Geisteswissenschaft

*) Vom Vortragenden nicht durchgesehene Nachschrift. Nachdruck verboten.

ist keineswegs etwas, was in der Gegenwart schon in weiteren Kreisen anerkannt oder irgendwie beliebt wäre. Im Gegenteil, diese Wissenschaft ist etwas, wovon man sagen kann, dass sie wohl noch zu den unbeliebtesten und unverstandensten Geistesströmungen der Gegenwart gehört, und insbesondere bei einem Thema, wie dem heutigen, kommen solche missverständlichen Auffassungen ganz besonders in Betracht; denn allzusehr ist noch die Meinung verbreitet, dass die Geisteswissenschaft eingreifen könnte in dieses oder jenes religiöse Bekenntnis, in das, was gerade vom Gesichtspunkte eines religiösen Bekenntnisses wert und teuer dieser oder jener Seele sein könnte. Das ist aber durchaus nicht der Fall, wie sich zeigen kann für den, der tiefer in die geisteswissenschaftliche Forschung sich einlassen will. Die Geisteswissenschaft will eine Wissenschaft sein, in einem gewissen Sinne die Fortsetzung dessen, was seit drei bis vier Jahrhunderten als die naturwissenschaftliche Denkungsweise in die menschliche Entwicklung eingelaufen ist. Sie muss nur das, was naturwissenschaftliche Denkungsweise ist, in anderer Weise von der Menschenseele heraus fruchtbar machen, als die Naturwissenschaft selber ihre Forschungsmethode fruchtbar machen kann. Denn diese Geisteswissenschaft hat es ja zu tun nicht mit irgend etwas, das durch die äusseren Sinne wahrzunehmen ist, sondern hat es zu tun mit dem, was mit der Welt des Geistigen. Nahe liegt es daher, auch die Fragen, welche auf das geistige Leben der Menschenseele sich beziehen, von diesem geisteswissenschaftlichen Standpunkte aus zu betrachten. Und es gibt gewiss für zahlreiche Seelen der Gegenwart keine Frage, welche im Geistesleben der Menschheit so wichtig sein könnte, wie die Frage, die das heutige Thema einschliesst: die Frage nach dem Christus Jesus.

49

Figure 50: Das Goetheanum, *the weekly journal
for Anthroposophy, February 15, 1942*

I cannot tell you how grateful I am for the journal. When the first ones arrived (the whole package of them, from January 6 on) I did not know how to contain my inner jubilation, and sense of riches. I would have liked to spread a white cloth and offer them up, these pages, as if on an altar. I shall never forget that you gave me *this* gift.[274]

From mid-February, the journal arrived in Limonest every Monday and was a "great, eagerly awaited highlight of the week."[275] When it arrived a few days late on one occasion, Maria described her annoyance at this as her "wonderful and sustaining dependency" on this weekly post—"Such a blessing from far away, linking the past with the present and so important in our poor life that has grown so seamless and uniform."[276] At her request, or of his own volition, her brother sent further items—the *Neue Zuercher Zeitung* and *Weltwoche* newspapers, but also a reproduction of the Dornach statue of Christ standing between adversary powers, which she had requested.

~

At the end of March 1942, shortly before Easter, her sick leave was to end, and Maria was due to return to Gurs. It was possible to extend her stay with a doctor's note, and Maria was by no means sure that her physical strength was ready to cope with Gurs. She still lived in a kind of intermediate state between here and there. All her friends and relatives were urging her to take further sick leave or even to escape. But she kept trying to reassure them, in all sorts of ways, that Gurs should not be seen only in a negative light. On February 23, she wrote to Maria Gnädinger in Bern:

> There is also a real attachment or loyalty that keeps us there. In a shared culture, with care from the best people in the *Assistance Protestante,* we Protestants in particular have a great deal of reason to be truly and lastingly thankful. Gurs is like an epitome of the desperate international situation. And therefore most love flows toward it from everywhere in the world. One senses this *so*

tangibly. Gurs as epitome. The strange landscape—the name. To begin with I heard the word abyss in it—*le gouffre*. But this also means "source," a spring of insight, a proving of the truth of the Word, giving rise to a spring from which flows the water of life, in close proximity to the abyss, and to death even. I preserve "Gurs" in me. Love. Without being tormented any longer by it as I was to begin with. I hope to be able to stay on here, but at the same time am gathering my strength so as not to be destroyed by a return there. Our life demands that we are always both "at home" and yet also "in a strange land." Is there really such a thing as to feel oneself truly rooted, protected in—a home?

At the end of February, she received a further gift from Basel— her brother sent her a vivid monograph on the painter Matthias Grünewald by Martin Hürlimann, published in 1939 by Atlantis Verlag in Berlin and Zürich. Maria contemplated the Grünewald pictures, especially the plates of the Isenheim altar, throughout the following weeks leading up to Easter: "We must inevitably regard this spring as something that raises us from the grave. Like Lazarus we have lain in the bonds of renunciation. And like Lazarus–John we must be reborn to deeper understanding and new tasks."[277]

Maria finally agreed to the Lagrange's efforts to extend her "sick leave," and once more consulted a physician in Lyon. The results of tests showed her to be suffering from a severe condition with advanced kidney disease and extremely high blood pressure, protein in the urine and a rapid, arrhythmic pulse ("my heart is like a butterfly—now fluttering, now quite still, and my days and nights are tormented by related ills"[278]). Despite being quartered at *le vieux logis* her physical state had worsened, and she knew she would not be able to survive conditions in Gurs. In her room, and during short walks in Limonest, in the daily rhythm she established for herself, she managed to cope, but how would she survive the barrack in the coming hot summer? She was overwhelmed by anxiety and fear of an intensity previously unknown to her, a sense of disquiet and state of inner tension whose torment only grew worse as February and March passed. She wavered between one extreme and the other, and on March 2 wrote to her brother:

> Really every single person [in Gurs] is needy and at the end of their strength. But—that is not what ultimately decides things. Cycles of time keep the circle closed. It is oddly difficult to free oneself from this circle—doubly difficult to place oneself back into it. It ought to be like a homecoming since one was so connected with the way of life there, with the people and the place. But looking at it from without, and free again, and blessed with the beauty of life, of nature—the silence—fear comes to wrap one in its grievous carapace. And because of this one loses the immediacy of these weeks. And grows cowardly. Surely every hour is a part of life; rescued unrepeatably—a treasure. Rescued or also—lost.

In the same letter she continues:

> And so again, and more than ever, I was able (unscathed) to gladly praise the power that could so often persuade me of the truth of the phrase "Fear not." So why, always, repeatedly—fear? Fear. Fear. It is the worst, most fatal and malicious of all evils. Time triumphs in it. I can also tell you that the deepest roots of misery— and of all illness—lie here. After all, one has time here to reflect and to contrast.

For a long time Maria had received no post in Limonest from her sister Luise. Although she knew that Luise, like her brother, had little understanding for her, she longed for her younger sister. She kept writing to her, aware that they might never see each other again:

> We are no longer young. And may one day succumb prematurely to the adversities of these times. And so I start to be plagued by homesickness.... And the shared vision of a planned future—that may no longer be realized—often constricts my heart in fear.[279]

~

Spring had now arrived in the village, and despite the severe inner pressures she increasingly suffered, Maria opened to all the changing

Figure 51: Mary and John, *by Matthias Grünewald (from Hürlimann,* Grünewald. Das Werk des Meisters Mathis Gothardt Neithardt, *p. 54)*

impressions of nature. Intense experience of the cycle of the year, a connection with the cosmos, continued to be a central aspect of her life. In March, she left her boarding house more often and took pleasure in all she saw, leaving her cares behind for a little while:

> The little village is so delightful. For hours at a time I wish you were here exploring with me and could send the children out into the great, wild park that ends in fields and meadows where two goats prance, one black and one white, and a bright little five-year-old girl runs about. Hens cackle happily through a farmyard. There is a spring that bubbles up there. And old walls. An old dog. And a proper bell calls people to their meals. It is like living in the past, in history.[280]

Physically she could not manage much and was unable to walk far without sitting down on a bench to recover ("It must have something to do with my uncertain state; with this culminating devotion to the spring at last, after passing through all kinds of stages, that calls forth in me the most profound longing to be still."[281]) In the second week of March she wrote to Toni Schwarz with longer reflections on herself and her life:

> The place where one's feet have found solid ground seeks to be filled with soul. And this can only happen if one doesn't just "stop" here to catch one's breath a moment but to—kneel. And to regard with lowered gaze the lofty reality of the hour and the day, the place and the blessing they bring.
>
> As the same life always accompanies us, from far distances, in higher circles.
>
> The sound of children singing can be heard in the nearby schoolhouse, beside the churchyard, where the town hall and the dear inn also stand (and where I usually take a coffee—or two—in the warmth). The gentle mellifluousness of the language makes a different impression from the songs our children sing. It always ends with *"C'est le jeu, c'est le jeu, c'est le jeu du mois de mai."* Years and years ago, as a young girl in Switzerland, I heard Joette Gilbert sing this song. Its light rhythm, its wafting words—touched

LIMONEST (Rhône) — Vue Générale

Figure 52: View of Limonest; postcard from Maria Krehbiel-Darmstädter

me so that I never forgot it. Here and now—my dear one—it comes to my ears again in young voices.

And strengthens my faith that there is a "playful" pattern in life that we continue in without knowing—always the rhythm that, once upon a time, we recognized as our own.

The only new things are the emphases, but not the notes themselves. *"Le jeu du mois de mai d'antan, il se joue en vous à votre insu pendant toute votre vie. Doux jeu douloureux du mois de Mai de la jeune verdure et de bien de morts."** Did you know that the greatest number of deaths occur in May? And that they give most pain to those who are left behind, since there is no place then for "black mourning"; and that few know how to practice "white, wise mourning"? But there are countries where mourning clothes are white. White like quartz, snow. And: transfiguration.

In G[urs], in the fall once, I was walking in the evening toward the Assis[ance]. And I thought: "Things are moving toward—fading and decay. It was fall. And within me I heard an answer. "No: not transience: transfiguration is the meaning of the transient."

I wrote to you about this. In the first two days in Lyon, when my "hunger" was no longer to be found in its proper place—not the usual emptiness in the stomach I suddenly realized: *"Le contraire de la faim ce n'est pas le rassasiement. Mais—le recueillement. On était toute trempée de la chaleur qui s'incline."*** The lack extinguished; one suddenly found oneself filled with devotion, love and joy. These, too, are real mercies, in the same way, even, as Goethe meant it.[282]

~

In the wasteland of Gurs, in the dry mud between the barrack, spring was something more intimated than actually seen. There the inmates often gazed with yearning into the far distance, to the Pyrenees or the blue of the sky. In Gurs, too, Maria had always succeeded in discovering the odd flower here and there—to the astonishment of the

---

*   "The game of past months of May keeps playing on in you secretly throughout your life. Gentle, sad game of the month of May, of the green grass and so many dead."

**   "The opposite of hunger is not being full. But instead—inner devotion. I was soaked through by the warmth that descended upon me."

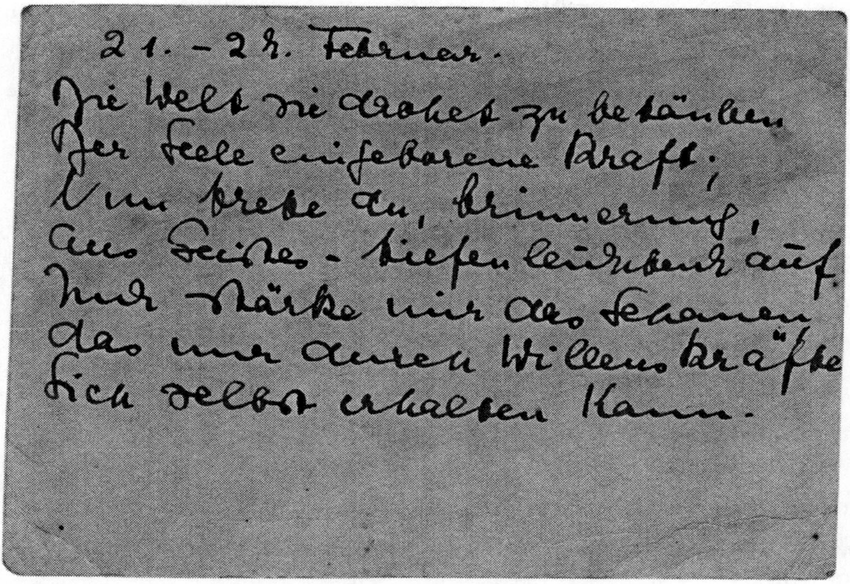

21. – 28. Februar.
Die Welt sie drohet zu betäuben
Der Seele eingeborene Kraft;
Nun trete du, Erinnerung,
Aus Geistes-tiefen leuchtend auf.
Und stärke mir das Schauen
das nur durch Willenskräfte
sich selbst erhalten kann.

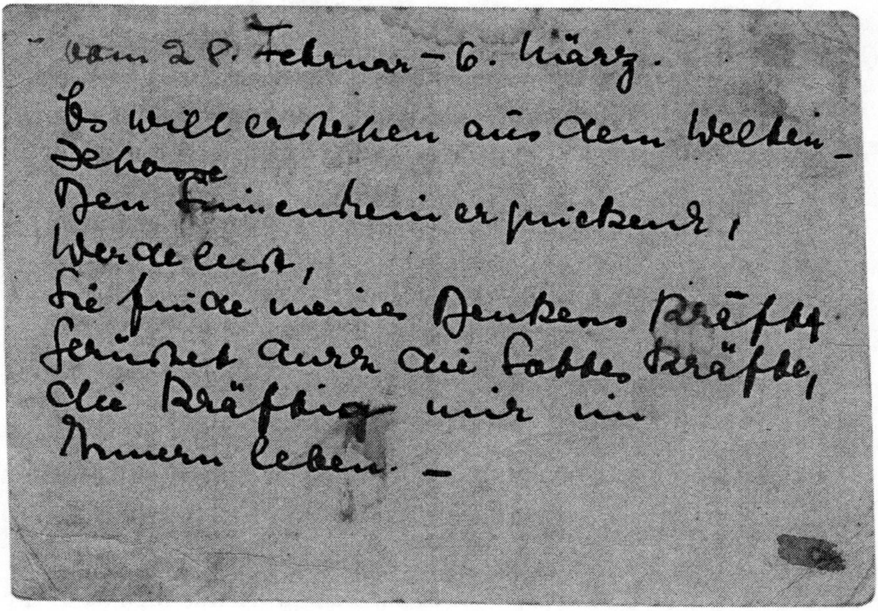

vom 28. Februar – 6. März.
Es will erstehen aus dem Welten-
schoße
Den Sinnenschein erquickend,
Werdelust,
Sie finde meine Denkens Kräfte
gerüstet durch die Gottes Kräfte,
die kräftig mir im
Innern leben. –

Figure 53: Weekly verses by Rudolf Steiner in Maria Krehbiel-Darmstädter's handwriting other barrack inmates. But in Limonest spring arrived with its incomparable wealth. Maria's window opened on a park where she would often turn her steps:

> Nature is already very beautiful, and the country seems to shimmer with the first enchantments of spring. The park, through which breezes blow, making its old trees creak and sway, at the same time releases a soft tapestry of flowers that sprout up everywhere. An old hill must be an "elf hill" since there, within the grey of winter grasses, are so many little nests of bright yellow. As if someone has dipped a brush in egg yolk and speckled it everywhere—the most poetic (and nourishing) sight. Here Easter is already waiting.[283]

Months later, looking back on this time, Maria wrote of the coming of spring in Limonest, which she had experienced so intensely, with its "magical garden land":

> The spring leapt from winter, as though fully formed; a sudden opening. And was there. With everything. Unknown to us northerners—that spring and summer flowers, blossoms, leaves, grasses, birds should suddenly all be there within a few days (days of brief weeks). And roses next to the last cowslips, lilacs next to peonies and flowering gorse and tulips (and here and there huge violets too). The nightingale sings both day and night. The cuckoo knows no shyness but is a near-by companion. And today the first golden oriole appeared. No, it is unheard of. One is breathless from accompanying and celebrating all this, and plucking it.[284]

~

The outer world was therefore heralding the approach of Easter. In the meantime Maria Krehbiel-Darmstädter now had access to the full texts of the Easter Epistles of the Act of Consecration, either from her own intensified memory or with the help of friends such as Maria Gnädinger, who eventually "tempered justice with mercy." Maria also copied out the epistle texts for Toni Schwarz, who had left Gurs with her mother in January, and gave them to her "for reflection." The Easter Epistles prepare Christian awareness for the passage into death and resurrection—and Maria knew that she herself might well be facing these experiences in the near future. In fact the Easter festival of 1942 was to be her last on Earth.

Despite her intense impressions of spring and her meditations, her anxiety, disquiet and restlessness did not fade, but remained as the expression of a creaturely response to danger and adversity. She battled with these feelings, and did not wish to entertain them, but was scarcely able to overcome them—also because her rhythmic system, her heartbeat and breathing, kept going haywire because of her illness.

On March 20, she wrote in a letter that, despite her physical state, she must soon return to Gurs. Eventually her return was arranged for *Palm Sunday.* Maria spoke of her approaching "entry" to Gurs as of a certain path into death. But then she developed a high temperature and flu—and Jean Lagrange was able to arrange postponement of her return.

In this confused situation, pressure on her initially subsided so that she could breathe a little again—as she told her friends. On March 26, she wrote to Toni Schwarz:

> It is nonsense if one is still restless in these circumstances. And so indeed it happened—was present even before these energetic efforts by my friends: suddenly there was calm in the place of restlessness. A still certainty took the place of all tormenting uncertainty. A different entity had seized the human, reflective place, making space for itself; and now it was displaced. A very great way beyond daytime and tiredness and fear. Upon a summit. As the barrier in G[urs] opened, one pictured all that one would feel. But there was nothing. The void. *Le vide.* But such that the new element stood ready to enter. At certain points in life, at the influx of this "void," we go far beyond what we had imagined. "Learn to sacrifice your thoughts to the divine." That is also Good Friday and Easter. There is much that seeks to speak to you.[285]

Before Easter she was very relieved to hear that Emil Bock had been released from the "protective custody camp" in Welzheim. She lived through the days of Easter with the relevant epistles, her memories of the Act of Consecration of Man, lecture texts by Rudolf Steiner and the Grünewald images. On Easter Sunday, April 5, 1942, she wrote again to Toni Schwarz:

> The great picture by Grünewald lies open on my bedside table, and has been like a missal for me through Easter week. I have never seen the luminous head of *Christus resurrexit* so majestic as here: light from light. Unreal and real. An unrepeatable creation.

~

Shortly before Easter she was once again "spared" because of her high fever—released from a state of existential fear and restlessness, a Gethsemane feeling of helplessness and abandonment. Her room at the *vieux logis* in Limonest was simultaneously a protected and a threatened space, that could be taken from her at any moment. But again she had been left unscathed. She was granted three extra months of sick leave.

For the first time she now wrote of the future, a time following the world war, and of what she then wished to undertake—against the backdrop of all her experiences and the needs of the time. On April 16, she also wrote to her brother:

> Ah, I'll be glad when this war has ended. And one is allowed to go anywhere again. Nurse others, dress wounds, of both body and soul. But of the soul still more.
>
> If anyone wishes to have me I would like to fly off somewhere in the world to help make good. To comfort. To say: that healing *is* possible after all. And that a fellow human being wishes to love.
>
> Have I ever told you the words of our sacrament of confession? "Learn to sacrifice your thoughts to the divine. And to receive your will from the grace of God. Thus will your soul feel peace. You will lovingly adore the revelation of God and show yourself loving to humankind. Love of God will enter your whole being, love to the human being in your heart."
>
> These concentrated words of the spirit are good helpers in dire adversity.

Figure 54: Head of the Resurrected Christ; The Isenheim Altarpiece
(detail) by Matthias Grünewald (from Hürlimann, Grünewald.
Das Werk des Meisters Mathis Gothardt Neithardt, *p. 97)*

Maria Krehbiel-Darmstädter often needed Rudolf Steiner's concentrated words of the spirit in the following months, and she was well aware of this. On January 20, the "final solution" to the Jewish question was agreed at the Nazi Wannsee conference near Berlin. Instead of deportation to Madagascar, Jews were now to be systematically murdered in concentration camps in the East. In the period before Easter, a train carrying Jewish prisoners had already been sent to Auschwitz from Compiègne in France. Neither the *Neue Zürcher Zeitung* nor *Die Weltwoche* reported this, and Maria was unaware of it. However, many newspaper reports did not bode well, and stricter conditions were put in place in Limonest for reporting to the police. Maria's inner intentions for the period after the war still held firm, however; and others too were turning their thoughts in this direction, including Rudolf Steiner's colleague in the field of medicine Ita Wegman, who had emigrated to Ascona and was preparing for the future at Casa Andrea Cristoforo.[286]

It was important for Maria to maintain her newfound peace although the danger did not grow any less but on the contrary grew more threatening. On April 16, 1942, she wrote to her brother again:

My new allowance of three months is again taking its inexorable path. Surrounded by looming uncertainties, we must, surely try to achieve *certitudes d'esprit*.* To be renewed daily we need these powers, that must be dynamic yet assured—like death! Yesterday I sought my quiet room and bed very early. Police regulations have tightened up again, and who knows what new decrees tomorrow will bring? But without agitation, torment or existential weariness I found a willingness—to conclude. The transition from an evening mood of this kind into a night, accepting that tomorrow will not come, no new earthly morning or day—would be a benign and gentle thing. Almost right. But to accept this mystic insight in a way that is both serious and simple, life's path must already have this quality (I don't say "suffering's path," for my experience down there [in Gurs] was so protected). And as far as I am concerned, there is no need to agonize about me.

---

* "Certainties of the spirit."

*Figure 55: Limonest, April 1942: Marguerite Delabarre
and Maria Krehbiel-Darmstädter (right)*

"Who knows what new decrees tomorrow will bring?" Two days later, in a letter to Margot Junod, Maria again described this evening mood of transition into death and an after-death, unearthly existence, and her willingness to conclude her own life in peace, and depart from it:

> I look upon all that is peaceful with such inward longing. To rest at last. A few days ago at evening—an overcast evening, one that really seemed to intimate the end of the world—I went to bed immediately after supper, at eight o'clock. The certainty that during this night at least one could lie there undisturbed, be where one is, let me nestle into the bed, wrapped me in layers, in blankets, in the evening's protectiveness, the safe, closed space that is so profoundly "mine." It wasn't anything resembling fear. Nor did restlessness or distress touch my inner being.
>
> And yet it was a yearning for home. No existential weariness. But a willingness to pass over, now, into another, stilled, uplifted existence. To know one's being directed to paths other than earthly compulsions. Oh, the evening was infinitely soft, tired (not tired of life) and lonely.

Limonest was a peaceful village in the zone of France not occupied by the Germans. Yet everything could change rapidly to "earthly compulsion" and become a "hunt to the death." Maria Krehbiel-Darmstädter would have been glad to know her being directed on "other paths," within other protective layers, and in another existence altogether. She read a great deal, including works by the French Catholic Charles Péguy, such as his book on the nature of hope ("I have bought this as a gift to myself, and "dedicated" it to these glorious, threatened holidays of mine."[287]) She was studying Paul Claudel and wished to "fathom" the spirit of France; but at the same time also read Adalbert Stifter's works *Solar Eclipse* and *Indian Summer,* which she had read before and thought very highly of ("Radiantly, I become aware how many of the old, best possessions of my life slowly rise up and incline toward me"[288]). Stifter's works had been available in the library of the *Assistance Protestante* at Gurs camp, and many people borrowed them, as Maria told Anneliese Herweck in a letter from Limonest:

> In the camp's extensive library we had...a few books by Stifter, and connoisseurs of his works read and reread them there, tried them and tested them. They "stood the test," like little else. Truly they are "equal to any situation." A sacred possession. An assured, royal treasure. As he writes in the foreword to the studies: "Let us seek to perceive the gentle law according to which the world is governed." This knowledge is more important now than ever, infinitely more precious, and—holding fast to this: there *is* a gentle law that is stronger than the harsh one.[289]

Via the weekly journal *Das Goetheanum,* Maria learned of a new book by the Swiss poet Albert Steffen, who had been close to Rudolf Steiner and was now chairman of the General Anthroposophical Society. She now asked her brother to procure this book, *Geistige Heimat* ["Spiritual Home"], for her. For Anneliese Herweck and Toni Schwarz she often copied out poems by Steffen that appeared in the Dornach weekly, and sometimes prose passages by him that spoke to her and were of contemporary relevance:

> The poet does not live without death, which comes closer to him than to others. He must continually take death into himself, since he grasps life where it becomes free—that is, in dying. His task is to seek out tirelessly illnesses, crimes, seemingly insoluble destinies so as to experience healing, catharsis, a word-mediated way out that passes through death and is reborn, and as spirit revelation addresses peoples of all tongues.
>
> To preserve intact the idea of humanity during a bomb attack; the image of an angel over the chaos of a city's devastated ruins; the spirit body of a dead person raising itself from a mass grave— grasped, seen and conveyed by a poet of the future, in contradiction to all supposed "war aims."
>
> For now the place of battle changes, when the dead enter the service of Michael, who overcomes the dragon:

> Upon the ray of light that pierces dark,
> your own name is inscribed.
> Above, the Sun that summons it
> below, the soul that listens to it.
> In Word become Human—O hark
> the whole world's resonant speech is heard.[290]

~

The time of Ascension and Pentecost came round again, commemorating the Christ being's ultimate and ongoing connection with the Earth that had begun with his death and resurrection. Maria Krehbiel-Darmstädter once again breathed in the powers of nature and absorbed them deeply: "This abundance is sweet. So mighty. And it makes one selfless, lets one sense the plenitude of times, of transfiguration and *pleroma*. And Ascension and Pentecost are prepared."[291] In a weekly verse for this period of the year, in the *Calendar of the Soul*, Rudolf Steiner had written:

> "I sense the essence of my essence,"
> so speaks feeling,
> joining in the Sun-illumined world
> with floods of light;
> feeling wants to give thinking
> warmth for clarity
> and closely join in oneness
> human beings and the world.[292]

It was thus that Maria absorbed the phenomena of nature, with sensibility united with "pouring light" in the "sunlit world"; and she tried to develop additional strength, Michaelic powers of the heart and thinking that she would need to go on living. At the end of May, after Pentecost, she wrote to Margot Junod:

Soon, after the second three months, I will be on the waiting perch again. But my sense of unsteady and fluctuating hold is directly connected with the inconceivable happiness that is granted to me.

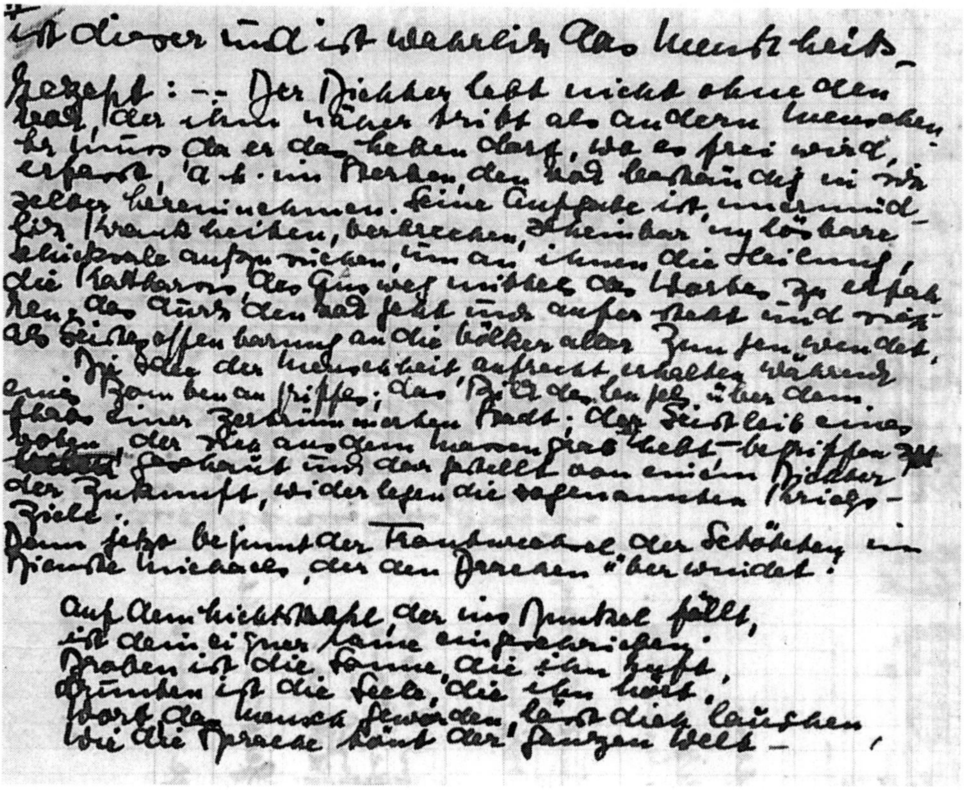

Figure 56: Maria Krehbiel-Darmstädter, texts by Albert Steffen
in a letter to Anneliese Herweck, July 13, 1942 (third page)

I'd like to give everyone a full sense of the rapturous beauty of my new country. And since it often seems kinder not to do this, I write my letters outside, even when this is made difficult by such things as the midday breeze. You're forced to stop your fluttering pages from flying into the fluttering leaves. I put a big paw on them and my hair streams wildly round my face. Sometimes an ant tickles along the bare skin of my legs since the meadow grass with its wealth of flowers and insects reaches half way up them.[293]

This sphere of experience was one Maria did not want to keep for herself alone but instead, as ever, tried to include her friends at Gurs in everything. She continued to write many letters each day to the camp, and her friends there wrote back to her, in efforts to maintain a "correspondence" between the different realities experienced in each place. Thus she wrote to Margot Junod:

I understand...the gesture that turns to all four directions of the compass with that drop of holy water. Ah, if only one could reach them, the suffering and exhausted ones. I am most concerned of all at my friends' exhaustion. How fortunate that the seasons intervene to give a natural and fortifying change. A friend—who was latterly my neighbor and to whom I must write especially often because "from one day to the next" she lost her brother there (a good, honest man, a little too soft; suffering somewhat too much from the usual tone of the camp)— writes to tell me that they now have permission to visit the little copse (a stand of trees, but poetic and mysterious). Until now it was guarded and strictly out of bounds since there is nothing beyond it (but freedom...). Hertha has also gone to see it. She was in shock to walk again among trees (and I have a park and a whole, wide, open countryside!). Her happiness was too great. Her heart could not bear it when she thought of her brother who lay nearby. And did not walk beside her.

And so she turned round after a few steps and returned home. Went back again.[294]

~

Figure 57: Maria Krehbiel-Darmstädter in Limonest, early summer 1942

Maria's second sick leave expired again after only four more weeks. Her friends in Lyon once again sought an extension, preparing the next application ("We filed a second application. Hopefully it will prove successful again. My Lagranges never doubt it; and Maria, by contrast is always ready to be taken back. Enrôlée; like a part of this time of battle to which, after all, one belongs as a fighter even if all one does is to endure, nothing but that. "Endure" is a magnificent word it seems to me."[295]) During this time Maria found a very fitting expression for her type of simultaneous hope and readiness in an artwork in Strasbourg Cathedral: the female figure of the "Synagoga" on the Romanesque South Portal, of which she had a postcard. She wrote to Toni Schwarz about this on May 30:

> One gazes on her with deep emotion and love: sanctified knowledge that is so truly embodied, is present as the eyes are. But she wears a blindfold. One can imagine that this is not a solid "bandage" as if the eyes were ailing (or missing) but instead a very narrow, light and even delicate protective veil—as if to guard and spare vision. And it is this that gives the figure her *hope*, for otherwise the acquiescing (conscience-stricken) "beaten"—as after a "battle"—nature of her being would be unbearable. Especially with the broken lance resting in her grasp. She still seems to shoulder it, remaining "faithful in loss" to it; and resembles a kind of Joan of Arc who embraces her death in the flames. Yet her waiting is no victory. The "ultimate" redemption of a portrayal of Christ, say, who sits upon the throne with staff and crown of thorns, subject to mockery and yet emanating such peace and victory over pain that this comfort outweighs the anguish, is not found here at all.
>
> The figure's right arm shoulders her broken dominion. But the left, oh the left, does not lie beside the delicate body but is *free*, in something like expectancy. Remarkable how the broken lance point lies gently against the lowered, gently inclining head. Almost like protection. And is this not so? The Jewish demise *is* its protection; in a scope of great, mystical dimensions....
>
> This work of art speaks again to our time. I will need to purchase several more copies of the postcard (though quite expensive).

*Figure 58: "Synagoga," stone carving on the exterior
of the Strasbourg Cathedral South Portal*

Its power and poignancy, I think, can suddenly become apparent to one or another group of people.

~

Maria Krehbiel-Darmstädter's perspectives were not easy to convey to others—not even to a fellow anthroposophist and esoteric Christian like Toni Schwarz. Her letters from Limonest repeatedly invoked—often unexpressed—spiritual experiences that were hard to communicate, and were frequently at the very limits of what language could utter. In mid-June 1942, she wrote:

> Recently, on a walk, I suddenly felt myself to be permeable to all that has been, is and will be. Everything is always ready, though not our capacity to absorb it. But when this capacity is composed simultaneously of renunciation and awareness, the stream can flow through, and no "separations" any longer exist. The exchange between "air" and "substance" (solidity) is such that a transformation through love occurs: transfiguration.[296]

Although Maria Krehbiel-Darmstädter was in this way prepared for accepting a great deal, in fact everything, that affected or impacted on her, she often reacted with deep despair to painful news from Gurs. As ever, people were dying there under merciless conditions, seemingly without any kind of "transformation through love" or "transfiguration," but instead in conditions of the most physically harsh kind. Maria never detached herself from this misery, never tried to relativize it in any way or to impose a redeeming metaphysical interpretation on it. For herself, for her own path of developing awareness in relation to danger and engulfment, and her possible fate and death as part of the tragic course of world destiny, she wrestled to achieve a stance that was appropriate to the situation, spiritually open yet at the same time inwardly secure. The suffering of others, though, impacted directly on her, agitated her and sometimes caused her great consternation. On hearing of further unexpected illness and deaths in Gurs at the end of the first week in June, she wrote to Margot Junod:

The pleasant day, my friends' solicitousness, the sunny weather, everything of my own, broke into splinters you can say. Vanished. And such deep, painful melancholy spread over me that days and nights passed in a state of restlessness like the one I experienced here to begin with. You know it: anguish.[297]

Soon after this she composed some poems about dying in Christ, the "Christ Sun that redeems human beings," and on June 18, 1942, four days before her fiftieth birthday, included these in a letter to her brother:

CEMETERY IN A FIELD OF GRAIN

Ashen arm serves up
Bread, the staff of life.
Graves rise from the grain,
Life is mixed with death...

Grave! Yet grave is crowned by cross.
Christ unmingles. Christ reconciles.

DEPARTURE FROM G.[URS]

Whether silent
Or in speech
You feel it placed upon your mouth:
Like a finger. Symbol that
Softly moves, a sign that points.

You recognize it.
Threefold known,
Touching brow and mouth and heart:
In the daylight (and so often at night)
From yourself to Him it led.

In admonition it descends:
A glowing coal now, wafer white.
And surrounds the cross's limbs,
Ringing them with solar light.

~

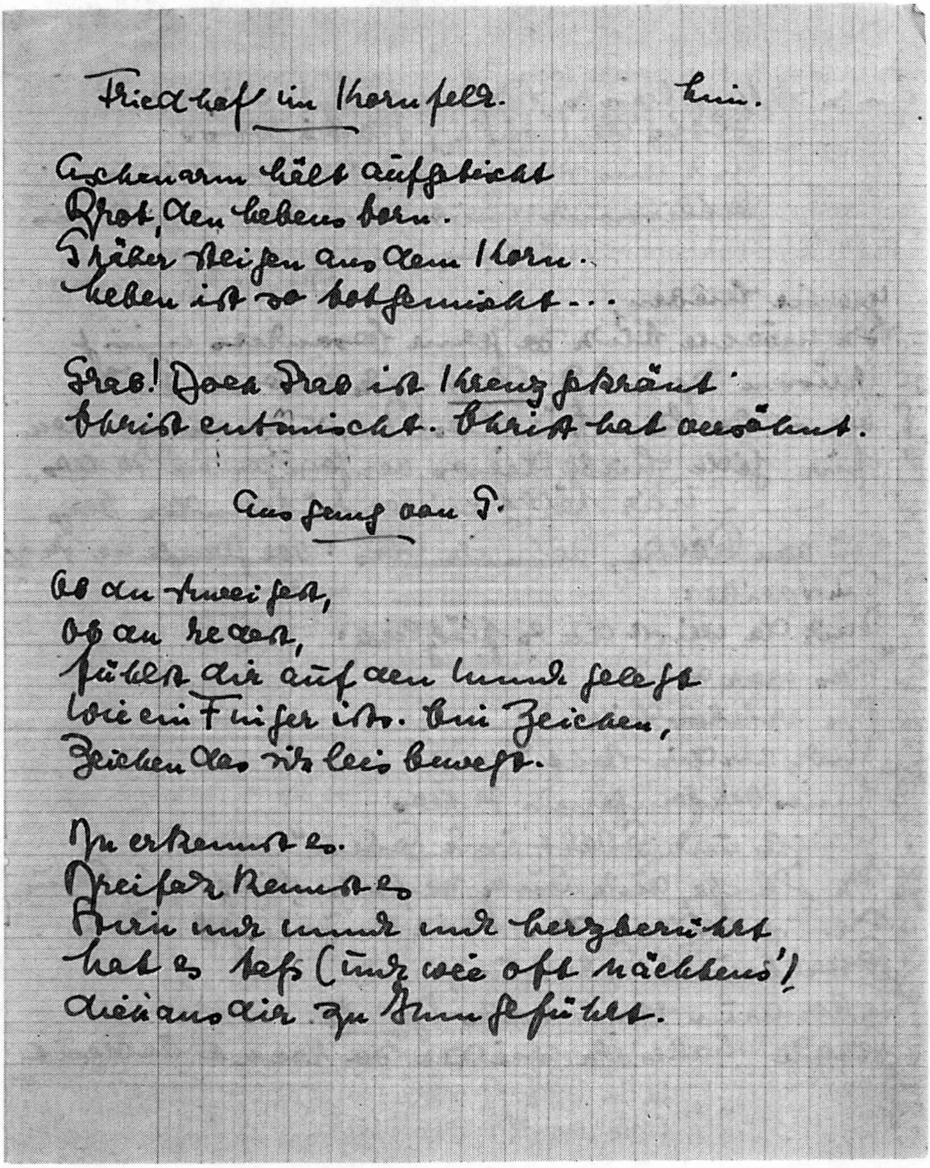

*Figure 59: Poems by Maria Krehbiel-Darmstädter, Limonest, June 1942
(translation on page 167)*

The post for her birthday on June 22 arrived a few days earlier—many letters from Gurs, and also from other friends, cards of congratulation and gifts (especially books), and roses from her landlady at the *vieux logis*. The other people in the boarding house knew nothing of her birthday—"It is not normal to remember or celebrate birthdays here."[298] Her real "community in adversity" remained the one in Gurs: "I continue to carry Gurs within me, and am unwilling to forget it, irrespective of my supposed state of health."[299]

June 22 was a day heavy with burden. On that day she received news from her brother that a friend of her youth, Elisabeth Eichler, had committed suicide in Mannheim in order to avoid deportation to the East. Elisabeth was the niece of Berta Altschul, the mother of Maria's dead fiancé Willy Altschul. In the meantime Bertha Altschul had crossed over the threshold at an internment camp in southern France, after being transferred from Gurs. Her husband, whom she had left behind in Mannheim in a state of grave illness on the morning of deportation, was no longer alive either. Now Elisabeth, too, had died—by her own hand, on April 25 in Mannheim, midway between Easter and Pentecost. Maria was in despair at this news. On July 19, 1942, she wrote to her brother:[300]

> And I sit here (momentarily) and look out at the wind-tossed park in sunshine, with a blue sky, and green so vigorous one imagines that all humanity could be renewed by it. I look out. And experience things—experience more than I say.

Thus St. John's arrived, "in the realm of Earth's guilt-laden / human seed in need of healing."[301]

～

At the end of June Maria had received a second, three-month extension to her stay in Limonest. "But urgent enquiries are apparently being made about when I am considering leaving the country, and what steps have been made to reach the United States."[302] The Lagranges were also asking—it really was high time, but there had been no news from the United States for months. On July 25, Maria wrote to Basel, "And—as I see it—this really is urgent now. The winter will be hard. And there are fears that we might all be collected again and sent to the East." These "fears" were real, and Elisabeth Eichler's death testified to the fact that transportations to eastern Europe had indeed begun. Many of the letters she received contained hints of this: rumors and suggestions that were going the rounds. Maria was pleased that all the children and teenagers at Gurs has meanwhile been accommodated in relative safety in French children's homes. On the other hand, she had received no news of Elisabeth Kasser for a long time, and was worried about her. She was still unsure whether she ought to be anxious about her own situation. On July 31 Maria wrote somewhat hesitantly to her cousin Anne Davidson, née Darmstädter, who was ten years older than she, and who, after emigrating from Berlin to Lisbon with her husband in 1933, had been supportive of Maria's efforts to emigrate, and was now urging her to act on her decision to do so:

> In the end one is just a leaf blown by the wind. And to bend without resistance is a kind of *power* of resistance. I mean, to be able to adapt to events, in whatever way one does so. A distinctive kind of readiness develops. And in the midst of doing whatever is necessary one withdraws from suffering through shouldering it without anguish, without lament or even complaint.
>
> We retain the liberty to assuage the suffering of our neighbor, our friend or comrade. A great, distant tranquility dawns amidst turmoil. And in the most extreme and uncertain destiny, the most effective power is the one that *sustains* us. So let us be comforted. And lead our human life to its goal.

In the "infinitely strange state" of her present life,[303] between spiritual trust in the future ("So let us... lead our human life to its goal") and the threat of "earthly compulsions," Maria wrote further poems that she sent to Margot Junod:

PALE BOUQUET

Pale bouquet. The colors blanched.
Form and nature here revealed—
Severely rises Master Death.

And the color, all the soft
Wealth that was, and now has faded,
Into higher essence resolved
Has found the way back to itself.

Star and stalk and thyrse and umbrel
Ring and radiance, bitter crown
Accomplish their sense-musing goal—
Offer to higher beauty all they own.

Yet the last few gleams and spots
Of luminous yellow, blue so full—
Go on shining for a long time still
In sweet burden of farewell.

MORNING

Out of dream there shines more pure
Something waking in the soul—
Seeking space in daylight to appear
Where deep inwardness unfolds
night's illumining commands.

Spirits hover at their threshold
Streaming, bearing brightness down:
And precious things are safely stowed.

Summer-sipping human being,
Open broadly, spread your wings!
Plunge in colors crystalline
All the world. These earthly things.[304]

After funeral bells had rung out for a funeral in the neighborhood, she sent Anneliese Herweck the following verses on July 25:

> Heavy blow
> The funeral bell.
> Making space
> Boom far, reverberate—
> Cloudless—
> In blue and green
> Sun enters, streams.
> And in-between
> Bell, air and Sun
> Changing realities converse....
> Pain, devotion
> Desire and bliss
> Resound into
> eternities.

~

Six weeks before she wrote these poems, on June 11, 1942, Adolf Eichmann had summoned deportation officials to Berlin from France, Belgium and Holland to discuss organizational requirements for further transportations to the East, following the Wannsee resolutions of January 20. ("In place of emigration, a further possible solution has arisen with the Führer's prior agreement—namely, to evacuate Jews to the East.... For the purposes of practical realization of the final solution, Europe will be combed through from West to East."[305]) SS captain Theodor Dannecker, head of the Gestapo's department for Jewish affairs in France, gave his agreement to Eichmann in Berlin to undertake immediate deportation of 100,000 Jews from France to concentration camps in Poland. In accordance with the Wannsee Conference decisions, a total of 865,000 Jews, including 700,000 from the unoccupied zone, were to be brought from France and murdered in Poland.

Dannecker, under whose command the first transportation from Compiègne to Auschwitz had been carried out on March 27, was

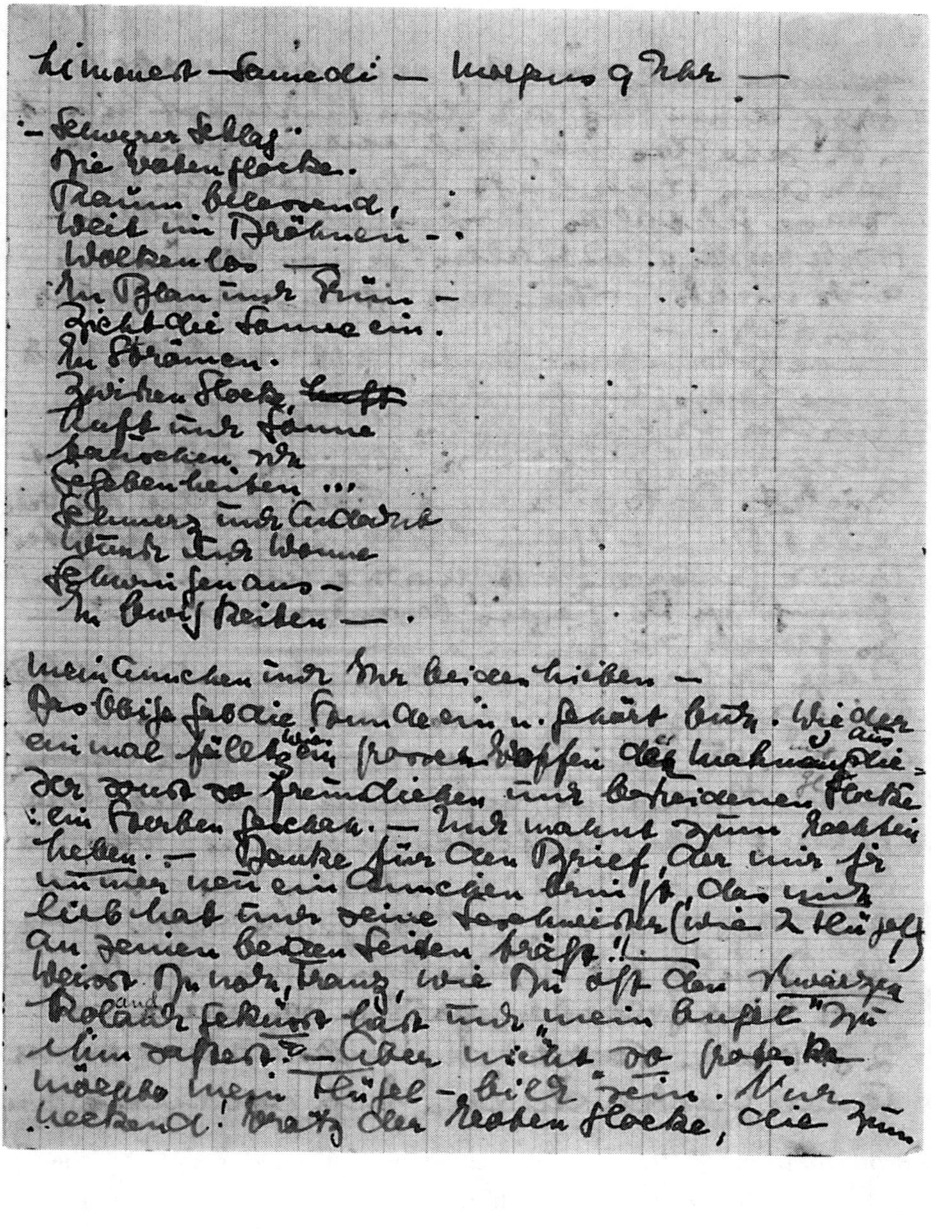

Figure 60: Maria Krehbiel-Darmstädter, "Heavy blow..."
(Limonest, July 1942)

urging the Vichy government to pass ever more draconian anti-Semitic laws. In July, he visited the French internment camps and informed the camp commandants of the forthcoming deportation of all Jews. "And there are fears that we might all be collected again and sent to the East," Maria wrote on July 25, 1942, five days after Dannecker visited Gurs, and showed his disappointment at the small number of Jews in the camp: "Gurs camp was something of a disappointment insofar as reports from the presently unoccupied zone had previously suggested there were at least 20,000 Jews there" (Dannecker[306]).

Soon after, Dannecker's lightning visit at end of July 1942, Gurs camp was surrounded in early August by French Special Branch police in black uniforms. Fear and panic ran through the barrack. News from Poland about the existence of death camps there, and the labor conditions in them, had long been going the rounds of the internees. At the time of the original deportation, October 22, 1940, the deportees in Mannheim had already feared they might be sent eastward. Now, just two years later, this threatened to become reality: "Everyone was afraid of being sent to Poland," wrote a Gurs survivor (Rolly Weil[307]) in her reminiscences of those early days of August. Many inmates were in despair and in a state of collapse, and there were numerous attempts at escape and suicide, some of the latter successful:

> All saw their approaching demise. No one wished to succumb to an uncertain fate. Better the death they could see than terrible new torments. In a few hours the hospital was filled with those who had attempted to slit veins in neck or wrist and were only just saved from bleeding to death. A few had taken poison but the dose was too low so that they too ended up in hospital in terrible pain.[308]

Jeanne Merle d'Aubigné and her colleagues in the *Assistance Protestante* stood by these depressed and stunned people to the end, as did Elsbeth Kasser. While they were able to soothe and help some, they were unable to prevent the first transport leaving Gurs on August 6, carrying inmates whose surnames started with the letters A—S. A total of 1,003 people were in the wagons, which arrived one day later at Drancy transit camp, ten kilometers north of Paris. Here their last paltry possessions were taken from them and their hair was shorn before the transportation continued. On August 10, sealed and completely overfilled cattle trucks rolled toward Auschwitz, provided with only a little water and food for the journey. The Gurs inmates arrived there five days later. Seven hundred and sixty-six people were taken straight to the gas chambers after the selection process, and their bodies incinerated. The others were accommodated in the Birkenau barrack and all but a few of them died soon afterward.

Further trains left Gurs on August 8 and 24 and on September 1—a total of 2,212 people who were transported from Gurs to Auschwitz via Drancy. In November, *Aufbau* magazine in New York published the names of deportees removed from the camp in southern France: "We can do nothing more than publish these names. We do not know the current location of these unfortunates, and have received no news of their fate."[309] On December 18, 1942, a week before Christmas, the journal also published an eye-witness report of the clearing of the camp.

~

When the deportation drama began in Gurs in early August, Maria Krehbiel-Darmstädter in Limonest as yet knew nothing of what was going on. Clearly, however, she had intimations through inwardly accompanying the people to whom she turned her thoughts and feelings day and night. After the night of July 31 and August 1, just before the French police surrounded the camp, she wrote to Toni Schwarz: "The past night was like a single memory of those times at home [in Mannheim] before the last days arrived."

A day later, in a letter to her brother, she stressed that she was now inwardly prepared for whatever would come, and again reassured the family:

> What this hour of the eons asks of us is to serve. In places where we can expect great need of it. In former times, when I wished to withdraw from things that were unpleasant, embarrassing or difficult (withdrawal *is* the first instinctive action of our nature)

Figure 61: Clearing Camp Gurs,
by Julius C. Turner, 1942

I was brought up short by reflecting that I therefore loved my neighbor less than myself! For another had to suffer in my place, and all "places" after all are occupied by living beings! Then it might as well be me as another, surely? This made many things much easier, and gave my weakness an aid for overcoming itself; and so it stopped in its *place,* so as: to go on existing. However this strikes you, you must completely quieten your anxieties about me; this has protected me wonderfully so far, and will continue to do so, I feel, if I know how to take my destined place without refusal.[310]

It does not seem likely that Franz Darmstädter was either able or willing to follow this train of thought. The Swiss *National-Zeitung* had reported back in July that the German government was arranging for internees in all camps in France to be relocated to Poland. If Maria's "destined place" remained unoccupied on the deportation lists, no one else would take it. Neighborly love was not called for here, but a final attempt to escape. Meanwhile, however, it had become still harder to escape to Switzerland. Almost all borders were closed, including those through the Jura mountains, in anticipation of the deportation from France to Poland that had now begun.

Maria had no news from Gurs in the following days, for no post left the camp, which was now surrounded by police. At the beginning of August Maria wrote a desperate letter[311] to Martha Besag, who had gone to a different camp with her mother and three daughters in July, and from there succeeded in fleeing into the woods. Maria was deeply concerned about everyone in Gurs, though she herself could be seized in Limonest at any moment and be sent to Drancy. Her surname began with K, and so she belonged in the first transportation: her absence from Gurs and her stay in Limonest were recorded. On August 5, as her Gurs friends were shuffling for many hours toward the camp exit in burning heat, Maria was still contemplating her return there, and wrote to friends in Mannheim and Heidelberg to say it was high time she returned, mentioning her worries that her health might not cope, but stressing that no exception should be made for her:

Figure 62: "Aufbau," December 18, 1942

For our vocation has committed us to suffering and adversity—and—we are no doubt only whole when we stand in the very midst of sacrifice and of being sacrificed. (And understand this as service to humanity and—as meaning and purpose.)

Ready willingness is a quality of opening, unfolding and enlarging the self. An expansion that brings our arms into the horizontal and our whole being into the form of a cross. But tensing up makes your arms sink, paralyses, accentuates the I at the cost of the not-I; and instead of gain it works to further our loss.

On that day (August 5, 1942) the Polish physician and teacher Janusz Korczak died at Treblinka death camp, where he had voluntarily accompanied Jewish orphans from the Warsaw ghetto.

Maria Krehbiel-Darmstädter was, similarly, prepared to return and to sacrifice herself in fraternal endeavor focused on the return of Christ—and on soul processes preparing this through the *sharing* of pain and suffering.[312] She was willing to return to Gurs, and from there to journey onward—wherever the others went. On August 10, she wrote again in explanation to Mannheim and Heidelberg:

> It's like this...one desires—once and for all—to be free of one's own existence—and has been willing to take upon oneself the care of strangers—or let us say, rather—of neighbors, to the best of one's powers; and so every call to embarking on this again must find us ready. The nature of this "mission" is the same as in ancient times. The unknown awaits us—and becomes our calling as soon as we have laid our hand (and heart. *Heart*) upon it.

~

Maria's situation in Limonest became ever more problematic. Her readiness to accept suffering, and thus also to share in deportation and death, was present in her and, in its own way, unshakable. But she had been separated from the Gurs community—largely against her will—and given "sick leave." If she had left the camp with the first deportation train on August 6 and gone to Drancy (either under the letter K for Krehbiel, or D for Darmstädter) she could have stood by the others in their hour of need—as Janusz Korczak had done—in her own, distinctive way. Now, though, she was alone at the *vieux logis* and, receiving no news from Gurs, was consumed with worry and fear for her friends there. On August 5, 1942, the same day she wrote the letter of strong will and Christian dedication to friends in Mannheim and Heidelberg, Maria also wrote to Toni Schwarz: "The disquiet that now encompasses us all is making us ill." Four days later she told Margot Junod:

> It is extraordinarily hard to *go on* living in this way from day to day. And my experience of fear, compassion, readiness for, and flight into nothing-but-extinction already exceeds anything I could have imagined.
>
> Everything is convulsed. And one withdraws. From the present and the future—and almost from the past. Nothing retains its brightness or meaning or form. Nothing of the inner being one has built up is equal to this.
>
> And what has so far been was all still "play." Even Gurs was just a nightmare next to this engulfing reality one cannot wake from.

This "engulfing reality" was the journey to Auschwitz, to the death waiting there: evil's perfected techniques of destruction, which it was impossible to countenance with tranquility. "Nothing of the inner being one has built up is equal to *this*." At this point (August 9) Maria Krehbiel-Darmstädter as yet knew no details of what was happening at Drancy (one day before the departure of the first cattle trucks containing Gurs inmates) nor of the true atmosphere of the Polish concentration camp, its gas chambers and crematoria. Yet her description was precise and accurate.

One more time she made efforts to contact her sister in the United States, and the Jewish refugee organization HICEM. At the beginning of August, two letters had finally arrived in Limonest from Luise Kayser, which she had written and sent off in May and July. Maria tried to reestablish her inner tranquility, writing to her brother on August 8:

You have to understand that I live in stillness and almost continual prayer. Thankful when a day ends. These beautiful, wonderfully lofty August days: I am relieved to see them incline toward evening; and the hours of the night are deep with sleep, like a refuge. Remarkably I never sleep better than in states of tension.

However, her grave concern about the fate of her friends, from whom no news was forthcoming, increasingly started to affect the nights. Never before in Limonest had Maria been without any news from Gurs. Now a great silence fell—no reply even from Jeanne Merle d'Aubigné. She heard nothing more from close friends and acquaintances in Gurs such as Hertha Heidelberger, Marie Kühn, Bertha Levi, Marta Schlesinger, Dr. Sokal and many others:

And instead of all the post, to see "none" arrive again is my daily signal to feel the utmost pain. Like the harsh clang of a gong on my heart. Right in the middle of it. And this wounded place remains with me through the day. Leaves behind as much disquiet as inner plea.[313]

On August 10—the day that many Gurs prisoners started their journey to Auschwitz in cattle trucks, to the grim death awaiting them—Maria wrote to Margot Junod: "There is no time left to fear what fate awaits ourselves when love for others' fate is all-pervasive. We pass over into the other."

~

But in Lausanne Margot Junod was expecting a child, and Maria also participated intensely in these events. In the same letter of August 10 she continued on this theme:

I will set down words here that our teacher once gave and that surfaced in my memory a few days ago.

> The weaving essence of light shines out
> through breadths of space
> to fill the world with being.
> The blessing of love warms through

> time's cycles—to invoke
> the revelation of all worlds.
> And spirit messengers unite
> the living essence of light
> with souls' revelation.
> And when the human being unites
> his own self with both—
> he lives within the lofty heights of spirit.

You will find the meaning implicit in the words; and if you learn them by heart they will serve you well—like angels—when the birth approaches.

These verses by Rudolf Steiner come from the mystery plays he wrote between 1910 and 1913. During these days and weeks in Limonest, Maria Krehbiel-Darmstädter came close to the plays again—and in a different way. The Dornach weekly published some remarkable reflections on Rudolf Steiner's dramatic works, part of the literary estate of his student, Mathilde Scholl.[314] Maria wrote about this to Toni Schwarz in a letter of August 12:

This compilation and esoteric nourishment is of inestimable value. And what one learns from it, in devoted reverence, is likewise sprinkled with healing medicine. We can sense here that *the* sacrament we have so long been deprived of is ceaselessly offered to us. Not just in "eating and drinking" but in every breath of air we take and in every spark of light we meet if awake and alert. We can notice this most strongly in the sinful depths atoned for in true insight, in the way this assuages fear—as one might remove a heavy, foul-smelling harness at evening from a tired, perspiring creature who deserves relief. It is our hope, our life and yearning, that we *do* deserve relief and mercy. And already the One drop descends on us to be the dew of our days and—the loftiness of our nights.

"If ye know these things, happy are ye if ye do them." The unspoken "it" hovers over our earthly existence like the cloth of Veronica.

> "Love between beings is like all love:
> affirming insight"[315]

*Figure 63: The first Goetheanum, Dornach, Switzerland;
begun 1913, destroyed by fire New Year's Eve 1922–23*

~

For a long while Franz Darmstädter in Basel had been insisting that Maria should make a concerted attempt to escape illegally to Switzerland. The distance from Lyon to the Swiss Juras was not far, and taking the initiative in this way would be better than passively waiting to be summoned and deported. But other people were advising Maria against this course of action. Her "Swiss plans," as she wrote to Toni Schwarz on August 12, had "faded entirely," adding on a humorous note:

> "Don't let anyone hear a peep out of you" is what we're being advised; and taking cover like this allows us to sound things out a little. And to be a kind of partridge hidden in a cornfield is not so bad. Where, on which picture (probably Flemish?) is the Madonna depicted with a partridge? These gentle fowl, defenceless in flocks—their cooing halfway between a dove and a cricket—seem somehow very close to the peace of Creation.

She also wrote about her inner state:

> Despite our good will none of us are yet ripe for our earnest, almost lofty destiny. And when terror grasps me, I flutter off to my dead parents, seeking there in the wrong place—for they are long gone from any earthly terror.

For the time being, therefore, everything remained in a strenuous and tense state of uncertainty from day to day and night to night:

> These days pass between hope and fear, and in deep, all-consuming compassion. Each day that passes without a summons is a victory. But only the night remains for relief. And in the morning it all starts again. One almost feels like turning night into day, so inward is the brief respite of dark and stillness, and so threatening the new, shimmering morning.[316]

On August 15, Maria told Margot Junod of her "days of terror," the question mark over her whole existence. She quoted a phrase by Goethe, "To exist one must relinquish one's existence," and added:

Surely it is good that one cannot look directly at one's heart. Can only sense it: the way it alternately contracts, convulses and expands. Caught in its own timidity and cowardice, or dissipating boundlessly in suffering on others' behalf.

It is not known whether she carried on writing to people in Gurs but it seems unlikely. By now she had heard of the (partial) clearance of the camp, and in mid-August told Rudolf Zeitler—whose aunt Martha Kühn had been interned at Gurs: "All I know for now is that G.[urs] is empty." But Maria remained in contact with people who, like her, had been allowed temporary leave of absence, including Luise Schwarz, a Protestant friend from Landau, who had been granted leave a few months back and was staying in Valence, in the Drome region. She too was soon to make a (successful) attempt at escaping to Switzerland:

My dear friend Luise—we have had no sign of life from each other for longer than usual. And in these times a sign of life has come to be worth a very great deal since it says that we remain in each other's thoughts, and that we have been able to extend our stay; and at the same time it shows that we desire nothing more ardently than to continue our modest life. Is this possible, or will we, today or tomorrow, be led on again to rejoin those we left behind? Who have now changed their dwelling place.

Such alarm lies around us all like a spell: we do not know where we are heading.

Then from far distant times we hear the words of St. Peter: "*You* have the words of eternal life."

And at this we begin to breathe again.

It is the light shining in the darkness.

And we become seeing through pain and anguish, adversity and wounds. Perhaps we overcome our weakness that seeks cover and refuge, while so many around us are left without protection, fearful and driven. And we can live then in expectancy of our tranquility, received by giving ourselves up to nothing but words of eternal life.

And maybe this will give us the true courage to accept and face new trials.

In a state like ours—continual uncertainty—we are really no longer "of this world"—we have long detached ourselves from house and home (though never from our native roots).

We find ourselves in the remarkable position of being able to survey everything. Nothing holds us back—we are so much at risk that we can fall—

But nor does anything restrict or constrict us. We can again find a breadth of soul such as those who have nothing possess— thus possessing all. I once read this:

> "Because the starry heavens now
> instead of parents have adopted you."

Isn't that beautiful? But still more beautiful because it is true, *true*. May we find peace in this truth.

M.[317]

The spirituality of esoteric Christianity, a source reopened by Rudolf Steiner in the twentieth century, continued to be the strength and substance that sustained Maria's life. She upheld this stance and outlook despite all hardship and distress, even if it had to be rediscovered anew each day—a situation no doubt that was familiar also to St. Peter and the other martyrs at the time of Christ, who had likewise borne "great resolve" in their souls. (Hölderlin wrote, "And yet now evening came the men/Were taken by surprise since they were full/Of great resolve, loved life beneath the Sun,/Not wishing to leave the countenance of the Lord/Which had become their home: it entered them/Deep as fire in iron. And he they loved/Was shadow now beside them."[318]) Even at the end of her "weak" and anxious letter to Margot Junod on August 15, Maria Krehbiel-Darmstädter took herself in hand again, writing:

We must all affirm our fate. And pursue its path. This is a fate that requires strong feet. But the feet received their consecrating sacrament. And thus: we can do this, we can walk on. To the inward, human help of friends, divine aid is added, and always comes. And always beyond understanding.

Figure 64: Rudolf Steiner's woodcarving of the face of Christ (Dornach)

Maria wished to cultivate a peaceful and loving stance toward the world—and thus also to her destiny within the world's realities. When gravely ill at the end of his life, and amidst severe attacks on himself and his work, her teacher Rudolf Steiner had written, "If we hold to Michael we cultivate love toward the outer world, and by this means find a relationship to our soul's inner world which leads us into union with Christ."[319] Maria, too, struggled to maintain this Michaelic love even in the most difficult times:

> Love, says the apostle, is patient and hopeful in all things. Has faith in all things. I am sure this love is also quite fearless. Even in uncertainty it creates its space of peace. In fear we are not within love. I always knew that I, that we, lack the capacity to stand the test of *coming* things. But we suddenly—simply—can cope with what *is*. And this enormous daring of "trust"—this: living under threat as in the greatest safety: gently. If only we could do this.[320]

~

From the second half of August 1942, Maria's letters to friends increasingly seemed like letters of farewell. She had the sense that every letter she wrote might be the last: "For this reason one gives each letter the kind of meaning and emphasis one really always ought to. For every day we live is a miracle, and every affirmation of one being by another must be authentic, full of warm truth."[321]

She now shared her worries, fear and weakness openly and directly with her brother—the whole uncertainty and fragility of her creaturely existence. Never before had she acknowledged this so fully—but never before, either, had her situation been so complex, since Gurs had been cleared and the transports were heading for Auschwitz. Consciously or semi-consciously she participated in much that was happening: "For each person who surfaces before my inner eye, then recedes again and fades into an indiscernible distance—is my close kin."[322] On August 18 she admitted to Franz Darmstädter:

These days are difficult and painful. I sit at my desk in an indescribable state of uncertainty. I have lost my connection with
almost all my friends from G[urs], whose lives have been suddenly
transformed, and thus torn from me.

Will we meet again tomorrow? It may only be a brief separation, and writing is superfluous—

For now, though, I stupidly hold onto the habit of many
months, and if no letters come with news, if everything remains
so empty, and there is nothing to do all day long—than—wait for
tomorrow and *hope*: then this is a trial that sucks the heart dry.

Naturally one seeks some occupation, darns a little, does a
bit of laundry, tidies one's room—looks through books—thinks
about what one—would leave here if—what one would let go of—
and so prepares oneself, though without really being able to do so,
and without managing—the authentic, great, tranquil matter of a
preparation that has been firmly resolved—which means: accepting what is to be. But in this way one weakens oneself by weakness! The breakthrough to sanctified acceptance of an unknown
departure (which in turn means only passing through to a higher
level of suffering and thus insight) is not successful. Not yet.

At the end of the letter she added:

We creatures are in need of redemption.

Instead of which new burdens are revealed to us, ones that others have already been tested by, which intensify our compassion—
until the entry into *our own* genuine, prepared suffering, comes
close to redemption...

The inner preparations Maria was making, which helped her find
inner strength, included the "Foundation Stone Meditation" which
Rudolf Steiner had first spoken during Christmastime 1923, and published a little later in the "members-only" part of *Das Goetheanum*
magazine. The first three sections of this meditation start with the
invocation "O human soul!" and describe the path toward deepening
the soul and permeating it with Christ, in connection with the spirit
hierarchies of the cosmos.[323] Referring to the lines of this long and
special mantra, Maria wrote to Toni Schwarz on August 21 about a

fear and breathlessness "that forgets that God has laid his name into every soul." She went on:

> We really therefore need do nothing other than—breathe. Out and in. In danger this sole remaining rhythm gives an answer to everything:
>
>> Practice spirit awareness in soul composure
>> where surging deeds of worlds' evolving
>> unite our own "I" with the "I" of worlds;
>> and you will truly feel
>> within the active working of the human soul.
>> For the will of Christ holds sway to all horizons
>> bestowing grace on souls in rhythms of worlds:
>> Let flame up, spirits, from the East,
>>> what through the West takes form.
>> This speaks: in Christ death becomes life.
>
> How fortunate that we may find refuge in such wisdom—breathing, perceiving. Receiving certainty of soul.

In the same letter, Maria reminded Toni Schwarz—who was likewise facing an uncertain future with her mother after being granted leave to stay in Beulieu (Dordogne)—of Friedrich Rittelmeyer's last sermon in Stuttgart on the theme of Christ walking on the water ("Fear not. I am."); and also of Christ's words of farewell: "In the world you have fear." And added her own words: "So may we hope to encounter peace in this world that has been overcome? You know it is the time of Christ's return."

Maria concluded her letter with the words of the Act of Consecration of Man:

> Remember: "We all approach you with our soul, O Christ, so that you may sacrifice us with yourself. And so your light may shine in our daylight. And you may take our part."
>
> Thanks again for all you have written and all you are. And be safe in God.

~

Maria Krehbiel-Darmstädter was more aware than many of her friends of the situation she now found herself in the second half of August— "for *the same* is happening, that will happen, everywhere."[324] "And though events may temporarily have rushed by us, none of us will be forgotten. It will gather all of. Not to take us home though, but to take us ever—further."[325]She knew that a hurried departure for America would no longer be possible ("My brother wrote in alarm that I should cable my sister urgently or apply for immigration to Switzerland. But all this is *'trop tard.'*"[326]) She also knew that all Jewish inmates of camps and barrack in the South of France would de deported to the East ("[Elli] Gellin [Rivesaltes] wrote today in complete *ignorance*, saying that she had been transferred to another *ilot*, but just for two weeks!!"[327]) Maria had received news that even the camps set up in Marseille for the emigration of Jews to America had been shut down, and that their inmates had been transported to Poland. They included people she knew from Gurs who, having secured permits for America, had been allowed to transfer to Marseille.

In this situation her physical condition continued to deteriorate. She found it difficult to eat, and felt much pain ("my stomach nerves rebel day and night"[328]). Years later Nelly Sachs wrote of the nature of "living under threat," its attendant conditions and inner impact.[329] These were the conditions Maria Krehbiel-Darmstädter was living in, and they grew worse week by week although outwardly—in Limonest—everything remained as it was. Deportation of Jews from France and their murder in gas chambers in Auschwitz (and elsewhere) continued apace however, undertaken brutally and systematically in the service of ahrimanic intelligence that Rudolf Steiner had described in his mystery dramas and in many lectures. Maria herself could be arrested at any moment—and sometimes she wished this dire moment would come so that she no longer had to wait anxiously for it to happen:

> Every bell makes my body tremble with terror. When the dog starts barking at a stranger's arrival. When an unknown man's voice is heard at the door. When—post—comes. And—when

none comes. Everything. Life has become nothing but pain again. And suffering surges so much [when] I feel that people remember me.[330]

Friends and relatives, and also many of those suffering persecution whom she knew—and who had received supportive letters from her to the end, sometimes containing meditations and prayers that they took with them to Auschwitz—kept Maria in their thoughts. She was an exemplary human being and a moral authority. Maria herself admired others, including the Jewish pediatrician Johanna Geissmar, who was already 63 when she was deported to Gurs and in [enforced] retirement, but had worked tirelessly as a physician in the camp and eventually voluntarily accompanied a transportation to Drancy out of concern for her patients and siblings.[331] Maria knew of this, and wrote to her brother on August 22, 1942:

> Dr. Geissm[ar] (Bertel's aunt), a fine physician, already fairly elderly, has so far refused to take a leave of absence, and now has voluntarily taken this new step upon herself. An extraordinary woman.... You can imagine what this signifies as moral support, comfort and help in the depths of gloom. I feel sure that sacrifices of this kind create an intensity that renders human nature radiant and bright. Then there are also the pious souls who take accept everything, really everything in humility from the hand of God. And who win the greatest victory because they refuse to allow themselves to be traduced into hate and fear. Instead they persist in hoping—and loving. I know such people and know that they are heard. There is something like transfiguration around this whole group—don't you too think this ultimately? There is a kind of overflowing abundance that makes others fall silent, and gives dull humanity a beneficial jolt.

Two days later she sent Toni Schwarz a meditation that Rudolf Steiner had given in the fall of 1914 during his "Samaritans Course," shortly after World War I broke out:

> Do you know this?

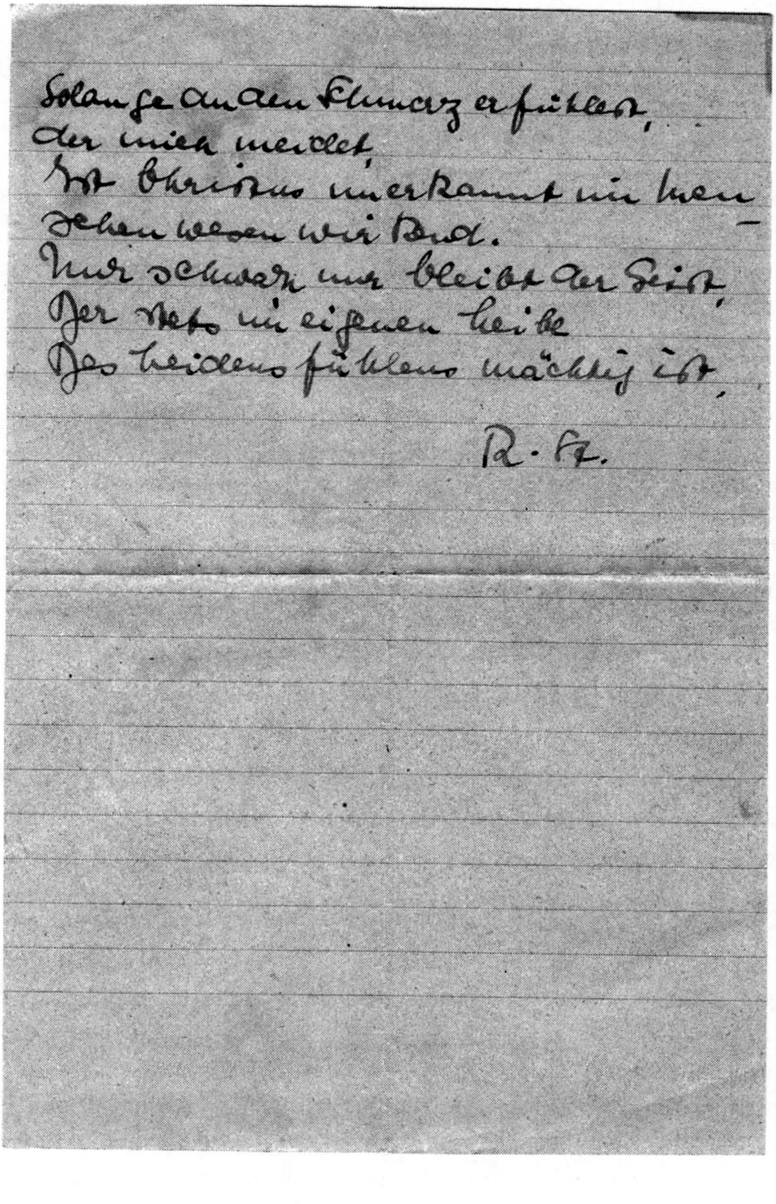

Figure 65: Verse by Rudolf Steiner
in Maria Krehbiel-Darmstädter's handwriting

As long as *you* feel the pain
that *I* am spared—Christ working in the human being
is unperceived.
And weak remains the spirit
that always only in its *own*
body is capable of suffering.—R. St.

In these days we live as if doubly. The others petition in us and continually yearn. Others' creaturely adversity has become our heartfelt concern—we are like mothers entrusted with the task of standing guard over pain! For these friends, on their own, do not cope with their pain. There is too much disappointment in it. And to welcome it ungrudgingly one needs to have renounced precisely what one has been unable to. One has just postponed life. And whoever has just lived provisionally these past two years, just getting through the months somehow, can see in the new that comes upon us nothing but despair and ending.[332]

Maria considered that sharing in the pain of others, and thus helping bear and be "guardian" to their destiny, was a task that present and future times were asking of us. She felt it to be possible that she herself had so far been spared the worst so as to participate in this way in the existential needs of many others. On August 18 she wrote to her brother in Basel [this seems to be a letter of August 21 she wrote to Toni Schwarz]:

But we do not yet know what part it is we must play: whether we belong to posterity, to those who have been spared or rescued, those whose part it is to pray, to serve at altars so that their pleas and compassion can *take effect* both day and night. Heart-rending grief gives rise to a disquiet that is not of this world. No, such things can never have been known before—And those who have been scattered and sent to oblivion—seem to have been torn from us. We who remain for the moment, who are still here, have a mission of mercy toward these torments, and must seek to "mend" the harrowing wounds that have been left.

Careworn and burdened by all these things, Maria Krehbiel-Darmstädter lay ill in bed in her room in Limonest at the end of

August. She suffered several heart attacks in her "great, agitated state of tension"[333] and—four weeks before Michaelmas—was temporarily overwhelmed by everything: "There is just too much suffering around me, and finally it settled on my chest like a rockfall. So close!"[334] Existential fear once again overcame her, crushing her physically and enforcing days of unwilling bed rest at the *vieux logis*. On September 15, she wrote to Toni Schwarz:

> And when there's a knock at the door, Moerike's gnome is suddenly beside me, and I ask him, "Who's banging so that my heart takes fright?" It is as if one were caught up in all kinds of enchanted dangers, and that giants, dragons, deep chasms, invisible evils and who knows what else all really *exist*. I experience all these things, though in fact in a quite different way from how they appear in the tales of Grimm, Andersen and others. But these tales somehow already contain them all.[335]

She tried to accept this situation, to lie "quietly by the margins" and to gather her strength and tranquility. ("First to regain my own composure, and then also: to be there for others"[336]). If she were deported, she wrote to her brother—reassuring both herself and her correspondent—this would reunite her with her friends in Gurs: "The worst thing of all would be cowardice; and surely it is not such a hopeless thing to meet my dear ones again, to work faithfully with them and to help them survive?"[337] Yet it was completely uncertain whether, if she were summoned, she would meet any of her old friends on the journey to Auschwitz, or if she would find them again when she arrived. Nor was it at all clear what kind of "faithful work" and "help" could be undertaken there.

Maria Krehbiel-Darmstädter possessed a lofty language and spiritualized ideals that bore future potency within them. At the same time, though, she had a clear and sober mind that could fully assess the current situation, and was given to few illusions, not even where her forthcoming deportation to the East was concerned.[338] She had to live in the tension between these two qualities, that were not contradictory, but the foundation of her life, and in doing so often had to summon all her powers. At the same time, even in the most dire circumstances, she knew that her friends in The Christian Community were holding her in their thoughts and prayers, and were sustaining her in a very real sense in Christ-devoted meditation. On August 29, she wrote to Toni Schwarz: "They encompass all of us with their loving prayers. I sense this. Today this sublime phrase came to my mind: "My thoughts are not your thoughts." And so let us allow *him* to have thoughts while we, we remain silent. Willingly silent."[339]

During this time Maria Krehbiel-Darmstädter received the surprising and very painful news that her close friend and godmother Karoline Schmitthenner had died. She wrote to her friend's husband and son from her sickbed:

My dear ones—

Before we grasp a truth, the truth itself takes hold of us. It undertakes its labor with a fullness of power that exceeds our own.

And so we give ourselves up to it.

Gradually our own self, riven by heartache, surfaces again. Suddenly we know this, for we have been transformed. And nothing is any longer as it once was. The direct experience must have done this to you, as the news of it did to me. One wishes to fall silent. And indeed we could be silent if we now stood together. But distance means this is not possible. And the tremulous desire to communicate sorrow is so great that one has to reach for a few words. We stand together in the very same pain of a loss we do not understand—my dear ones. Though there are bonds of kinship here (even ones that have grown mystical—for god-parenthood is such a deep reality) the connection exceeds even that. What connects us, and what no death can prevent, is the great secret of friendship—which is a choice, and was forged in Heaven so as to become reality on Earth.

It was granted us to accompany, and thus know one another from an early, early age. And now the eternal part of us has resolved and absorbed a great deal of our own temporal nature. That is quite clear.

When parents die, one suddenly becomes a generation older. When what is most precious is then increasingly lost to us, we acquire ever more of a house and home in the high realm beyond. And we approach the threshold to sample it. The power of resistance, the desire to remain on Earth, grows weaker. In farewell we have received a greeting that goes on beckoning to us—

Let us, who were close to her, not speak of the dangers that might have threatened her, of the losses, sorrows and pain that she was "spared." After all, we know that from the world of spirit the soul participates in everything that happens to us, both good and ill. But there is something new now. We now have one more "intercessor"—and—you my beloved ones must inevitably feel the strength that kindles anew there for us and—ministers to us....

There is still much I would like to say to you. But I cannot and dare not. I, too, was ill, and still am. And this delayed the new beginning of work. But I am sure that many rigors and trials await us. And the time now comes when loss liberates itself from loss. Let us bless those who have reached a safer haven, and ask them for their helping love.[340]

~

After the death of her friend Karoline, and in the depressing hopelessness of her situation, Maria's strength and powers of resistance waned. On September 10, she told her brother that she was beginning to understand Elisabeth Eichler's suicide in view of the deportations to the East: "For the first time I 'grasp' Elisabeth E. But—this is also impacting on us for a second time, isn't it." She wrote things she had always previously avoided, which gave utterance to her frailty: "There's much more I could say; or rather: I have nothing *to say*. I only wish I could lean my tired heart up against this letter. So that you could feel me, have me, as I am—live—and—how hard all of this is."

A few days later, close to September 15, she wrote as follows to Margot Junod about her inner state, her feelings and thoughts:

It is good of you to say that you need my letters and that they touch you. In saying this you call forth words from me that would otherwise have stayed frozen, because they are *no longer* heard or needed by those to whom they most closely belong. At night, by the window, under the sky of fall, when the trees lament and my heart is uppermost in me (as though born forcibly outward from something within), these words emerge. Shadows and specters and realities; and ask for love, but this time differently.

And one is not equal to this love!! For one buckles fearfully, makes oneself small and hides, yearns for nothing but concealment. And they wish one were wide open, free. Entirely ready. Fully accepting. Now I know what the form of the cross implies: but it's not something I can do—spread my arms out, ready to receive—fear of pain and vulnerabilities holds sway in my soul.

Perhaps. Perhaps, at the moment one has to, one learns this all of a sudden.

Constricted breathing, wary looking, hesitant walking: that's the life I lead now. Lead with such shame—and pleadingly seek renewal, and the reinvigoration that befits me.

She also wrote to Maria Gnädinger that day:

My heart isn't really *in* my body any more—that is, between my ribs and under my skin. It is quite naked and free. And utterly vulnerable and utterly—curable at the same time. "Practice spirit awareness in soul equilibrium"—that is what one should do, finally, and after so many trials, *ought* to be able to. And when the time arrives (a time so difficult, for now I see that I have only so far climbed the lower slopes)—then, when this God time has arrived: how unfit one is.

All my strength it seems has been blown away. And I cling tight as if in fear of going under. I cling on: to fear. For me this has been the most evil and terrible torment: to know the great phrase, "Fear not, I am"—and yet to let myself be driven as if I did not.

The indescribable misery in this sense of loneliness, the caving in to fear and helplessness and compassion, and the pure fear of death: was terrible and—remains so.

It seems to me that to daily and hourly face "decisions" is one of the cruelest kinds of torture. Only now do I really know what "night" is. When nothing happens—except stillness and starlight. And the trees blow in the wind. But when you sit at the window the departed emerge in mourning from the depths of the park— pleading that we think of them and bless them. They draw you

Figure 66: The Archangel Michael (twelfth century)

after. And leave you quaking. It is hard to go on living with others who are not suffering. You yourself are "somewhere else." And you stare upon this peace that inhabits the world in almost harmonious accord with strife.

Yes, if life were not a path of initiation, how could one ever dare to go on?...

Willing sacrifice is more difficult than anything. You live in a trembling that is prayer for—preservation. But if this cannot be, one would wish it to come *soon,* for these days are like a secret, violent theft one snatches hold of and with which one—cannot flee.

~

Then Maria pulled herself up again. As her strength slowly returned, and Michaelmas approached, she started to cope better with existential fear:

> I once read something that is very true—that courage is not lack of fear, but a quality that we can have despite our weakness because courage wishes it. Because it decides to augment itself with what it lacks. And does so, my dear ones, from a higher armory. The extra inches one adds to one's imperfect form are not drawn from earthly repositories.
>
> And it's true. When one stretches this hand out toward strength, we do also receive it. (September 19[341])

She gave her agreement for the attempt at flight to Switzerland proposed by the Lagranges. The end of October was agreed as the date for this.

Nine days before Michaelmas she wrote to the worried Toni Schwarz with sentences by the philosopher Johann Gottlieb Fichte (from his "Instructions for a Blessed Life"):

> True life and its blessedness consist of union with what is eternal and not; but the eternal can only and solely be grasped through thought and is accessible to us by no other means. The One and non-transient reality is grasped as the ground that clarifies our being and the world. And so true life and its bliss consists in thoughts, that is, in a certain view of ourselves and the world, as

emerging from the inner and inwardly concealed divine being; nor can a doctrine of bliss be anything other than a doctrine of knowledge, for there is indeed no other doctrine than one of knowledge. Life rests in the spirit, within the intrinsic vitality of thought; for without the spirit nothing truly exists. To truly live means to think truly and to perceive the truth.

Toni Schwarz, who painted delicate watercolors, was considerably more despondent and anxious than Maria Krehbiel-Darmstädter, and turned frequently to her, seeking her proximity and advice. In Gurs, already, Maria, as a well informed, spiritually advanced teacher of Anthroposophy, had often enlightened Toni about spiritual-scientific matters with an eye to her pastoral care. In mid-September 1942, Toni Schwarz again wrote of her numerous anxieties, evidently also for the fate of Jewish children living in French institutions whose parents had been deported. Maria once again replied to her:

> You ask about the children who are suddenly deprived of "parental love." There is a greater love that encompasses them, taking them up into the great, absorbing sphere of love of the world of spirit; and people are sent: the helpers (who may be angels) and who can love above and beyond ties of blood.
>
> Steffen says that we should be comforted: "Because the starry heavens now—instead of parents have adopted us."
>
> The *truth* of this truth was something we could glimpse in Gurs when we found ourselves between Heaven and Earth, suddenly experiencing ourselves, to begin with, in a hovering state of the greatest "surrender."
>
> What awaits us we do not know. But this "stranger"—the fate awaiting us—can also be an angel. And if he raises his sword and sunders what is inseparable on Earth, it will fly together again in the realm beyond Earth. What has been divided will find itself again—in the sanctity of greatest refuge. If we—like Abraham—wish to sacrifice;—today such sacrifices must be accepted in a real sense. There is a Something that calls upon us to work with Christ for atonement. And behold: which people is chosen for this? The blindfold is loosening.[342]

Only seldom in the past had Maria written expressly about the Jewish people—at most about the "Synagoga" figure in Strasbourg and her embodiment of hope and acceptance. She felt no sense of belonging to the Jewish religion although, in a transformed guise, it was incorporated into her esoteric Christianity. Now she outlined to Toni Schwarz her view of greater historical and spiritual contexts as distinct from external events—as a path of sacrifice by the Jewish people who had once prepared and made possible the incarnation of the son of God: a path accompanying the present and returning Christ. Despite her fear, Maria was willing to take this path of sacrifice for the sake of humanity, however absurd, cruel and seemingly pointless it was. The archetype of the *Synagoga* in Strasbourg Cathedral continued to hover before her—as an image of the injured yet willingly self-surrendering human being in a time of turmoil and new beginning.

To support Toni Schwarz psychologically, however, Maria Krehbiel-Darmstädter was also able to express the humorous aspect of her being, her capacity for gentle irony at her own expense—which linked her with Christian Morgenstern, another pupil of Rudolf Steiner's who meant a great deal to her.[343] On September 20, just five days after the dark thoughts she had expressed in letters to Margot Junod and Maria Gnädinger, she wrote to Toni out of the blue about her own weakness and the situation she was in:

> I think of myself like a dwarf fan palm we always had at home, standing "apart." It even had a silver-colored cachepot. It was always rather feeble and at risk from mites, placed faraway from the other plants in the bright veranda that together created a collective beauty. Standing separate it seemed or was meant to seem very select. There it stood, in the close air of the "best room"— beside curtained windows, beautifully bound books and silver candlesticks; all too close to plush carpets and elegance.
>
> Only when it joined the rest of the plants during cleaning or hosing, liberated from its silver dress, could one see what a frail weakling it was, shamefully degenerate. Yet my mother loved

"him" tenderly. And when he died a new crown prince succeeded to the throne.

That's about how I feel here.

(And *Palma Kunkel** would have made a verse of this gibberish.)

~

Maria spent Michaelmas alone in Limonest, reflecting on the nature of Michael and seeking to absorb his strength into her being so as to endure whatever was to come. Two days before Michaelmas day, on September 27, Thomas Mann had addressed the German people via BBC radio from his exile in the United States, focusing attention sharply on the Nazis' persecution of Jews: "These torments stop at nothing. The latest, demented decision is to destroy and eradicate all Jews in Europe." Reference was also made to the transportations from Drancy to Auschwitz: "In Paris, sixteen thousand Jews were herded together within a few days, loaded in cattle trucks and taken away."[344]

Physically, Maria Krehbiel-Darmstädter was in a very bad state at this time. At the beginning of October, shortly before the date agreed for her flight, she sent packages to friends, Toni Schwarz in particular, containing her remaining possessions, papers and pictures—including the image of *Il Reddentore*—and her journals and books. She wrote to her brother asking him to arrange for the Dornach weekly to stop being sent to Limonest. Time was pressing—roundups and deportations were now also taking place in cities in the unoccupied zone of France. Maria received from Drancy a letter from Berta Levi—a barrack companion of hers in Gurs—shortly before she was sent on to the East. The Lagranges, who were increasingly working for the French Resistance, seemed on edge ("my always radiant friends have lost their lovely aura and live nervously"[345]). In Switzerland both Franz Darmstädter and Father Gnädinger and his wife were making one more attempt to arrange a legal immigration permit for Maria, but this was turned down.[346] The escape plan was again postponed to await more favorable conditions. On October 19, Maria wrote to

* One of the poetic personages of Christian Morgenstern.—Tr.

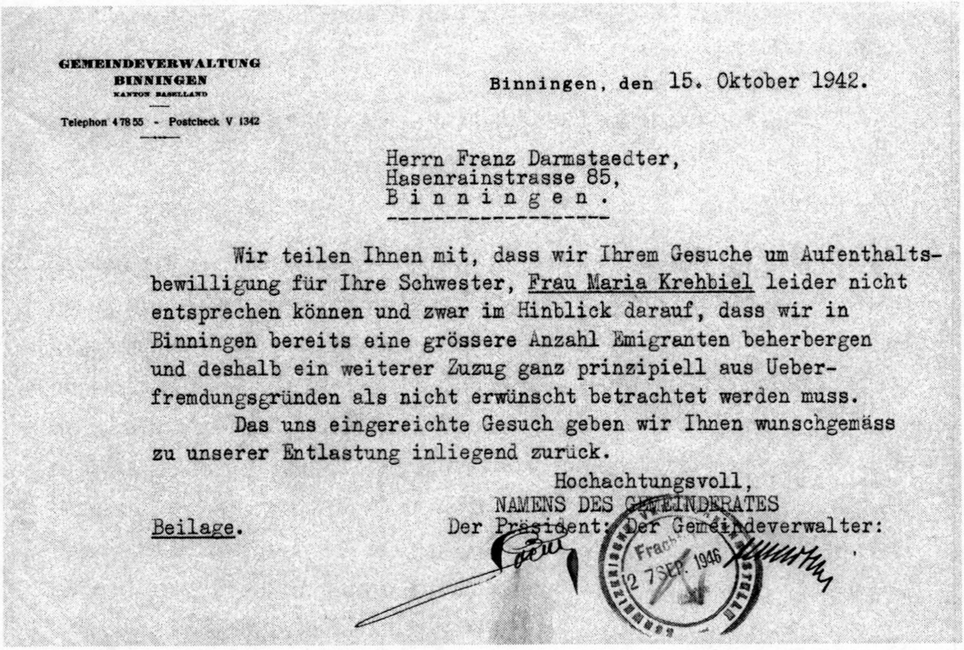

GEMEINDEVERWALTUNG
BINNINGEN
KANTON BASELLAND

Telephon 478 55 - Postcheck V 1342

Binningen, den 15. Oktober 1942.

Herrn Franz Darmstaedter,
Hasenrainstrasse 85,
B i n n i n g e n.

    Wir teilen Ihnen mit, dass wir Ihrem Gesuche um Aufenthalts-
bewilligung für Ihre Schwester, Frau Maria Krehbiel leider nicht
entsprechen können und zwar im Hinblick darauf, dass wir in
Binningen bereits eine grössere Anzahl Emigranten beherbergen
und deshalb ein weiterer Zuzug ganz prinzipiell aus Ueber-
fremdungsgründen als nicht erwünscht betrachtet werden muss.
    Das uns eingereichte Gesuch geben wir Ihnen wunschgemäss
zu unserer Entlastung inliegend zurück.

                   Hochachtungsvoll,
               NAMENS DES GEMEINDERATES

Beilage.   Der Präsident: Der Gemeindeverwalter:

Figure 67: Letter from Binningen district authority, Switzerland, to Franz Darmstädter, October 15, 1942, in reply to his letter of the 10th (see note 346). It rejects his application for a residence permit for his sister, owing to the "large number of immigrants already accommodated in Binningen."

Basel: "My situation is a strange one. No longer so fearful as in previous weeks, but no less agitated. Waiting without acting makes me long for action and work." Five days later Jean Lagrange was arrested, making things all the more difficult. Hilda Lagrange was now alone, and winter was coming.

On October 24, 1942, the day Jean Lagrange was arrested, Maria received a summons at the *vieux logis* to attend a consultation with the police doctor to check whether her state of health would allow her arrest and detention. She wrote to Toni Schwarz that day: "There's a sense that decisions have to be made. Let us hope that we will not be painfully and permanently separated and condemned to silence." Two days later she saw the police doctor in Lyon:

> Endless hours of waiting. And I almost sank into unconsciousness. The lovely book I wished to read had no power over me—there is a kind of tension that simply extinguishes the best in us. And *that* is the most terrible thing.
>
> I think that things improved after that. When I got outside, my feet did not easily find their way. Tears darkened my gaze. What a *single* kind gesture can do for us. Oh, the unstoppable collapse of barriers, walls and caverns. One is still quite soft after all. And receptive. And has faith in kindness and goodness.[347]

In another letter she wrote about the end of her medical examination: "At last I stumbled out. But still feeling the doctor's hand on my shoulder. The gesture of mercy. Let us hope. For this examination was of decisive importance."[348]

The medical report stated she was not fit for camp internment.

Yet things remained uncertain and unpromising. Where could she now turn? A little while back, at the urging of friends and against her original intention, she had agreed to attempt to cross into Switzerland illegally to escape the threat of deportation. Then Jean Lagrange was arrested, and the plan had finally collapsed. It was nearly November: heavy storms were battering the country bringing empty, grey, sad days along with worries about Hilda and Jean Lagrange who had done so much for her. "I am so close to falling into melancholy and forsakenness," she wrote.[349] Maria's heart was badly affected by high blood pressure—owing to her kidney disease—and the stress of her whole situation. Her breathing was labored and she found it hard to stand upright: "I notice how my will and capacity grow weaker."[350] Often, in great agitation, she took refuge in literature as a last haven ("Devouring books wherever I find them—sadly, haphazardly and at random."[351]) On the last day of October she wrote about her situation to Maria Gnädinger in Bern:

> The last few months have been one long effort to survive, but not fully, intentionally lived. That's bad. I add each day to the next. Like playing dominoes, the dots have to match—but they are always the same sad dots; and the lack of activity or peace remains constant. And joyless. And of "no use" to the soul. The experience seems never either to clarify into crystal or ignite in flames. Oh, how difficult.
>
> I read my piles of books and cannot choose which of them to read. But time passes, and in this way you live other lives, appalled or inspired, or share other fates. Scarcely do you return to your own again than you find yourself taking fright as if facing ruin...
>
> Each day I try to hold fast to optimism and composure for an hour or so. (Especially if a coffee gives me a leg-up—it has become my purest elixir and I have it so rarely.) Then anguish returns the rest of the time, gnawing at you like a deadly disease...Pain for the others—agitation about one's own fate. And then it is fall. And All Souls.

She again asked Maria Gnädinger for a reproduction of *Il Reddentore* by Vincenzo Foppa: "Longing for the altar is great. And since G[urs] I have found no means to engage in the communion rite."[352]

Three days later, on November 4, she wrote again to Toni Schwarz, telling her about All Souls Day, and also writing in a more direct and open way than previously about her last few weeks:

> The most beautiful, stillest day, golden and blue. I picked dande-lions at around midday, standing up at the top of the park where there is a far, open view: to the church firstly and in the distance

Figure 68: The Resurrected Christ *by Vincenzo Foppa*

the Lyon mountain ranges—my tightly armored heart cast off a few weights that hour and confided in itself—as you, as your intrinsic being, the love rooted in Him, counselled me—

Yes. As all "human aid" fell away, I [realized I] had long sensed, as a premonition, that it was not the right thing (for me) to place not only all hope but also all "faith," really, on this [her flight]. This grew gradually for me. We so easily submit to the influence of beloved people, raising them to "divine" status; my conscience *knew* this, but "Maria" did not wish to believe it.

But when things collapsed, in one way and another, really more than I can tell: all that had been constructed—I had the clear sense of coming closer to truth, the source, my real home. My deep feeling of forsakenness was precisely what created a home for me in grace and mercy. And within me formed the words of a prayer to Christ: *"Cest toi maintenant qui doit tout te charger de moi."** You understand this....

Not that I was close enough to feel Him within me—no doubt that would require still many renunciations and—catastrophes perhaps. But I knew where I stood once more. The sole clear orientation. It seemed to me that I was able to make one more choice, almost without my will. As one finds the way home again, quite naturally, after getting lost, without thinking about it. The path was there all the time and waiting. It is not for nothing that our feet are a sacred symbol. Wiser than our thoughts, they follow their creator's path.

But how pierced by woe and illusion as soon as knowledge bends down and touches its own "feet." Only the revelation that feet once bore the holiest wounds, that they hearkened with such such unspeakable obedience—can let us hope that love is greater than death, than aberration and atrocity....

Poverty is the necessary gift today. And so I offer only that. Of myself.

As on many previous occasions, she again wrote out passages for Toni Schwarz from lectures by Rudolf Steiner, most probably from her own notebook. This was the last letter written from her room in

---

* It is you now who must take sole charge of me.

Limonest, shortly before—after all—attempting to flee. The words of her teacher bore the character of a farewell and a bequest:

It is extremely important in all esoteric development that we arrange things in a way that ensures two things we possess in ordinary life are not lost—but that we can easily lose in esoteric schooling if the latter is not properly governed. If it is rightly governed and directed, we will not lose them. The first is this: that we do not lose recall of all we have experienced in our present incarnation, as this is normally retained in our memories. The structure and coherence of our memory must not be destroyed. This coherence of memory is something greatly enhanced in the realm of esotericism as compared with ordinary life. In ordinary life we understand memory to be the faculty whereby we can look back on our life and retain awareness of important events in it. But in esotericism, in addition, right memory means that we assign importance imbued with feeling only to what we have actually accomplished in the past, thus valuing ourselves only insofar as our past deeds allow this.

It is important to understand this very accurately my dear friends! This is something of very great importance. If, through his esoteric schooling a person were induced to suddenly tell himself: "I am the reembodiment of this or that spirit"—devoid of any justification for this arising from what he has actually accomplished previously, what he has already brought into existence in the physical world [in his current life], then in an esoteric sense this would be a disruption of his memory. It is an important principle in esoteric training to attribute no value to oneself other than what arises from accomplishments in the physical world during the present incarnation. This is extremely important. All other value must arise from a foundation of higher development that initially comes about by standing on the solid ground of regarding oneself as no more than one's accomplishments in this incarnation. An objective view of things shows this to be natural, for what we have achieved in our present incarnation is also the fruit of former incarnations: it is what karma has so far made of us. What karma is still to make of us is something we must still allow to develop and cannot yet be included in our self-evaluation. Thus we will only rightly evaluate ourselves as we embark on esoteric development if we see our value in terms of the past we retain in memory. This is one element we must preserve so that our I does not grow somnolent as our astral body awakens.

The second thing that we should not lose as modern human beings is the degree of conscience we possess in the outer, physical world. This again is something extremely important to observe. You will often have witnessed someone undergoing esoteric development without this being directed and governed in the right way. In this case you will often find that the person concerned has a less acute sense of conscience that he had before his esoteric schooling began. Previously, his upbringing and social context governed him, ensuring that he would not do certain things. After embarking on esoteric development, some people who might previously not have lied may begin to do so, and take a less serious view of matters of conscience than before. We must not lose the least degree of conscience we have acquired. Our memory must be such that we draw our value only from consideration of what we have so far actually become rather than by "borrowing" this credit from the future, from what we may still do in future; and conscience must be retained to the degree already acquired in the very ordinary, mundane world. If we preserve these two elements in our awareness— our healthy memory that does not give us an illusory sense of being other than what has emerged through our accomplishments, and our conscience that does not allow us to take matters of morality more lightly than we did in the past, but if anything to take them more seriously—then our I will never be able to fall asleep once our astral body has awakened. Then we bear the coherence of our "I" into the world in which we awaken with our astral body, as if in waking sleep, maintaining our awareness in a state where the astral body is liberated from the physical and etheric body.[353]

In precisely the same way as the event in Palestine occurred on the physical plane at the beginning of our modern time reckoning, so the office of judge passes to Christ Jesus in our era in the next higher world. And it is this fact that works into the physical world, upon the physical world, in such a way that the human being will develop a sense that all he does creates something for which he will need to account to Christ. This sense, arising henceforth in a very natural way during humanity's evolution, will be transformed so that it pervades the soul with a light that gradually emanates from the human being himself and that will illumine the figure of Christ within the etheric world. And the more this feeling—which will be loftier in significance than abstract conscience—develops, the more visible will the etheric figure of Christ be in forthcoming centuries.[354]

Let us picture what happens when we pass through the portal of death. The physical form we saw when we looked in a mirror or had a photograph taken, is no longer there. And we are not interested in it either. But the cosmic archetype, inscribed into the ether, is what we now look upon. Yes, this was rooted in our own ether body during our lifetime but we did not perceive it. On Earth it is contained in our physical being but is invisible to us. But now we see the nature of our own form, though it is also a luminous image we perceive. The image radiates powers and this has a very specific consequence. You see, what the image radiates has the same kind of effect as a luminous body—though this is meant now in an etheric sense. The Sun shines physically, while this cosmically perceived image of the human being shines spiritually; and since it is a spiritual image it has the power to illumine other things as well. Here, in earthly life, you can place someone in the sun for as long as you like, but though his hair and so forth will shine, his deeds, both good and bad, will not be illumined as qualities. But the luminous image of his own form that a person perceives in the world of spirit after passing through death radiates a spiritual light that illumines his moral deeds. And so, after death, in this cosmic image, we approach something that illumines our own moral deeds. This was concealed within us during our life on Earth and resounded softly in us as conscience. Now, after death, we gain an objective view of it. We know that this is our own self, and that this must surround us after death. Here we are remorseless with ourselves. You see, this illumining quality is now no longer so comfortably determined by the excuses we found here for our transgressions and our tendency to accentuate our good deeds, but rather, what shines forth from us there is an inexorable judge who illumines the actual worth of our actions with a clear light. Conscience itself becomes a cosmic impulse that works externally upon us after our death.[355]

Of what use is Ahriman? Very useful indeed within the sensory world: he helps every soul. You see, he helps every soul to carry upward into higher worlds as much as possible of what unfolds in the world of senses, and can only unfold there. The world of senses is after all there for a purpose. It is not just maya. It exists so that events can unfold there and beings can experience things. What unfolds, and what is experienced, needs to be borne upward into the supersensible world. And the power enabling what is valuable in the sense world to be borne upward into eternities, is that of Ahriman. Giving each moment back to eternity is made possible by Ahriman's power.[356]

In a phone call with friends of the Lagranges, Maria was persuaded to attempt to escape. She left *le vieux logis* one day after writing the letter to Toni Schwarz, but returned in the evening because the agreed rendezvous failed due to a misunderstanding. On the following day, November 5, 1942, she left the house again for another attempt, and never returned.

~

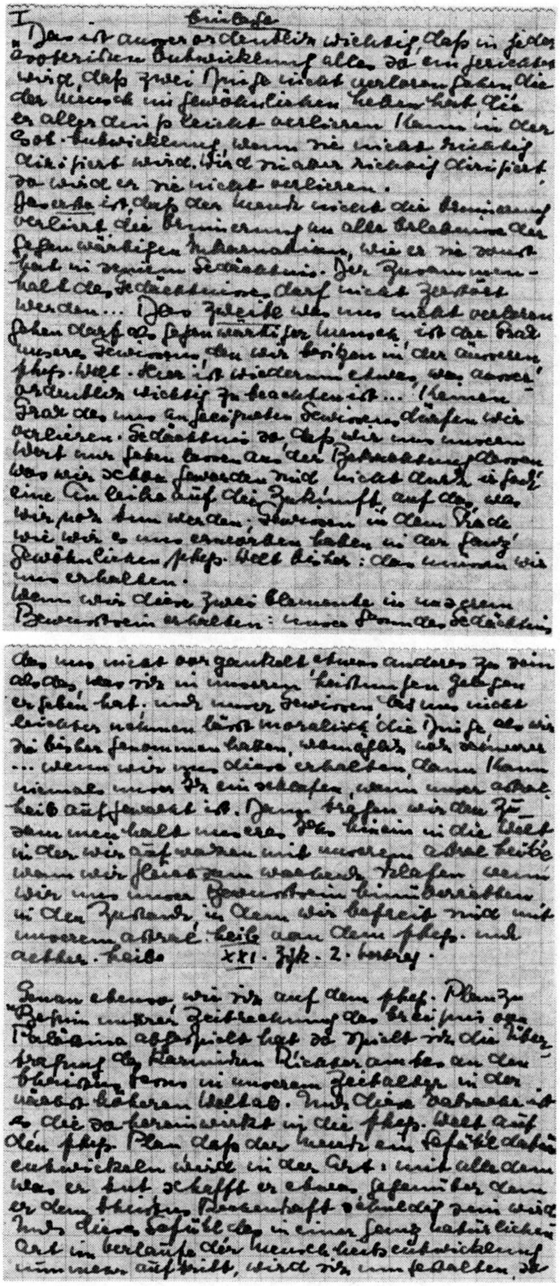

Figure 69: Maria Krehbiel-Darmstädter: passages from lectures by Rudolf Steiner, enclosed in a letter of November 3, 1942

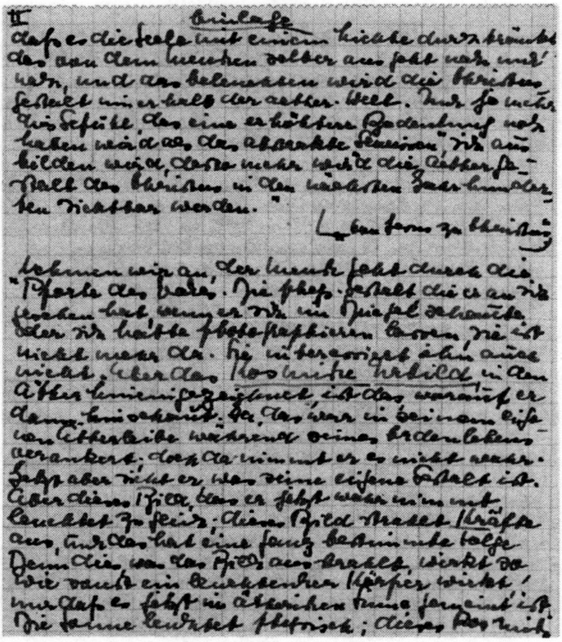

II Beilage

daß es die Seele mit einem Lichte durchleuchtet, das von dem Menschen selber ausgeht nach und nach, und das beleuchten wird die Christus-Gestalt innerhalb der Aether-Welt. Und je mehr sich das Gefühl, das eine erhöhtere Bedeutung noch haben wird als das abstrakte „Gewissen", sich ausbilden wird, desto mehr wird die Aethergestalt des Christus in den nächsten Jahrhunderten sichtbar werden."

Von Jesus zu Christus

Nehmen wir an, der Mensch geht durch die „Pforte des Todes". Die phys. Gestalt, die er an sich gesehen hat, wenn er sich im Spiegel schaute, oder sich hätte photographieren lassen, sie ist nicht mehr da. Sie interessiert ihn auch nicht, aber das kosmische Urbild, in den Äther hineingezeichnet, ist das, worauf er dann hinschaut. Ja, das war in seinem eigenen Ätherleibe während seines Erdenlebens verankert, doch da nimmt er es nicht wahr. Jetzt aber sieht er, was seine eigene Gestalt ist. Aber dieses Bild, das er jetzt wahrnimmt, leuchtet geistig; dieses Bild strahlt Kräfte aus, und das hat eine ganz bestimmte Folge. Denn die, von dem Bild ausstrahlt, wirkt so wie sonst ein leuchtender Körper wirkt, nur daß es jetzt im ätherischen Sinne gemeint ist. Die Sonne leuchtet physisch; dieses kosmisch

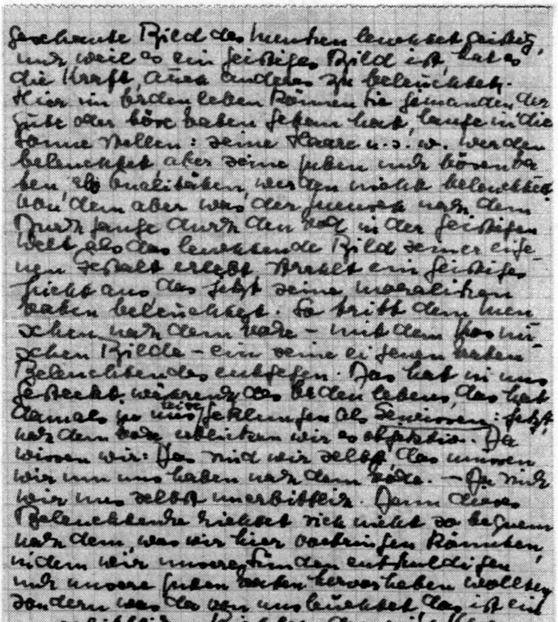

geschaute Bild des Menschen leuchtet geistig, und weil es ein geistiges Bild ist, hat es die Kraft, auch anderes zu beleuchten. Hier im Erdenleben können Sie jemanden, der Gutes oder Böses getan hat, in die Sonne stellen: seine Haare u.s.w. werden beleuchtet, aber seine guten und bösen Taten, Eigenschaften, werden nicht beleuchtet von dem. Aber was der Mensch nach dem Durchgang durch den Tod in der geistigen Welt als das leuchtende Bild seiner eigenen Gestalt erlebt, strahlt ein geistiges Licht aus, das jetzt seine moralischen Taten beleuchtet. So tritt dem Menschen nach dem Tode – mit dem kosmischen Bilde – ein seine eigenen Taten Beleuchtendes entgegen. Das hat in uns gesteckt während des Erdenlebens, das hat damals in uns geklungen als Gewissen; jetzt nach dem Tode erblicken wir es objektiv. Da wissen wir: So sind wir selbst, das nennen wir in uns haben nach dem Tode. — So sind wir uns selbst unerbittlich. Denn dieses Beleuchtende richtet sich nicht so bequem nach dem, was wir hier ergreifen können, indem wir unsere Sünden entschuldigen und unsere guten Taten hervorheben wollen, sondern was da von uns leuchtet, das ist ein unerbittlicher Richter, der mit klarem

*Figure 70: Maria Krehbiel-Darmstädter in Drancy
at the end of 1942 or beginning of 1943*

4.

Drancy and Auschwitz

"Here below we have no peace.
But future peace we seek."
Adieu, Maria. Who is yours.
Maria Krehbiel-Darmstädter, February 6, 1943

On November 5, shortly before her train departed from Lyon for Lons-le-Saunier, a center of resistance 120 kilometers to the North in the department of Jura—the new agreed meeting place with an escape agent—Maria wrote to Toni Schwarz on one of the latter's own watercolor postcards of a ship. She wrote as follows, in French:

My dear friend

I am taking your little pink lifeboat for my embarkation. A double embarkation both in thoughts and realities. I am trying this once more. Will it be the right thing this time? Let's hope so. But let us be tranquil above all and dwell in the desired surrender, for which my whole being so yearns. I think of Verlaine's wonderful verses. These: *Les sanglots longs / des violons / de l'automne / blessent mon coeur / d'une langueur monotone. / Tout suffoquant / et blême / quand sonne l'heure, / je me souvien / des jours anciens / et je pleure. / Et je m'en vai / au vent mauvais / qui m'emporte / de ça, de là / pareil a là / feuille morte.**

I learned this poem as a young girl at my Swiss boarding school, and never forgot it. Since then my season-steps have been colored

---

*   The long sobs / of the violins of autumn / wound my heart with their monotonous melancholy. / Scarce able to breathe / and pale / when the hour chimes / I remember / days of old / and I weep. /And I take my way with the insidious wind / that carries me / this way and that / just like / the dead leaf.

by this sense of "being carried off." As much music as melancholy. It's true. Hold my hand for you have long held my heart. This is no letter and needs no reply. I will write again soon.
Maria

On the sixth, I think of my mother's birthday. Farewell until we meet again. Let us pray strongly for each other. Leave the pullover, or wait.

But the attempted flight encountered further difficulties and the escape agent vanished in Lons-le-Saunier. In the end, Maria had to hide away in a hotel for two weeks, largely alone and without safety or protection, knowing that the Gestapo were looking for her. She appeared passive and resigned, beleaguered and lonely.[357] She wrote to Margot Junod on November 17: "*Croyez-moi que jamais avant je n'ai pensé avec une force aussi intense, und force douloureuse a vous tout. Combien j'aimerais vous embrasser!*"* Her room in Limonest had been a last earthly home for her. Now she had finally been uprooted and left vulnerably exposed.

Lons-le-Saunier lay just seventy kilometers from the Swiss border: the destination was close yet seemed almost unattainable. Maria continued to feel great agitation and ambivalence about the rightness and significance of this action, her "private" escape. We know little about her during this period. In the end she was able to leave with a group of Dutch émigrés, and reach Switzerland, before her fate took its ultimate turn: "We were already on Swiss soil and turned right instead of left at a fork in the road. Knocking on a house door we were met by Germans, and were arrested and imprisoned."[358]

～

Maria Krehbiel-Darmstädter told the truth about herself and was taken to Drancy, the Gestapo's horseshoe-shaped collection and transit camp near Paris, in which up to 7,000 people waited to be transported on to the East, to Auschwitz and Lublin-Majdanek

---

* Believe me that never before have I thought with such intensity and painful power of all of you. How I wish I could embrace you.

From Drancy, on December 3, 1942—four weeks after she tried to flee—she wrote to an acquaintance in Limonest and asked her to send a few essentials, again possibly both for herself and others ("since *we* are in sore need"), including a grey bag, blankets, boots, her fur coat, rucksack, pajamas, handkerchief, soap, thermos flask and socks—and "all my plates and the bowl from Gurs." She asked her friend to inform Father Toureille of her circumstances, and merely remarked on them:

> The previous gentle months and the year before it now seem to me like enviable dreams. One has to defend oneself with the last reserves of one's being; and without the serene patience that draws on God alone, no doubt I would soon falter.

Maria was housed in very cramped conditions in Block 15 of the huge transit camp. The sixty people she shared this space with were Polish Jews waiting for compulsory repatriation to the country that was no longer their home, and their death in a Nazi death camp run by the "General Government." Four weeks later Maria Krehbiel-Darmstädter wrote of her relations with this group: "Here again, in a camp, all love me. They address me as "Madame Mère Maria". Things are not so good here as in Gurs. It is dirty and noisy."[359] Despite the difficult circumstances and her embattled state, Maria Krehbiel-Darmstädter's generosity of spirit affected the people around her in Drancy, too. Clearly, *Mère Maria* was once again able to offer them help and support.

On December 10, she wrote a hurried note to Marie Baum asking whether it was possible to send a copy of the "Aryan ID" of Emil Krehbiel, her divorced husband, and to inform Walter Schmitthenner and his uncle Paul Schmitthenner, who was minister of culture in Baden and an influential party official. Apparently she had again been urgently advised in Drancy to try every means to save herself before being sent to Auschwitz. She told Marie Baum that there was hope that a petition from Schmitthenner, and the existence of her divorced husband's Aryan ID, might be of some use; but she also added: "If

Figure 71: The inner yard at Camp Drancy

not, be tranquil at my fate. I strive to surrender myself and to walk on bravely where life leads. May God protect us all."

Six days later, on December 16, 1942, Margot Junod, who had also received news from Maria, wrote to Franz Darmstädter:

> After all forebodings, a brief, desolate card informed me today that Marie's attempt to flee has failed. She is in a reception camp and will be deported to Poland. The exact address on December 3 was Camp de Drancy près de Paris, bloc 14, escalier 4, chambre 7. This camp must be far worse than Gurs and M. has no money or any belongings. Though Father Freudenberg thinks the outlook is hopeless, we will go on trying everything. But I am so afraid that this may have been the last news we will hear of her.[360]

As an army officer, Walter Schmitthenner—Maria's godson—succeeded in visiting Drancy on January 6, 1943, the feast of Epiphany. Alone with him she was able to tell him about her failed escape bid. And said:

> Perhaps this was the right thing. I didn't have a good feeling about my attempt to flee with the escape agent. It was a skewed undertaking to try to evade my duty of being wherever human beings must suffer. I was not pursuing this with my heartfelt agreement. And it is right that things worked out differently.[361]

Maria struck Walter Schmitthenner as being wasted and ill, careworn by her experiences over the past two years and her illness. He succeeded in getting her admitted temporarily to Hospital Rothschild in Paris. Yet her farewell to him was definitive: "Greet everyone, all of them. My husband, his wife, his child. Please give him this [a volume containing the Gospel of St. Matthew]—I have nothing else. Frau Dr. Baum, everyone. The country, the houses." She spoke of her "invisible community" of people and left him with this memorable phrase: "Tell everyone: I am a good representative of Germany." She bore Germany in her heart, she said.[362] Schmitthenner brought with him to Drancy from Emil Krehbiel a book containing notes on Anthroposophy, which Maria Krehbiel-Darmstädter had written by hand at the time of her engagement and given to her future husband. "Ah yes," she said, "I know this: I am very pleased to see it again here."[363]

The Germany, Maria bore within her and wished to "represent" was a different realm from the one that was in the process of sending her—along with millions of others—to their death in the gas chamber. The spiritual Germany she referred to was one Maria Krehbiel-Darmstädter did not relinquish. It encompassed the humanistic culture of German idealism and its furtherance through Rudolf Steiner's anthroposophic Spiritual Science—true insight into human nature and the world encompassing science, art and religion. As a Jew by birth Maria shared the fate of the people of Israel who—as she saw it—bore the real destiny of humanity, the "form of what is human" (Celan[364]). The Nazis program of murder and destruction, seemingly dictated solely by fanatical anti-Semitism and racism, was in a sense directed against the human being as such and the Representative of Humanity (Christ); and was thus also an attack on the "other Germany" and its Christological heart. Maria Krehbiel-Darmstädter's deep connections with this other Germany and also to Judaism—as the realm of prophets and of Jesus of Nazareth, of preparation for all that the future held—were spiritual in nature, profoundly pondered and consistently adhered to. Friedrich Rittelmeyer once had a dream in which he asked Rudolf Steiner how the text of the Act of Consecration of Man had come to be written down. Steiner replied: "I had to go to a place where the German language was taught in mantric form."[365] To the very end, Maria Krehbiel-Darmstädter felt herself pledged and indebted to this super-geographical Germany *"sans adresse."* "The German spirit has not brought to completion / What it must still create in world evolution," wrote Rudolf Steiner at the beginning of a verse about a country whose spiritual task was a matter of profound concern to him.[366]

~

*Figure 72: Rudolf Steiner's bust of Christ
(modeling clay, the Goetheanum, Dornach, 1915)*

Maria was able to stay at Hospital Rothschild for a few weeks, and to recover a little. She received news from Margot Junod who told her among other things of the birth of her daughter. Maria wrote her a postcard on January 20, 1943: "Here, where I am treated as a sick prisoner, the tender news I received from you is the most effective medicine. News so full of the deepest solace: that we remain connected."

Writing of her own situation, she went on:

Ever more spiritualized due to lack of spoken words and correspondence, you increase in the realm of thought, gathering yourself in an almost permanent prayer. Although I am once again in a large ward, the noise is just a sort of confusion that no longer disturbs my reflections; I am so used to it. I am strictly confined to bed because of my blood pressure and heart condition, and this is an immeasurable difference compared with the past, tortured weeks. This sudden relaxation is almost like a blow. Almost. But the wonderful thing about the transfer here [is that it] keeps me, at the same time, in continuous worship. I never cease pondering on the goodness of God and of my friends.

She was only rarely allowed to write—one postcard every two weeks.

The last message Toni Schwarz received from Maria Krehbiel-Darmstädter came once more from the camp at Drancy, and was dated February 5, 1943. She wrote (in French) about her sudden return from Hospital Rothschild to the camp, and of her disappointment and weariness:

More weakened than anything by the treatment, which kept me in bed the whole time; and then this weakness of soul, you know. And for the first time I feel myself growing weak, both physically and spiritually. Erika and her fate fill me with agitation for good reason. You understand what I mean, and that these words are for you. Addressed to you so as to thank you once more for this whole friendship, deep support in these hours when the light seems extinguished...the trials—will one endure them? With the help of the Lord who has unlimited power: I know this. But I still lack it.

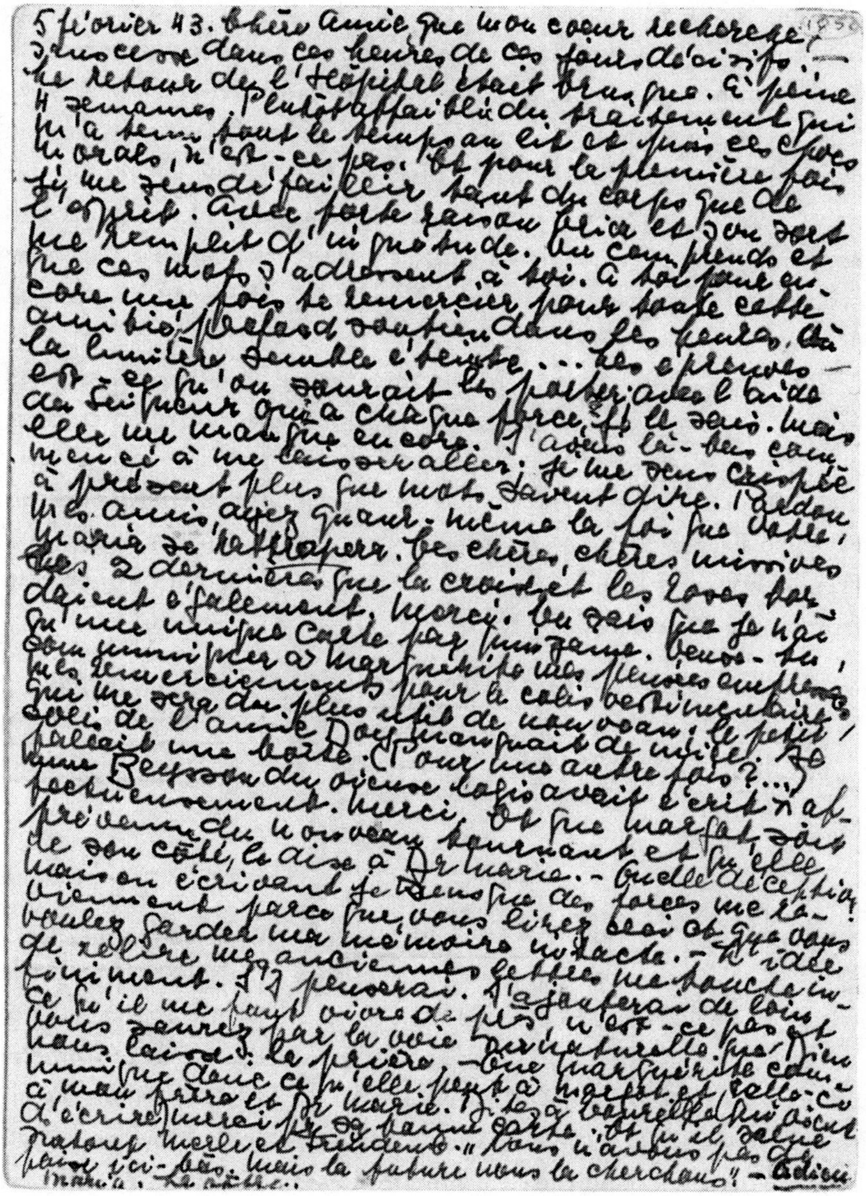

*Figure 73: Maria Krehbiel-Darmstädter's postcard
to Toni Schwarz. Drancy, February 5, 1943*

Once again Maria expressed concern for the fate of a friend, the solicitor Erika Sinauer from Freiburg, who had been deported to Gurs with her and Toni Schwarz. She too had been given sick leave from Gurs a few months after Maria, and gone to stay in the Drôme department, where Maria wrote often to her. At the end of August there were no further replies from her. Maria did not know what had happened to her—though she had a hunch: Erika Sinauer had been arrested and deported to the East via Drancy. She had already been dead for months.

Through Toni Schwarz, Maria also turned to other friends and took her farewell: "In writing, I feel my strength returning because you will read this, and because you wish to preserve my memory intact." She thanked everyone and also asked her greetings to be conveyed to Father Toureille (who had written to her in Drancy), Adolf Freudenberg and Jeanne Merle d'Aubigné. She ended with a quotation from St. Paul's letter to the Hebrews:

> *Nous n'avons pas de paix ici-bàs. Mais la future nous la cherchons.*
> *Adieu.* Maria. La vôtre.
> (Here below we have no peace. But future peace we seek.
> *Farewell.* Maria. Who is yours.)

~

Six days after her postcard to Toni Schwarz, on February 11, 1943, Maria Krehbiel-Darmstädter was transported to Auschwitz in a cattle truck. The truck remained sealed for the whole journey. Maria may not have been aware, therefore, that the train passed close to Mannheim on its journey through Germany. Two days later, on February 13, the train halted at the Alte Judenrampe, a platform between the village of Auschwitz and the extermination camp Birkenau. After being forced to leave the cattle truck, Maria and her companions underwent a "selection" right on the platform. Of the 998 Jews who arrived with her transport from Drancy, only a few young people capable of work—including fifty-three women—were selected for work and later

Thank you for visiting the
Allen County Public Library

Barcode: 31833066237055
Title: From Gurs to Auschwitwitz : th...
Type: BOOK
Due date: 11/20/2013,23:59

Total items checked out: 1

Telephone Renewal: 421-1240
Website Renewal: www.acpl.info

accommodated in the camp barrack. The others were transported immediately by trucks (or had to walk) to the gas chambers, "Bunker 1" or "Bunker 2," located almost three kilometers from the platform. They all died there, including Maria Krehbiel-Darmstädter, whose name does not appear on any arrival lists (and thus was not selected for work).

Around six months before she died at Auschwitz, Maria had written in a letter:

> *"Il ne faut pas savoir le matin où l'on couchera le soir."*[*] This is nothing other than the path to truth and life, the intrinsic nature of initiation. To possess as if one possesses nothing. To regard everything one has and is as only being lent; and what does this require other than to take wing, to lift the sole of the foot from the ground...shake off the dust when the spiritual journey begins? You may think my words a riddle. And—there's no more I can say to you....
>
> We will be transformed from one clarity into another. And "wandering" from one pain into the next we are the people of God whose path is, as ever, the path to God. Cast out and willing to suffer, we are victorious in pursuing a devotional obedience. The lamb is the symbol of a willingness to follow a path that is *essential* if we are to prevail. Without violence, speechless—pervaded only by the strength of gentleness, the strength of the path to be followed. The love of God passes all understanding—is this true? It *is* true. It equips us to be children, and to fulfil our sacrifice "in the Father."[367]

---

[*] One should not know in the morning where one will lay one's head at night

Figure 74: The gate of Auschwitz-Birkenau

Part II

"No Separation Where Love of Being and Truth in Christ Prevail"

Excerpts from letters
by Maria Krehbiel-Darmstädter
1940–1943

*Figure 75: Maria Krehbiel-Darmstädter with a seagull;
at the house of Hilda and Jacques Lagrange, Lyon, January 1942*

Camp de Gurs, November 6, 1940
To Margot Junod, her family and friends

My dearest friends and relatives—

You must have heard the news of our sudden departure from Baden. For the past two weeks we have been the guests of France. Naturally ill-equipped, and now under harsh and arduous circumstances: direct help would be needed. It appears that immigration to America is proceeding rapidly, and I must inform my sister and cousin for the purpose of obtaining renewed sureties from them. If one has relatives who can pay the necessary minimum each month, one can leave the camp and live in unoccupied France until the immigration permit for America arrives. All these steps have to be taken but naturally they take time. Dear Margot, I hope with all my heart that your parents are still living peacefully. (There are numerous Belgians in the next *ilot*—ah, their sad appearance, and so strenuous to try to survive.) There is a mess facility here, but the food is scarce and not nutritious. Would it be possible to send a few concentrated and nutritious food items? Butter, cheese, tea and something to quench thirst since the water here is undrinkable. (We can't cook but get something to eat three times a day.) Many people are sick. Writing paper, ink pens and above all strong boots or Wellingtons since the paths between the barrack we're allowed to walk about on are muddy. It often rains but the early afternoons are often bright and very warm. Because of the mountains. And the nights are very cold. I am afraid, my dear, that it's not possible to send parcels, except perhaps through the Red Cross? We'd be so glad to have some woollen things (all very thin since there's so little room!) and a ski suit would be ideal. But let's leave fears and complaints aside. You know that I am fortunate to be alone in all this, with my neighbor as my relative. And one has an opportunity to help in so many circumstances—the poor people, the poor, old people. One has to keep one's courage up and stay healthy. Having learned humility previously means drawing now on a wonderful source of strength. But the farewells! The dear friends one has had to take leave from forever, without permitted contact except via the Red Cross. Maut, can you write to Dr. Hanna Glaser. L 12, 18 in M? She is half-Aryan and has been allowed to stay: her mother's maiden name is Darmst, a distant relative. We are friends, and she can pass on the news you give her to other friends. Please send to all my warmest thoughts and say that I remain peaceful at heart despite everything. Send me your news. How is the little one? How are you all? When did you last get news of Claire and Hans? And please, do tell Georg or Hans's mother where I am! I embrace you all very warmly. Your friend and godmother Maria Krehbiel.

~

Camp de Gurs, November 19, 1940
To her brother and his family

My dear ones

My address will no doubt not be news to you. We have been living here for the past 4 weeks—many people together in the difficult conditions of life in a barrack. Physical and soul powers are sorely tried, and without wishing to cause you anxiety I hope you might endeavor to ease our plight.

I know for a fact that gifts from loved ones are permitted; and from Bern in greater amounts than just two kilos. But even that would be wonderful!

The most important would be concentrated, nutritious foods. Then charcoal and alcohol for medicinal purposes (much diarrhea and bronchial conditions .) Warm gloves, warm socks, warm vests etc.

Please write and send items and tell me how things are for you, and your views. Can we get to the United States from here? I will write to Lulu. Maybe there's some way of helping everyone here.

Thank God I have been able to overcome some health problems, and there is huge opportunity for giving loving service to others. (Our sole wealth.)

With loving greetings to you all—from your sister
Maria Krehbiel

~

Camp de Gurs, November 27, 1940
To Anneliese Herweck and her family

Dear, precious Annelies and you other loved ones—

By now you will have received the first letter I sent to Bex-Gryon?... And from Margot, I hope, more news of my situation.

I am very thankful to say that there's nothing worse to report! The weather is sunny and the dreadful footpaths are drying up a little. It is bitterly cold at night. I think how good it would be to have mother's plaid here with me, a sleeping bag, a fleece. One starts wishing for things, knowing them to be beyond reach, and then tries to summon *from within* the warmth one lacks, the absence of protection.

Deep feelings—and simple ones—pass through you here. Things to do with life and death. What one wrestles with is not to lose love for one's neighbor.... "Naked" egoism initially wants nothing but to live.

The unaccustomed fact of living so closely together with others in noisy misfortune is not yet something that is taken for granted. Despite wishing and good intentions and efforts: one must not give oneself up to illusory hopes of speedy liberation.

I find myself hoping for letters—which are like gentle blessings. The writing paper you sent was very welcome. Perhaps you could also some time send those lightweight, airmail envelopes?

Everything is relatively expensive yet one has to pay for what is most urgently needed. And procure everything available (mostly fruit) that can keep us healthy.

Naturally we look forward to getting a parcel with essentials and food. Maybe at Christmas?

Sunday is the first of Advent. I have two candles with me. Also a picture of the Madonna. My little corner is the outermost one in the hut, the coldest—but also the most secluded and quietest, and this is a great help to me in bearing up. A beautiful angel, faithfully included in my thoughts, hovers over this spot. I have a picture of my teacher R. St. and of Margot's little Jean-Christoph, which I was so glad to receive a few days ago as a loving greeting.

Please, to save postage, send Margot my thanks this time. I had just finished writing when her letter arrived.

Dear Annelies, you see that I wrote to your friends too straight away. The reply, which must be very painful for you, I simply enclose here....

I am very pleased about your move. Hopefully you can stay there until you can all leave. We just don't know what will happen, do we?

You can say that my house was in good order when I left. For a long time I had only the absolute essentials—which then one thought of as "the absolute essentials," but was of course luxury compared to here. But I was always ready for this kind of upheaval. And mourn deeply what I left behind. Without despair.

I faithfully embrace you.

M.

Could you include a reply postal voucher?

~

Camp de Gurs, December 8, 1940
To Margot Junot

Days of heavy downpour again, a crush in the barrack, darkness, poverty. When these equinoctial storms are unleashed over us with thunder and lightning, distinct individuality is almost extinguished by creaturely need.

And what strange misery when you have to go out into rain and storm to relieve yourself, at night, too. The least blade of grass your foot treads on is drowning in forlorn wet.

How well my parents lie. How glad I am that these beloved ones have found safety both above and beneath the earth.

And how hard to wrestle through to the good. A long wait in rain and storm when parcels—so much longed for—are distributed. Yesterday a greeting came from your friends in Lyon: a parcel with charcoal for medicine. One of the medicines we most need. So did they get my letter I wonder, or did you alert them to the need?

The dullest days have arrived now. Before Christmas. It was impossible to attend Mass today. One has a strong inward sense of *the necessity of* participating in preparations. Lying awake at night, I gather around me the best feelings I can.

~

Camp de Gurs, December 12, 1940
To her brother and his family

My state of health has not improved, owing to the dire weather (downpours, flooded paths, the cold and darkness: a Pyrenean winter). But thank God I have still managed to conquer the worst (severe cold, diarrhea, weakness). I have a ravenous hunger! As most do here. The air and maybe the unaccustomed conditions and other things gnaw at you so that you'd like to be always eating, and buy yourself foods—not cheap—from the mess. Fruit, biscuits, dates and figs are the usual thing. Once we had preserved fruit. The greatest lack is fats. I feel I have lost weight—but I'm cheerful and:—grateful to be so. Amidst the miseries you can't survive without egoism,—yet conscience comes into play. Often your body is flooded with a sense of gratitude that gives it unusual strength. Shouldn't I therefore give to others? Everyone has their particular role in the barrack community. Mine is chiefly to mediate and help with the elderly. Of whom there are so many more than younger or young people. Your heart goes out to the poor elderly!

How peaceful, dear brother, it is to think of the grave where our parents lie under the little birch tree in quiet seclusion.

For me the most incisive experience here was: the area set aside for the ever-increasing rows of graves in the cemetery. There are many of my acquaintances there already. I saw it once (you can only go there when people close to you are buried) in its magnificent position and so also perceived the whole nature of this situation here. The camp is surrounded by the most interesting ring of mountains, also a far view of eternal snows; but from the camp itself you can witness only what is very close at hand—and terribly earthly.

You have to look *up* to gain more than anguish and fear… all life is purchased at such a cost, every need such a problem. Where all is lacking and one lives "under the open heavens."

But—where difficulty is *so* weighty, suddenly it is lifted and the clouds part.

Christmas here—is really an experience of the utmost impoverishment. Wooden joists and straw and night and the sense of being forlorn—how strong the certainty of conquering light has to become. And how happy he who has the gift of memories of celebration and altar and annunciation.

I am so glad that you three have a lovely home again and can celebrate there. Dear Kläre, dear Franz, dear Boppa, I embrace you with all my grateful love and inward Christmas spirit. Don't torture yourself with worry about me, please. Just enjoy giving me pleasure with the loving kindness of your parcels (Flannels. Almonds, artificial honey—the solid but spreadable kind). You can decide what to put in. Woolen socks and tights, a rubber-band belt, a strainer and sugar, instant coffee (Nescafé) some tea, cocoa; that probably doesn't need mentioning, and flour—perhaps containing milk and fat?—to dissolve in hot water to make a nutritious porridge sometimes.

~

Camp de Gurs, January 10, 1941
To Maria Gnädinger and the friends in Bern

Dear friends

I was profoundly glad to get the journal you sent, and today your letter dear Maria.

I wonder if you have any idea what it means to me to keep in touch here with our communal support, its sacred healing? The grace that speaks of the "bread that does not feed us" is continually true. We eat and drink spirit, and cannot live otherwise. The most wonderful signs in the heavens and the clouds just a little way above the darkest atmosphere of Earth are experiences that offer continual healing.

And this is needed. Also to share with others. How glad I would be to expound vigorously of such things. But even that is not necessary. Living here is a service—and: we are served. Everyone who comes, as you do now to me, is a messenger of the good, of bright solace.

Christmas here was a deeply moving experience. We also have our Protestant and Catholic worship. We have a wonderful priest, the greatness of whose inward devotion at the Christmas Eve service would have moved you.... I also found here a member of Dold[inger]'s parish—Miss Schwarz; she paints beautifully and I sometimes meet her. She would be very grateful if you would write to Herr Dold. about her circumstances. Please.

It is so good that you want to send us spiritual nourishment and even loving parcels...we also have other faithful people, almost a radiant circle who stand watch over us. So don't exhaust your resources! But every word you send will be so gratefully received, with a reminder of our indestructible, joyful and vigorous connection. Please send special greetings to Hansele, who is new to me. Send me the picture of the resurrected Christ.

In close bonds of old, Maria K.

~

Camp de Gurs, January 27, 1941
To her brother and his family

I have got to know, and am still getting to know a huge number of people here, partly through my role of "responsibility" for the Protestants in my *ilot*. And since funds and gifts arrive, there is always something to be done, to discuss, someone to visit or look after. And love to be given to all. It is wonderful what one becomes acquainted with here and learns to understand. Oh what a strange place in the world this is!

A place where people are worn down and edified in equal measure. Outside of the usual "earthly order." And therefore a very important place of the greatest furtherance and super-temporal phenomena. Residing here therefore confronts us with new tasks! Spring days have already arrived. Sudden outbreaks of the warmest, flooding light and red dawns—during which we drink our coffee by the open door. Fold our hands round our hot cups, eat our precious bread with reverence.... This is a "gift" since none earn anything here! And the starry nights, when you walk out lonely to the toilet, a long way off! So strangely still—all in quiet repose. And the dividing fence becomes a protective hedge. God still loves us after all. It is often enough to make your heart break.

~

Camp de Gurs, March 5, 1941
To Margot Junot

An important visit at present from the priest in charge of serving the French camps, Mr. Toureille. I gave you his address in December, and he did not return until now (Father Freud[enberg] is continually in touch with him.) We have had fine gatherings—for worship and just to meet and talk, and I am deeply, warmly grateful for them.

You know, the length of time, growing habituation—which wears one down mentally—physical weariness, spring fatigue: all these weaken one's élan and this makes me unhappy! But then comes renewal at just the right moment—and you live anew, with new willingness, finding new dedication and new loving kindness. As if nourished anew—Margot, My dear. You can understand this, I know, for what else should we live from and survive on? Simply enduring is not at all enough to cope with what is and is to be. For we are, no doubt, in for the long haul here. No point in having illusions about it.

How shall I say this? The sick leave is also a problem—in principle, not just its length. The regions in France that used to be open have now been forced to close their doors. And the open ones are far off, and how can one obtain a Cert. d'Hébergement [visitor's residence permit] there? Despite this, of course, I will faithfully pursue the path we embarked on until the application is accepted—or turned down. At any rate, the sick leave would be of limited duration. And I am deeply thankful to have the comfort of accepting *everything*, whatever comes. There are unlikely to be any great changes here. Perhaps increasing tasks for the individual in relation to his community. Well here we are—while the world's history unfolds.

It is a strange fact that we are so marginalized yet a part of this history.

Also that despite everything we live as if—richly endowed. A stream of love flows round us, and we witness great loyalty. The grace, "It's not the bread that feeds us, what feeds us in the bread, is God's eternal Word" bears such majestic truth within it: it really is so fortifying. For God speaks here. And we are the fortunate possessors of His Word.

~

Camp de Gurs, mid-March 1941
To Ida Deutsch

Dear, good Aunt Idel

How pleased and surprised I was to get your letter, sounding so warm as you always did in the past.

We know each other well enough to be kind to each other, don't we? Yet back then, of course, we went through some experiences together. How long ago that was, after what happened and bore us away to such a distance.... The inexpressible and tumultuous nature of those events has not yet faded entirely, although of course we accustom ourselves to things and so they are soothed. It's astonishing what people can endure. First, if you have to. Then if you surrender to it and gain insight as well. These always come upon you, "choose" you like a kind of grace. And then you stand, much moved, before your own destiny, as if before a secret half revealed and half concealed. Where you live as if in a place of responsibility—: you might say, toward humanity. So great a test we undergo; and greater the love that arches over it.... Visible in the elemental powers, the phenomena of the heavens—the distant, sharply outlined mountain ranges. These latter in gloomy, ancient, volcanic foreboding; some in quiet, though far-off, luminous majesty. At a very great distance snowy peaks rise even, as if married with cloud, wind and light.

But the soil, the earth here, is strangely mud-like, very rapidly softened so that you sink right into it; and this makes for the greatest difficulty, requiring great attention, confinement and a gaze—fixed—on the ground. This and all kinds of privation must be admitted. A *waiting* hangs over us all here...what may Heaven still intend for us? But all of us who suffer here, who endure and keep faith, would wish to be worthy of blessing. Aunt Idel, I'd like you to know that.

~

Camp de Gurs, March 19, 1941
To Laure Wagner, Margot Junod
and the friends in Heidelberg and Mannheim

You have no idea how quickly time passes here in all kinds of work and organization and continual interruptions from visitors. If you have a responsible role you have to counsel many who ask you things. I am often fairly weary in consequence, but also often content—so much so that I don't even wish to leave but am learning to regard this place as the most fitting for me. You might say that my whole former life seems to have equipped me to serve here and stand the test. Even in purely physical terms. The limitations and constrictions here become *rich* in renunciation—and also offer a freedom that cheers and strengthens you. It is as though a juice were pressed out of you that in turn has a regenerating effect, like a refreshing drink. Do I keep repeating myself?

At night, when the winds blow or the profound stillness stands there in our streets in its infinite depth, the stars moving across the heavens and the Moon rising and setting, then—often having to go out—you experience such connection with the sublime. And in the grey wasteland of ground and barrack: these colors in the sky, sometimes almost grandiose in their splendor, at other times delicate and faint to the point of vanishing. And the chain of mountains. Inexpressible the gratitude one feels for this luminosity and anchorage of the mountains conveyed to eye and spirit. These things are more important than all else here: the water flowing in the basins that gives you the sense each morning that everything can be washed away. Unheard of—to bathe your face in the water like this, to let it flow and to sip it and slurp it (despite it being not at all "healthy" in quality, and wine being recommended to us instead). Here you have a sense of life that has no resemblance to the past. You slowly become one with nature: a single violet, a piece of moss, two daisies on a makeshift table with a white napkin are the focus of rapture for many of our poor inmates.

Someone brought them in from outside. But at the edge of our paths, too, the grass sprouts so greenly. So green. And soon it will be Easter.

~

Camp de Gurs, around March 20 1941
To Maria Gnädinger

My dear Maria

Your good little letter stroked my heart like a good, helpful bow, and enticed soft sounds from it. Now they're fading, but not without being heard I think? They know of us, and that we make efforts to anchor the place where our feet have had to gain purchase. The place where spirit stands. In the special, difficult magnificence of this Pyr. landscape we have whole armies of manifold elemental qualities: they help us with their scintillating beauty, at other times—do battle with us. Glorious days of sunshine, terrible days of rain; the heavens full of sights such as I have never, ever seen before—the chain of mountains both so solid and so changing is most beloved of all to us. Feelings of redemption are medicine here, you see, and the sacramental must thrive because we need it so very much. Love—suffering and adversity are submerged in the infinite. We are taken up, received. I have never yet lost this certainty.

But leaving, seeking a different abode: this is increasingly impossible. After all, one is just a tiny sliver in the encompassing whole, and cannot expect special dispensation. And—believe me—seen from this perspective it is even better to remain where one is. Impossible to explain this better. My dear ones, who have made such efforts, I hope you will forgive if all your labors go awry. (But, by the way, very young children and old people have moved to a different camp.) I have reached the point of seeing that change does not—change very much. Just new exertions, transits, journeys, losses etc. I have grown to love a great deal here…above all our *Eglise universelle* protest. [Universal Protestant Church], as the great prison chaplain Toureille embodies it—and established it here. We have fine, yes even magnificent moments. And communion services: the plates, cups, bread and bottles of our daily life—touched by something close to the most sacred. How, how can I explain this? The poverty of the greatest wealth—love. Here, too, we are preparing for Easter. Flowers brought in from outside: violets, a clump of moss, catkins and—little Hansel's daisies, my dear! Also picked in the meadows. By others. Sweet joys for us, tender care, a white handkerchief is like the richest silk, a box for a table. "He who speaks the 'I' within me is my shepherd."

~

Camp de Gurs, April 11, 1941 (Good Friday)
To her sister and family

My dear ones, dearest Fritze

Your good letters, so full of warm loyalty and concern, and so festively adorned with the golden pansy—they brought me Easter joy. The big pansy is now the aura for the angel I have standing over my camp bed. You may be pleased to know this, and it is wonderful that such a delicate flower survived all the travels and censorship. A special strengthening, also for one's own weakness and situation! My dear ones, can you understand this?

By now you will have heard that my departure permit was turned down as all circumstances are unfavorable, and the efforts of outsiders simply aren't sufficient; and people of average age, specifically, are excluded from transfers to other camps. I continue to complain of nothing. I dedicate my eyes and ears to the grandeur of destiny, seeking to wrest from it what is useful. Thinking in the traditional sense has little purpose here. But: loving, acting, giving joy, receiving joy wherever it can be found, and being comforted in the depths of one's soul.

The festive days we celebrate here are earnest and rich in impressions in a way that many feel, and in response to which they change. But sadly not all. Most are too accustomed to complaint and haste, and get nowhere with either, and cannot overcome the void! For this reason I intentionally take care not to make convulsive exertions that can have such disheartening repercussions when the deadlines repeatedly expire....

Thank you for all the love and devotion you send me in thoughts and deeds. Please also understand my stance: of staying calm and composed in order to survive this time!

Yesterday we had a profound, beautiful musical event [at the Assistance Protestante]. And during the great Beethoven Op. 18, I wandered in my mind through our old house [Werdestrasse 48]. I visited and blessed each room, the stairs, the basement and garden, and was completely at home. I took all of you with me, lovingly.

And was certain of your love when, at the end, I found myself here again. So alone and—not at all forsaken—

A faithful embrace from—your Maria.

~

Camp de Gurs, around April 25, 1941
To Margot Junod and Kläre Hennig

Please don't think that there is no beauty here, where I am physically and—with all my being, too.

I could write whole pages about the landscape, which has a liminal quality. Not merely interesting in meteorological terms but also wonderful in its geology. (It would be good to read Goethe's scientific writings here.) I have never known a more changeable landscape. All gifts of threat and blessing strewn from the heavens. Cloud formations, and heavy, damp mists, paint endless worlds of magic as recompense for the sufferings they bring. The shocks and wonders such as sunrise and sunset bring us almost daily, are rare on Earth. The snow peaks tower over our confines like the noble, mighty railings of godhead. How far away? We do not calculate this. They are distant like our homeland, which we still nevertheless possess.

Believe me, strengthened, prompted in this way, we find a quite natural outlook. It is quite different here from my experience long ago when a vast starry night in the Black Forest in winter overwhelmed me so that I trembled in creaturely impotence. In the early dawn the new day pulls me up and out. There I stand—deep stillness. Being alone. Rare gift. Precious. Indescribably savored. And blessing falls with the dew and encompasses you in inexpressible beauty. We have the reality of God here, and His Creation stands there waiting for the human being who is "given up" to it. That blessing flows from pain shows that we—are alive. And therefore being able to thank is something wholly blissful here.

And the arrival of friends' love that enables us to continue living beyond the present moment: in letters—parcels. Oh, how much good it does. And whoever has none must be eagerly given some of the others' treasure.

Our religious care—which I am permitted to contribute to in a small group—is likewise marvelous. Suitably sober. Deep. Calvinist in tone with wonderful sermons. The ritual element in it as if our life, by its very nature, were *intended to be a rite!* . . .

I also go sometimes to [the Catholic] services because I need the sacrament. But we also had communion celebrations unforgettable in their communal spirit.

Yes, summer is coming. I have the strength to live out the time that must pass until an end arrives.

~

Camp de Gurs, June 25, 1941
To her sister and family

My birthday passed like that of an artist—I was given so many portfolios, pictures, ornaments—even here they flourish. Although I wasn't so aware of it, I may well come to feel this birthday in Gurs to have been a very stirring, moving experience. Almost hourly, people came, as it were, to refresh their congratulations. With a sense of pride. And with rare and precious flower arrangements: a whole sheaf of lilies and white roses and wild orchids and lovely heather.

The last, fiery summer days are upon us now, with glorious dawns, and evenings and nights all spent outside the barrack. Already on the eve of my birthday a real folk festival started up; I was fetched by our lovely barrack child who led me by the hand in my fantastic garment (a bright-blue coat strewn with white flowers, white stockings, yellow clogs—my hair grown very long but still curly. And over all, a sunset painted in every color. And a barrack poem and musical serenade.) And many, tiny gifts, a lucky yellow pig made from a lemon, a little woven basket, perfectly endearing with nougat and an egg and fig bread.

And a cross of lilies, painted, on which were written the words: "Behold, I am with you always, even unto the ends of the Earth." Such a surprise. And several other striking, intimate things.... Children, we are poor with a strange, child-hearted nakedness that is close to fairy tale; and sometimes it seems as if we are very, very rich.

Your good wishes, your love, your help—in both material and inner ways—they enable me, you see, to endure and to hope. If I sometimes burden you with the weariness that also comes to the fore—we nevertheless *have to* embrace what is here. And it is so unspeakably hard—and still harder, to separate out one's own individual destiny and—to save oneself.

It's preferable to be brave and full of patience. Especially since those around you need this so much. Your tender letters that paint a picture for me of a far, far distant home: it's like standing in front of that little vista in the Schwetzingen garden, the "End of the World." You can never decipher it. A lattice before it.

Keep me in your loving thoughts.

~

Camp de Gurs, beginning of July 1941
To the friends in Mannheim and Heidelberg

My dear ones

It is a long way to you. Summer, which shifts our life outdoors more, into nature, withdraws from us a part of our strength of awareness and restraint. It feels like a kind of melting, connected with the fear of loss. A sense of sacrifice developed strongly in these weeks. We ought to practice voluntarily relinquishing what is involuntarily torn from us. Then comes pain at the world's suffering, which likewise reaches like destruction deep into your inner being. And insight into the love that is needed becomes so all-embracing that the vision of the Cross, of the grave, of Resurrection, becomes the sole real activity of your being.

Where do we start to be "ourselves," and where do we cease to be this? ...

St. John's tide: a time of humility and lament. The seriousness and mission of cosmic worlds. It is the crowning transition we pass through. How wondrous that one's soles burn with sensitivity.

This only as a sign of life and love.

Your Maria

~

Camp de Gurs, around July 15, 1941
To the friends in Mannheim and Heidelberg

My dear ones, it is Sunday—and bright thanks to you for what has flowed out to me again from you. The picture of the *Disputa*, concentrated as if into an "essence" by the small form. And also the intense garnering of what is great—here like nowhere else.... The whole dome of the heavens serves, indeed, as overflowing and Earth blessing. And the altar! The absent or empty center—here given back. It is a deep, deep reassurance to have this reproduction here. So that one enlarges it for oneself and renews one's powers through it;—like cleansing oneself, my dear ones, after long days of bitter isolation. Actually, I imagine the altar as standing on the steps that lead down to the old, deserted cemetery where my parents lie. Behind it lies the land of home: the sky of home, the trees and river—the far towers. And you, you dear ones, so precious to me, more so than anyone I have here. Although—and I say this in gratitude—there are people here with whom the same feeling, the same reverence, yes, the same knowledge connects me. But who could pass to me the gifts that you can? Today came like—nourishment. And I have to gaze upon the sacrament, and the benediction of the white figure of Christ who stands there as if—"eternally in my soul."...

Do not think me too effusive if I lean myself against you, wondering at the living possessions of your souls and feeling the coldness and heat of life being soothed and healed. Please share in this with my gratitude.

Morgenstern's "Washing of the Feet," if you could copy it down, would be a real gift for me. On the table I sometimes have an artwork, or a verse and exhortation, along with all the stones: little treasures I've found, witness to ancient eras, contexts and cultures. The land here is filled with meaning going a very long way back. And history rises from mountains and wasteland: sometimes threatening, sometimes, like heroism, Michaelically rejuvenating—with glinting spear. R[ittelmeyer's] saying: "Holy spirit, make us into human beings" always seems to lift and draw up the will. And all our defeats and failures continually make beggars of us. Beggars in spirit, who are to be satisfied. To be rejuvenated in the most heavenly love. Utterly, and in a completely individual way for each!

Your sister

Maria

Yes, the St. Francis card arrived, Laure. But didn't you get my last message that it had? And the letters?

~

Camp de Gurs, around July 16, 1941
To Margot Junod

Dear heart....

I received the *Disputa* and letter (and wrote to thank Laure). Deeply moved by this new possession. For me it is a gateway, despite the small size of the reproduction—yet its significance is lofty and exemplary. A high portal of meaning. That is often the hardest thing: that you feel the meaning of what happens to gradually fade from you because the new, sustaining element has ceased and become habit, whose paralyzing effect pervades everything. From my early youth my prayer was this: not to lose the strength to be renewed—eternal renewal in the life of spirit. As this becomes visible in the rhythms of the cosmos. The best means is this: to experience the dawn. The quietest time, before anything has begun to stir in the huts; when you walk drunken with sleep, and soundless hearing becomes a "humming in the ears of spirit." The passage, that wonderful one in Faust—do you know it? "Rise ever to higher realms, grow ever unobserved." It's part of the last choruses, the blessed choirs. What would become of us if renewal did not itself raise us as if on—broad, strong wings? For we ourselves alone: we cannot do it, Margot....

I send all the powers of my greeting to you, beloved, dear people. Maria

～

Camp de Gurs, end of September 1941
To her sister

Every afternoon—is the "quiet hour," which we usually spend sleeping, writing or reading—as a truly sacred moment. Sometimes a Sunday like today arrives—misty and drizzly. And one can take a book so lovely in conception (by Hilty: "Happiness"—not known to me before, and so close to our ideas) and then a wonderful mood of peace arises, one not of this world....

From here we have not much to give, nothing at all, compared to the rich love and help our friends send so actively toward us. All the more delicate then is one's sense of "possession," all the more inward the desire to give back something of what is trying to spread such grace around us. There's a kind of sacrifice in this: to give away that same "stillness," quietness, emptiness almost. I wonder if you can recognize, love and—accept the "mysticism" of this outlook and the essence of this conduct? It is September now, and soon it will be October. A full year. And in retrospect the grace of this survival seems unfathomable. I have been preserved—here. By powers that are no doubt as tough as diamond, but express cosmic majesty and love as clearly as a mirror.

It seems to me now that I am sitting as if alone in this afternoon stillness on my "luggage"—upon the moment of peace, laden with everything that makes me weak; and poured over me all that gives gladness.

My dear ones. Is there really such a thing as "separation." We are all in life together, pursue the paths of being and having to be, the nights and the days and the paths to our goal. Novalis says we are "always heading for home."

"Praise daily the Lord. He lays a burden upon us, but He also aids us." In the weekly catechism sessions that I am permitted to accompany, and translate into German, we trace the paths of the Prophets. I learn a great deal from this. Because in the old days we had no real instruction in these things. And so this—not strict either—but proper instruction is truly beneficial. Naturally I am pleased to start on the New Test. but the Old strikes me as so venerable. I learn to respect my past, to "see" my forefathers and parents. And to understand your nature and the inspiration of your art. And to greet you.

～

Camp de Gurs, October 11, 1941
To Margot and Jean-Michel Junod

My Margot, Jean-Michel, you kind, beloved godchild. This moment is so precious. Saturday afternoon, whole swathes of my barrack are empty, friends having gone out and about. The weather—in the past few days gloriously fine—is changing. As yet the sky is streaked with blue, and the weather dry and mild. The door is open. I lie in my quarters to nurse my bad leg. And fly to you with heart's haste and wings of joy. You see, while I'm writing it seems I'm with you, by your "hearth." Which would be—and is—the deepest sense of homely comfort. Receive me, you receive me. And here I am. The red flower cloth, despite not going so well with my thin, yellow face, is like cheerfulness around me. I like wearing it best of all because it wakens the will so well. And all my comrades love it greatly. I could easily give it away hundreds of times. But I myself still need its power to cheer. The green socks really relax my feet. I so much like the fact that you can spy me from afar like this, as if with binoculars; for in this way you also "shine" on me, day in, day out. Though no letters come.

For weeks now very little post has reached me. Yet this does not make me feel forsaken, though I miss the little flames of joy that letters kindle. I hear from you by other means. There is an inward, unbreakable bond of love, which works in tranquility, acts in the breath of the day. In the rhythm of the hours. In acquiescence and empowerment. In waking and in sleep. I wish you to be my next-of-kin and I'll arrange this soon. Are you willing? And in each of your palms, you three, I'll inscribe a gentle reminder. Oh, inmost act from furthest closeness.

I recently got word that Hilda confidently wrote to a supervisory office here. I do not yet know what this message means, whether it guarantees my convalescence. And after many failures one also becomes patient, to wait and see. Willing, it's true. Very willing after my strength has waned and the bitter, merciless winter awaits me. But this isn't impatience. No urgency; no imperative. No despair.

What is right for me will happen, I am sure of it. What has developed in us, crystallized out in each of us as a new, smaller I, a perhaps harder being, yet one grown more transparent: it has a power of surrender from which it lives—and where it springs. Despite this solidity: a springing source. We are made of the very essence of devotion. The most profound thing we learn is a fearlessness that we would never, never otherwise have learned.

Margot, do you know a painting by Bellini. Theresa, the great St. Theresa the covering of whose heart the angel removes so as to lodge the arrow in it. It is as if he disrobes her of fear to endow her with the gift of certain pain. Yet this wounding is—love. Once upon a time I chose this depiction to open to other, more wondrous beauty. "There is no fear in love; but perfect love casteth out fear: because fear hath torment. He that feareth is not made perfect in love." This is in the first epistle of John.

And would you believe it, I found the book by Karl Hiltys here. Donated to the big, still growing YMCA library—the several volumes of his collection "Happiness." I came upon them by chance. And since then I want to find out more about him, especially his exegesis of the Gospels and his letters. And something else I read and am thinking *for you*: the little book of Kierkegaard (three discourses): "At the Foot of the Altar," published by Beck in Munich. Please Margot, since I am *unable* to give it to you, please buy it "on my behalf." I'm sure it's not expensive. And—I was delighted in a different way, but likewise infinitely, by *Journey to the East* by Hermann Hesse. Read it, I beg you, my precious ones. And then a little request. Mauti, I don't have a photo of you. And—a dear, old friend would be so pleased to have a nice one of me. Do you perhaps have one you can spare from the old days at Bodenhof? That you could send me.

For now, good night. The quiet has changed into general tumult now. But I was with you.

Maria

(I have enough letter paper. But no envelopes, forgive me.)

~

Camp de Gurs, October 22, 1941
To Rudolf Zeitler

Dear Doctor, your kind card gave me great pleasure. A great deal of comfort in those few words. And a sense of familiarity. It is as you say: one must guard against fear and hatred. But love must increase. And we can try to do this at the most intransigent place in our life. Yet we cannot give ourselves this power: the authentic power of love must first have raised and graced us before we can achieve anything with our supposed "own" powers. Which is why we are also in an— Advent stance. And hope. It is terribly wearing to endure and be compelled by daily imperatives. And in every breath a help is also close and promised. We live and do so for the sake of others if we learn true sacrifice. And here too affirm the destiny God gives.

In warm and affectionate greetings, and in the repeated assurance that Aunt Maria is loved and kept safe in our thoughts,

Your Maria Krehbiel.

~

Camp de Gurs, November 15, 1941
To Margot Junod

My Margot—

Now fall is deep in the landscape, tingeing both sky and earth. Here a fading and falling silent—there a blossoming, flaring. The night and the stars are starting to lead us toward Christmas. How often I'm forced outside, damp and cold—and then this: to look up. And stand silent. "There's peace still"—to experience this. Then back to my three pillows: "The indispensable" (father), the "inseparable" (mother), the "extra personal one" (my godchild)! You know we can't live from what is merely essential. And that extra things here—are a saving grace. To grow soft. To feel love still after all. To feel found. I wake up a lot at night. And then I live entirely from the stillness and promise. I listen to my heartbeat that is like a memory of having

253

once lived in earlier times, of having already lasted a long time. And for how long still? Kläre is around me—the children. Hans. Can you tell me how they are? Can you give something to them? Advent and Christmas are the homely times. And the Bodenhof lies quiet in moonlight. Walking down the avenue; slowly blessing. When I come back from supper, which is a gift renewed daily—for health reasons and salt-free—at the Assist[ance] Prot[estante], I hear a tawny owl calling. (There were many tawny owls in the park.) On their way South, migrating birds fly over us. It seems that a few tender singers remain here with us, for at sunrise and sunset new voices are fluting; the Robin sings a tireless song that stays engraved in the air the whole day long.

Such a song, like strength. (There were many singing birds in the park where you grew up.) Dear Margot, I want to go on giving things to you always; want to come and pile the things of "beauty" here on your lap. New...bearable. Greater than the terror that daily surfaces and is a messenger of the world, and howls like pain. Ah, greater still is the gentle "law"; it overpowers and suffuses. And that is why now, at this place in this letter, want to ask about what is preoccupying me. So much. Geomeys—what is happening with them—what has become of them? And the parents—is there news. Unbearable? And Fréd[éric] L[ewien].

Also my ones at home. Oh, my dear, would you ask once more of *one* of them about—*all* of them?

Thousands of questions arise and gaze upon me after they've been asked. What does Hölderlin say in a late poem? "Flags clatter in the wind." I used to hear in this the moaning spin of weather vanes.[*] But today. All flags are streaming iron and sharpness heading toward extinction. Woe-iron.

Please give a sign of love to those who think of me. The blue time of Advent (all our orphaned altars used to cover themselves in blue through to Christmas) makes us yearn and ponder. How grateful I was to receive the greetings from Switzerland, from my Bern community.

---

[*] In German, a weather vane is called a "weather flag" (*Wetterfahne*). —TR.

Do you have the address of the priest couple there, who, in their own way, have been surrounding and protected the isolated? If you ever go to Bern do visit them. S[ister] Elsbeth Kasser also brought greetings from there. And now Hilda too should send some [greetings]. I await this each day, for after all she wrote that I'll have my share to distribute.

But no doubt she hesitated, for so far it is still uncertain where I will be. We're still waiting for the final word on this. The penultimate word, no less important however, signifies rejection of our attempt, since permission for the so-called new arrivals (one year is "nothing") is generally being turned down. Now they seem to have decided on, or rather conceived, another project. A house near to Hilda has been sold, where a number of people able to pay are to live together—not exactly free, but in a safer, more protected winter refuge. But this hasn't been allowed yet either although everything is ready, and—as I'm told— was only the list of residents for another house, i.e., a second one that hasn't been bought yet. The costs of accommodation sound very high. And experience suggests it will be quite some time before these things come to something—and in the end therefore Marseille *could* come sooner than that. I imagine that the good Lagr[anges] will make the right decision. A Lulu telegram tells me that they may be counting on January for [transfer to Marseille]. Only once it's all been approved in W[ashington] can a place be booked on a specific ship and then the consul can approve travel to Marseille. Please don't be worried or pained by the thought I may stay here in Gurs for the winter. I myself am not at all. All the back and forth, and tension, and rejection, ripens one into endurance and quiet hope to await what will come. Then, the most important thing: there are worse places of suffering in the world. And the battlefields make an end of so much life that one's own keeps becoming less important. Time passes one way or another—it's just that when I gaze over to you—when little Jean-Christopher begins speaking and runs through the avenues—as I remember Ele and Moni doing—when I recall the blue lake, when I think how you all live on into the future and work and labor, then it seems sometimes as if my heart would burst, Margot. But you all include me in your life, your good life, authentic and true—Isn't that so.

And now I embrace all three of you in my two arms.

Maria.

Could you send me a nice photo—of myself, for an old friend here who very much wishes it??

Just now, surprisingly, comes a resumption of the process for liberating those who have sufficient means for it. No use to me. Communal liberation in hotels.

~

Camp de Gurs, November 24, 1941
To her sister

How long ago is it? Thirteen years since we celebrated the wedding at the Castle Hotel? Do you remember it Lulu? Will K[rehbiel] still think of it?

After downpours, darkness, gloomy fall weather, comfortless incarceration, it is such a bright day now. Sunshine sparkling on everything, enticing tenderness from us. Who does that pointillist technique? Monet—Sisley? The true, inward artistic spirit wishes always to awaken to the light, and makes use of the tiniest sliver or last strand of light and color to live.

Sometimes one seems to have lost all words. The confusion of noise around you stops you writing as you should, and makes words burst forth half-formed. Continual semi-obscurities intrude into your joy in writing. I with my chessboard as writing desk have a place by the door and more opportunity than many. And my own small window. The hut boasts a little "Christmas window": small, square, unbreakable, finely interwoven with a kind of wire. Like a little attic window. Can't be opened, but outside a shutter can be raised and lowered. Cut out of the roofboard. What a fortunate, proud possession!

And soon it will be Christmas. At all events, I'll write a little Christmas letter now already since you never, ever know in life whether and when and how you might get another opportunity. We just lost several young women and are in a somber mood. At the same time we keep thinking we might be leaving. Our now homely Gurs is to be largely dismantled and its inmates allocated to better winter quarters. But a transport is unsettling. Involves a severe drain on one's strength and, as strange as it may sound, you cling to what you know, to the place you've "made your own." And I have no will for anything other than real lib[eration], as my friends have been laboring so long for now. Or the desire to reach Marseille! For this too it takes so long not only for all the papers to be approved but for the—paid—place on a specific ship to be allocated, i.e., on a specific date! At the office for emigrants here I have been repeatedly urged to ask you which shipping company has received the payment and the booking. Then it could be set in motion. You know that I have not generally been in favor of "pushing harder" when matters are already in hand. But—it's also possible to prevent things happening if one doesn't give them sufficient momentum. I know you're helping things stay in motion with your feelings and wishes, and this strengthens me, comforts me as I wait. People who actually live in Washington have sometimes been able to speed things up for their loved ones by locating the papers and dispatching them. Yet that is really something I don't feel comfortable with....

And so Christmas is approaching. The second! And no doubt the last that we will celebrate apart?? Here we are not forsaken as long as we stay close to one another as we have so far, in fond comradeship and sometimes also in true friendship. The chance event that brought me together with Hertha Heidelberger here (she lost a very good, faithful brother) has made us good friends. We help each other. She is fairly lonely... Her Aunt Wertheimer, whose only daughter stayed in M[annheim], is now in Marseille, finally on the way to her daughter, and will write to you when she arrives over there....

After a year, all of us in the camp experience what brought us here, and the protection we have received, as grace.... We think with great grief of those who stayed behind; those who remain.... Those who must leave now have more difficult things to endure. I wonder how the Geomeys are? And Felix and his wife no doubt enjoy less peace than we do, despite everything. The quiet of the nights. The freedom to roam about without danger in the daytime—

What will people say to one another and—to others—about the great cosmic protection that arches over us like a giant bell, and rings. Swings and rings as admonition but also promise, that quietly resonates as absolution and fades away—or will do one day—as—peace…World peace. Let this unspeakable hope make my letter a Christmastide one. This joy—it can only be born from God…

Greetings to all three of you from the depths of my heart.

From Maria.

~

Camp de Gurs, November 29, 1941 (first Sunday in Advent)
To the friends in Mannheim and Heidelberg

All my dears—

On the eve of the period that shimmers blue from altars (which for all of us have become ever more spiritual altars) I received news from you as I had so long been hoping. And now I'm replying. Our souls grow contemplative, don't they, as we stand before our lives. And spiritual intimations dawn on us, and peace. The veil that conceals the future from us—shimmering through heart and mind—is full of the certainty of revelation. And this is why—as Novalis sang in his Mary song—we can have the heavens smiling in our soul. Not of course unclouded. Cold, a night that comes early and cannot be brightened, the creeping damp that cannot be dried—these often constrict our days and hours. They draw us together into the narrow confines that lodge and shelter us. In this last, admonishing earthly encampment, as in the first—we are made equal again, despite the divergences of fate and outlook that become apparent.

Our patients, who undergo the altitude cure so necessary to them are—almost unteachable. It may of course be connected with their illness. A phrase I used to find extraordinary, is after all magnificent and heartening. And its wisdom is of a nature that, once experienced, acts like revelation: 1 John 3:18–19. Becoming free of fear is the thing.

The old fairytale of the child with a shirt full of stars prophesies to us ever anew, sends us—mountain-breathless, sorely tried climbers— a message of Heaven's proximity.

I send you this star as Christmas sign. It is so light, isn't it. So empty? No. It is inexpressibly full of *love's space*, blessed remembrance—healing wishes. It cannot be "filled" at all. No substance, no color, no earthly content is gathered in its five points. Nothing but Christmas connection and communion. That bond—forged in the past—the circle that encompasses us, continues to work and act, my precious ones. Its center is *the sun* that is born at the midnight hour. Surely we should rejoice at this! Christmas joy is the threshold to a whole year full of solace. So let us continue to sustain it. Even if my request for a vacation meets with a negative reply—I'm still waiting for an answer, but no doubt it's a vain hope. Before I didn't want to take this opportunity, and so I have my come-uppance now, since everything has become more difficult; and anyway, one feels oneself that any kind of change (even for the "good") will use up so much energy. Long journeys with all the discomfort they entail is something we're wary of here. And I am willing to wait until my sister is at last allowed to call me to her, because she needs me then. It will be February or March? I am not impatient. "Working while waiting" is a meaningful stance. And love endures all—gives strength for all—gifts us with daily, inward surprises.... I do not yet want to take my leave from you. But here is the end of another sheet and—we remain present to one another after all. The Advent wreath will also be woven here, will be with me. Even red candles are hung up here. And green holly and red wool to bind it. And a great, great need for light. And for this light—

Bound to you in sisterly love, with all that I have.

Maria

~

Camp de Gurs, December 8, 1941
To Rudolf Zeitler

Dear friend Zeitler

Did you know that—in reference to "Heinrich the birdman"—we call you *Rudolf the Zeitler**? We both like that so much. And I'm saying this without particular reason, probably just because you write in your letter that you often fail to write! And to respond. And so things suddenly grow—quiet around you. And then you realize this. And you keep an eye out. Suddenly someone is there. As if by appointment. A hand takes hold of yours. No doubt you know the poem by Conrad Ferdinand Meyer, "In nights of grief": the hand that reaches out, we know it don't we? And this hand quietens bitter loneliness, and sweetens it as something we seek.

I have no reason (for we—who live in exceptional circumstances—may, it seems to me, write everything lovingly from the heart)—no need to ask your forgiveness for the natural outpouring of thoughts and reflections. You have understood the first thing, and will understand the rest of what we write to each other. At Advent, in our beloved Christian Community, we have these words: "Our souls grow contemplative. Before the eye of spirit, peace unfolds. The sway of the Father's ground of cosmic being can be heard in the ground of our soul." I have the clear conviction that in your being you accompany the festival times and—are accompanied by them. I hope that you experience Christmas. Not enduring but borne up. But struck by light. Wishes of this kind come toward you and find a means of entry.

It is a lovely thing that your dear aunt has become my dear friend. We try to lighten each other's existence and also bring joy to one another. For such things keep us alive, despite all the grave privations that are so harsh in winter. The terrible weather and other things

---

*   in an old German poem Heinrich is a birdcatcher elevated to royal status. *Zeitler, containing the word Zeit (time), suggests someone who comes only at intervals, but also at just the right time.*

that plague us. Yet the birth of Christ took place amidst deep poverty, which is precisely what intensifies its immediacy—brings help. Helps with such solace that using this possession only makes it go on and on growing. Don't be afraid for us, since that will weaken us: have reflective confidence about us, as that strengthens us. We cannot dispense with such help. The void is near enough. And our longing is to be filled with the fullness of the spirit.

Here is a Christmas sign; it wants to settle on a little tree or branch in your room, and do its service as a bird, foretelling the rose's flowering.

Our letters, wrested from lack of light and warmth, beg forgiveness, dear Rudolf, for their deficiencies.

Good greetings
Maria Krehbiel

~

Camp de Gurs, second week in Advent 1941
To Margot Junod

Beloved little sister
Today it is *my* turn to give you pleasure. It flies toward you on Christmas wings and—only gives back to you something in recompense for all, all that you and Lagr[anges] have tried and worked for and hoped for—and sacrificed for, over a whole year. Yesterday I was told that the *demande* has been allowed and (for three months initially) I have been granted *permission de santé* to go where Hilda wished me to, and where her faithful love has so long desired to see me. I myself know neither the exact location or address, but post can now go through Hilda at all times. Asked when I envisaged taking this leave, I requested to go between Christmas and New Year, partly so as to go on helping prepare our communal Christmas festival here, and to celebrate it in my "intimate circle" (they are finding it [the thought of my departure] difficult), and partly also because a new

period arrives organically with the new year. And one should let things come to a natural end without haste.

Dear Margot. My thanks come from deep within—and are both serious and joyous. It cannot be otherwise. There is something of grandeur in what "has been" here as well as in what is to remain here—after me. Looking back, though, elicits not sorrow alone—nor gratitude alone.

What *exists* here signifies a part of the human condition full of knowledge and insight. Thus, full of grace and truth. My hope is to remain equal to this so that—when released—we do not forget and cast it behind us. But so that we keep deep faith with it in our further life. These last days have sought to release me back into "life." But on the other hand, the same days have swiftly carried off from life some older relatives (on my father's side) whom I found here. As people tend to depart here. This juxtaposition and pulling apart of events is a shock. You will understand this, and the gravity that comes over me and keeps me in its thrall, although otherwise inclined to rejoice on my own behalf. But this time in this world is really no longer in any way just pure gift. It bears such a generally tragic character that a single individual cannot delight fully in what he is given but instead feels prompted immediately to do nothing other than "make redress." ...

So, enough for today, Margot, Jean-Michel, Jean-Christophe. With loving thanks from

Maria.

One more Christmas request—that Laure Wagner write home by return of post so that her anxious friends can celebrate with joy and relief.

~

Lyon, January 3, 1942
To Martha Besag

Dear Martha—my thoughts have long since arrived with you before these greetings come to alight on your bed.

Everything I experience is so self-evident for the world yet for us is it *so* extraordinary to rediscover it all. It has to be said that one feels the year that does not "count"—yet counts more than previous ones—in bones and muscles that have to relearn the climbing of stairs. It has to be said that one feels this year—spent in a far-off place—like a burning wound. Yet—like one that must be kept secret.

The world does not care to hear about sad and gloomy things more than just the once. And after a couple of days one stops speaking of it. One just replies to occasional questions. For you see, the world outside, the world here, also has its own cares, anxieties, haste and problems— Yes, it has more of them than we do who battle with the elements and physical needs, but otherwise stand at the margins. Almost indifferently. Grown, as a crowd, very private. Very impersonal as an individual. All this is new: to turn right round again and become an individual once more and—largely to think of things in the same way.

I won't speak much, Martha, of the comforts of life that pretty much surround me at present, since my relatives' excellent friends are taking care of the larger and smaller details of my "return." I won't speak of this because it so quickly becomes something "natural"— this wonderfully civilized eating and drinking—and also because it is so far out of your reach, and unattainable for you all. By day already I have adjusted to it. But at night. Then I'm plagued by pain for all of you and feel a sense of reproach at my "enjoyment" while you go without. And then I want to pack a thousand little parcels. But I have no *tiquets** and no boxes, and I can't yet cope with the vast city; and can't ask my hosts to take this on as well, on top of everything else.

---

* This probably refers to the rationing "ticket" system at that time. —Tr.

I still have a hunk of bread I brought with me from "home," which I eat religiously. (Though of course the bread here is much better.) I could not move straight to Limonest but am permitted to stay here for 8 days. In the hotel. With mimosas and white violets on the table. Martha.

I bury my head on your bed. Don't forget that I do not forget you all. Greetings to your hut. I'll write again soon.

M.

~

Lyon, January 3, 1942
To Margot Junod

My dear Margot

I could never have imagined how it would be, to find myself suddenly with your friends, amidst the life of the world—and—to find myself "alone" again. There are three different things. All three disconcertingly different from what one, from what someone else, from what even you, heart of my life, could believe. It is hard. It is big. It is so much—that words cannot express it. No calls, fanfares, fame, fortune or praise sound forth from it. But instead. Instead it is: like emptiness. Like lying flat on the ground. Deep. Humble—alone. Despite all the variety. And despite the fervent busy-ness and the protective and wonderful care from your friends. If we should see each other again, Margot, then I can tell you how everything, everything is—

Discharged again into the world! The climbing of steps that one can no longer manage. Getting along on the sidewalk and paying attention in the hum of the big city. Speech in just *one* language, the fact of having left one's friends behind—and being forsaken by them. For this utter difference inevitably means a rapidly increasing separation. And all *douceur de la vie* seems like theft: what one brings to one's mouth like religion, and what one no longer speaks of after a few days because the unprecedented and shocking is in fact "nothing" for others who, in the meantime, also stand amidst their own unprecedented experience.

Yes. It seems we have spent a "seven sleepers" time* or—a period of extreme wakefulness; perhaps. We were sick and removed from mundane labors

People tell me I am healthy and can live again as others do. But I cannot yet do this.

The only thing I am capable of at present is not "distancing" myself, too greatly from ordinary daily life. Margot. Suddenly you see yourself in the mirror of a big shop window—see yourself as "apparition."

All this would still be bearable. But at night memories of the others rise up—the sad, yearning ones who remained behind. The ones who—were far more impatient than I. And the pain of their pain lies down questioningly beside me.

Whether and how I can cope with this. What I sacrifice, whether I am faithful! Not just in "little parcels" that they await so eagerly from me, but are so hard to accomplish without tiquets, without "my own" money—for now I have a much more acute sense of living on my friends' resources; while before one seemed to be naturally in charge of life's requirements. There's restlessness in this state—sometimes a sense of happiness, or of wonder or of suffering; yet it all seems like a dream. It is: thankfulness, Margot. Which is like—incredulity that one is now really somewhere else from where one was all the time. Yet "outside," less protected than before. Because one's personal life has begun again and one must acknowledge oneself to be "alien," facing alien people, an alien world.

The magnificent thing about this, which is so hard, so new, so—learnable?—is all that you have given and accomplished for me. Even the rich, gentle, joyous treasures received from you (the fur coat even!); I arranged it with Hilda today. And am so happy to live newly in this new life. It wraps itself protectively around me.

---

* This refers to a legend about a long period of sleep or unconsciousness into which seven apostles fell

Please give your parents my warm greetings. For here of course I can talk about all of you who know and love one another. My friends, though, are truly wondrous.

I hold you all in my intense embrace and hope to receive post from you soon.

Maria

~

Limonest, January 17, 1942
To Toni Schwarz

My dear Toni

I ought to be writing to some other folk, for I haven't yet come full circle even though I've been writing one to tow letters each day. Is that my "work" now? It seems so, and I can't find any other where I am at present. The house is meagerly occupied by old people, or rather ancient ones, who, however, are left to themselves and find "sufficiency" in their own company. At most an old Ital[ian] lady, once a member of the Salvation Army and a Protestant (but no longer quite awake) would be terribly pleased if I often came to see her in her room; which is crammed with things and colder than others. But in fact I myself am still for now something of a lone wolf who—finds nothing more gratifying than to hear the "lock clicking shut behind her." And: to just sit there. Or sometimes to stand in front of the big mirror, asking: "Is this me?" Or to spend half the morning in bed. Usually until ten-thirty. Catching up on sleep. For at night, you see, proper sleep doesn't come despite the perfection of the good bed. I have a nightstand (with cupboard), and an Indian lamp on top. Then I tidy my room myself, drink half a cup of wine with an anxiously rationed hunk of bread (for life is very simple. Impossible to buy it). And then it's midday, and lunchtime. A little mocha cup full of coffee. But now I have boiling water almost daily for my tea in the thermos. Around seven there is a modest supper. It's cheap, too: 35 frs. And the little room is lovely, and the whole thing pleasant and—close to the city. I wrote so much about my room furnishings to Luise Schw[arz]. She'll tell you more whenever you wish, my dear.

On one of my first nights here I dreamed of these three people: R[udolf] St[einer]—Ri[ttelmeyer]—Dold[inger]. I was only able to "offer" something to Dold[inger]. He gratefully accepted an egg and ate it. The two others—very serious, had to "fulfil the unreduced burden of their work."

My dear. The first "color study" wants to be yours, and this slim little letter craftily conceals it. The soft peach blossom is the color of my room. With grey, pearl-grey paint work on doors and windows....

Please greet yours and mine. Thanks for your letter.

[Maria]

~

Limonest, January 18, 1942
To the friends in Mannheim and Heidelberg

Today, in the early morning in bed I saw that there is no use in simply putting on this new dress of a different life "over the top" of the old one. Anxiously, and even sorrowfully I kept thinking all this time that—yes—I should really cling tight to my old, grey nurses' uniform?

The misery of my forsaken patients pursues me reproachfully, and I've allowed restlessness and worry to take hold. Especially at night when I realize how protected, soft, warm and safe I lie, and ought to be resting in such unspeakable comfort—without the night vigils, without the strain of going out, without sharing the torment of my patients' pain and cold.

I believed that I owed them that. For it was hard enough already to wrestle my way through to decide on this sick leave. To "sacrifice" the habitual work of an habitual life—and to accept the good respite, also considered so necessary by my doctor. And, despite their regret, how eager and without envy my friends were to release me. They said I would be better able to serve once I had regained my strength, and many other kind things. But I could see only that I was leaving them—most of them—with no improvement in their condition. And in winter as well, when they are always more severely tested, as lies of course in the nature of suffering. And I had to ask whom I would still find there on my return. And yet I went. No longer knowing that there is so much other life, so much beauty in the landscape, so much "ordinary daily life," so much bright sunshine in the world. Unaccustomed I wandered around—grown alien to the world and lopsided—in my friends' big city. I met new people, the busy circumstances of a city, and situations I felt unequal to which—were simply forced upon me (for daily life, taking hold of you again immediately, makes no allowances for fragility). There was scarcely time to make a "transition" from living excluded, on the margins, to the naturalness of inclusion in this daily life.

Such warm-hearted friends this young couple are, and I owe them so much for their actions and concern; yet each person has his own life to navigate. And soon—after the first, tender reception I received—both my narratives and my dull-witted silences were met with a "strong return to the daily schedule." This may have been a very wise thing, and right, the natural path back to health. But initially it made me very sad—suddenly I no longer had my companions with me who would best have understood every experience. No response was forthcoming, to my amazement—

The thing is, in our distant altitude we are scarcely able any longer to take naturally what is quite natural. It is as if we've "come from the country." But then every tiny detail is experienced with shattering impact and—kneeling one wishes to offer it up before an altar.

~

Limonest, March 13, 1942
To friends in Heidelberg and Mannheim

My dear friends

Life here is perfect in an almost improbable way. I so long to tell you about it. But telling wouldn't be adequate. Rather, with bated breath, I want to show you everything. Never before in my life have I found myself in a situation like this, that leaves nothing to be desired. A stirring condition but one that also includes bliss. I must not consider how long these gifts may endure. For duration is not something they are—ultimately—endowed with. Some people live all their lives here, but they seem not to know it. And one must have lived—as I have—in an entirely different way, immersed in vocation and destiny, in order—to understand. To allow and embrace it. My hands are always open. Like vessels. And now drops of the spring also fall into them. The park alone is lovely—with a white and a black goat, a couple of hens. Today there's a smell in the air of burned leaves and wood—everything's a little misty. And the near mountains seem to be fading away. As all this will one day again. Here and there you can imagine you're with Hete in the wild park, or looking out of the window at Dr. Marie's house.* And so every path grows vivid. A small garden statue on a tall column already quite green—is a goddess half lowering a jug, to dispense? There's no water. But the genius of the place gives forth a few infinitely quiet drops of some precious substance, a magic elixir. And these drops find their way into your heart, so that it begins praying. A singing, delicate thanking encompasses this phase of my life. Making me young through memories and old in awareness of the wisdom that's called for.

Things can come to an end here as soon as tomorrow. The vacation that started in such anxiety has expired. And my friends and the doctor are seeking a further one. My health has not returned. In fact, sickness has come to the fore properly through my resting. My heart is like a butterfly—now fluttering, now quite still, and my days and nights are tormented by related ills. But this can be endured, though no direct treatment is possible. Rest will have to act as a substitute.

My patients [in Gurs] write frequent, moving letters so that half my time is spent in answering. When I'm doing this it seems to me I'm "at work," and that is good.

---

*   Hete Aschenbrenner—a friend of Maria Krehbiel-Darmstädter since the 1920s, and a member of Mannheim Christian Community. Dr. Marie Baum, see page 29. —Tr.

I have received such fine books, and they also contribute to the perfection here. And the heavens, rainbows and Madonnas in them, all the spiritual qualities, resonant colors, against the backdrop of the beauty of these gardens and landscape; they seem, don't they, to show forth our riches.

And I always come to you empty-handed. Despite the birthdays and the wishes that I'd also, sometime, like to clad in raiment. You will just have to take what is yours from my old reserves of love. Please do so, all my dearest ones. I send infinite greetings to my godchildren....

Be blessed and stay close to me. M[aria]

~

Limonest, March 20, 1942
To Toni Schwarz

My dear little Tone. Your whole being was so vivid to me in the letter—I could see the little car, the colors, landscape, rainbows, sunshine. Dordogne, and questions.

Here—in Limonest—we haven't had even half a rainbow, though many other pleasurable things. First and foremost, there's *a whole* hill in the wild park! Wild, because the fresh wind thrashes about in old trees. And because last fall's mouldy leaves and the snow-weary grasses of the winter lie there so haphazardly. On the hill in question, yolk-yellow and green nests of primroses are brightly sprinkled. A pre-Easter, cavalier feeling. You could say this wild garden beauty has been left "untrimmed"—refusing to be reined in or assuaged even by the small goddess with the cautious, gentle gaze, who, inclining from her old, green column, is bashfully pouring out the contents of her amphora. The old trees surround her in a rough kind of semi-circle, like knights doing obeisance.

Yet none of this stops the cavorting of either the little white goat or the brown, nor of cheerful little Adeline, who is five. The grey "elf hill" itself, where the yellow primulas blossom and birds twitter, participates least of all, however, in such festive frolics.

Furthermore, there's a large folly open to the four winds, with stone benches and a view over all of Limonest. Here grow white violets and cowslips. And nearby rustles the fountain; and vineyards—hills adorned with the symbol of all good growth—incline piously around the church with its Easter Lamb.

Here one should gaze upon the work by Grünewald. And the timeless, ultimate measure of beauty becomes the hour of your own existence—a gentle spring rain sprinkles branches and benches. The colors of the sky keep changing in intensity. But when sky puts its glacier-blue face to the window in the mornings, and the pink hyacinth, with its baby offshoot, still a little green, shines out so lost in dreams upon my bed and breakfast, then one thinks that nothing can be better. And Gurs seems like the grey wall upon which memory flames and begs: keep me, me, with you. In love. "Learn to surrender your thoughts to the divine." You understand. Love can only stream if it does so through the "open wound."

The two epistles for Passiontide I wanted to give you for contemplation. And for Good Friday to Easter.

~

Limonest, March 27, 1942
To Maria Gnädinger

Thank you for news of our friends. And for letting me know that some of them, such as our esteemed B[ock] have returned home.... Do you know any more about D[oldinger]'s life? Is he still suffering so much? And the publishing company? Yes. "Learn to surrender your thoughts to the divine." The words of the confession sacrament surface unexpectedly at many places in life. To keep faith—is all that we can do. But—can we only always do this? Forgetfulness is so much encouraged by the passing and clamoring of time. Without doing "violence" to ourselves we must keep faith through steady practice. Oh, how these things become apparent in relation to my poor G[urs] and the year that is past. How often memory seeks to flee and find "its peace." Or the reverse—how often does the agony of sympathy make my heart stop. Yes—but this is not right. "Learn to surrender your thoughts to the divine." That is right.

This month, though, this great month of remembrance, all sorts of things are occurring.

My "expired vacation" has given me much trouble. Fear and questions about what is the right thing to do have turned this month into a torment instead of a time of tranquil relaxation.

My friends in Lyon have taken all necessary, permitted steps, and all steps their love and concern suggested. My dear, what excellent people these are, the friends of my Margot in Lausanne. Their assistance means that living in their proximity becomes an infinite source of joyous gratitude. But nevertheless: these inner conflicts.

Fear and hope, the most contrary feelings, come to the fore at times of tension such as this. There are plentiful feelings of shame. The "recompense" you wish to make for the gift you are once more expecting, is so utterly inadequate. Really nothing at all.

Nevertheless, hope returns. And reaches out toward a gentle destiny. Because it is spring. Easter approaches. And the inexpressible freshness of a new season smiles upon us.

~

Limonest, around April 8, 1942
To Walter Schmitthenner

It is difficult to express your thoughts in letters—thoughts you take from your shoulders like a burden where two roads diverge, to have a breather and pause for thought. Or that you remove from round your neck (almost like a necklace) to offer up reverently. The Cross is always at a crossroads, pointing in one and another direction. But asking first that you "divest" yourself.

Your letter, my dear godson, has something of greatness for me. And how hard to answer it on the circuitous postal route, seen by other eyes and taken in other hands. In their speechless existence, word-thoughts have long since accomplished what we can only attempt: the conveying of a message. The bearing of testimony. And the hovering nature of their task can be lost en route; simply by being touched. Like something too easy—like something—whose intrinsic life withdraws or is extinguished. Something: too essential to express. You know. In every life there are the fleeting moments of: "Now all is well." Their peace is fulfillment and spiritual solace. The infinite gentleness of this certainty is the stillness of greatest ripeness. One step further—and we no longer live. Your letter, though, exhaled something of this perfection. There is no shame for us in the fact that I say this "to your face" from far, so faraway. Oh, I do know indeed that we may speak and reveal "it." But to fix it on paper like this is hard. Yet has to be. (The risk, if genuine, only a failure to express, for the knowledge itself after all is safe as in a protecting mantle.)

My dear. You say you experience our belonging together as a mirror. Eye to eye. When I started to read you, my whole being drew together and focused as though in a pivotal point. This was what I had so far lacked here until now—to be "called," summoned. Every true call summons us from the grave. And Lazarus is our exemplar. He stands up. At the summons. He is not only awoken: he also heeds the call. And stands up—and is another. This, my dear—to be touched, gently. On the shoulder. By the angel (or one's "best friend") makes you as though new. Full with Easter. You will grow green, standing there. Put forth fresh green like our great, wild park that, without "cultivation" (since it has wrested itself free of human care)—has gone back into nature and now walks forth into meadow and field, path and far horizons. Opening to the source and the vineyard. Yet still a radiant garden; things blossom in such infinite loveliness there, and the little goddess on her column always reminds me of Goethe's *genius loci* in Weimar...There, though, it is the resting snake....

Your summons, my child (and wise man) gathered my being together and I heed it, as if it came from far further away—from still greater realms. But you are the messenger.

Back then, after my great journey into new territory, the first "call" from people was unspeakably touching for me. In the silence lasting weeks one almost had the sense of being a different soul in a different embodiment, and no longer having any memory.

But then one evening the first "summons" arrived—being called by name and emerging from the crowd to answer. It was a letter from people who have now grown so close to me, who took on responsibility for my care here. (And this accord with them, in my vacation here, is also greater than I can intimate.)

You write that you see our connection as fellowship in the same faithful cause. We heed the call of the times. And take a stand. Certain that this is our task. Beyond all doubt.

One thing one has to know is that there is no "interim period" that one just has to "get through." There is only meaningful existence. Every hour is time: a time to live. And made free so that it can be filled with "us." There is no empty, reverberating space or dream. We are this... To be entirely in the little portion of life, of the day—of the hour: of the action. Of sacrifice. That's the thing. And we are ripe for it. My dear child. The skin of our being is ready, and both the sharp and gentle beams pierce it to flow forth.... We want—to be permitted—to sacrifice ourselves. And to love. This is what you say.

Every detail you tell me, your studies, and that you are now moving toward summer and enlisting: O, how I absorb it. And wish to nurture it. The picture of the child with the big eyes was added to your letter. It seems nothing other than inevitable. And now we travel onward. But we feel the pledge.

Maria.

~

Limonest, April 18–19, 1942
To Toni Schwarz

My dear, we would no doubt be safer, more protected, in one of the collection houses, wouldn't we. Times are such that we do not know how and where the next moment will take us. And the few inches of ground we occupy can so easily be contested. Since the beginning I've been "busily" pondering these things, weighing them up; and have been unable to come down on one side or the other of the balance. Although I sense that the gift of this vacation has been given me for this "purpose," indeed perhaps as trial.

It is not the freedom "from" but the freedom "to" that we've been able to attain. And I do think that the moment that takes me back into a closed-off "something" will be almost a relief. And so you are far more "free" than I am. And so I disappointed my Toni, did I? At any rate, my friends [Lagranges] are seriously talking about leaving. And I will quite simply be unhappy to lose them. Today, separations are losses. If people don't know each other so deeply and so well as we do—and came to do. To stand in the same destiny does surely give a different intimacy and unity. To look together from the same spiritual striving does really give rise to this buoyant permanence in relationships. But other ties, of warmth and friendship, certainly exist. Similarity of outlook, a shared taste in art and literature.... But a world sunders us where rel[igious] life takes a conscious part in our life; yes, *it exists*. And there, in these beautiful people at whom we are inwardly amazed—it is lacking...is lacking after all. This aspect, which forms an infinite, heart source of community with quite simple souls. To *give* them *any of it* is completely, is impossible. My dear one, it is another kind of existence that is engendered. Here in Limonest, too, the house with its residents is multifarious and divergent. "Shot through" with the "colors of souls" who live here—and use it. That's the thing: all too easily and certainly you use what nourishes you, what sustains you and gives you lodging. As if this "has to be," the miracle of protection—of earth-bearing and enduring. And the recompense we give for this?? Cultivation of the earth? No doubt, but only so as to take still more from it again (for the seed is so much less than the accruing harvest). But gifts to the earth and the heavens? My dear: gratitude, prayer, churches—yes. But the purity today of building and establishing edifices with love? Where joy is to live in the foundation stone, and a sense of eternity can announce itself in dialog with the infinite? As in olden times this lived intrinsically in cathedrals and, more recently, in the essence of our building [the Goetheanum]? But most recently there is only pomposity. And vessels of vanity, raising grandiose idols (or serving as cinema screens). Yes, there is such impoverishment that we no longer grasp the miracle of the spring in its exquisite splendor. But just as something to bask in. (Or some even grow "embarrassed," unable to know how to deal with a "thing" without evident use or produce. Not "consumable." Merely fullness of growth...hope.)

If I go on like this, my own thoughts will take up all the space and prevent me copying down the wonderful things Péguy says about "hope." In connection, specifically, with the spring and April. Victor Hugo, too, has a wonderful poem about the sower. Here it is; for you. I could go on a long time in this vein. Messages go back and forth between us, don't they. Yet are still not enough to convey all that we might share between us in our sisterhood. Thus I feel more, and more clearly than I can put into words, house-healing and allure (in the healing and wholesomeness of the house) that surround you, nurture you, hover around you and—sip at you. The time of wings has arrived everywhere. Florets float about. Innocence and admonition. Butterflies tremble through the air. And if you sit still, they settle beside you by the edge of the path and taste the sunshine. ("The flower is the butterfly bound by the earth." "The butterfly is the plant freed by the cosmos." R[udolf] St[einer].) By mistake, I wrote "belighted" instead of "freed."* But one might sense what "belighted" means. Something like: pollinate with joy?...

Your little cool-blue chamber is cosily cramped and so completely— sufficient. Window-door! Lovely. And the whitewashed veranda running the length of the house also already gives me pleasure. Boxes for geraniums. And facing South. The morning is lovely for me here. Light. Because the Sun shines in. The afternoon, though, more earnest.

---

*   *Befreut* instead of *befreit*. *Befreut* does not exist as such but closely resembles *erfreut* (delighted). —TR.

Green-golden reflections on sunny days. Blue-green shadows. A grave twilight almost on overcast days. The trees in the park, the grass pushing up with its primula embroideries now and—distant murmur of the residents who sit around chatting; and laughing too. And faint bleating of goats and the noise of saws cutting wood. Repeatedly the useful wood is being sawn or chopped. These things accompany my letters. When I'm at home.

~

Limonest, May 16, 1942
To Margot Junod

Did I already tell you what our park is like in May? The park here I mean. How thickly green it is, a rich green, so abundant it almost hurts. Lush profusion at these times of misery makes comfortless nakedness all the more painful. And just as one would delight in putting a horde of dirty children in a giant bathtub, so you feel you're immersing all your friends (yes, with their whole barrack, too) in this aromatic green expanse. "Green" it seems to me is not "strictly" a color like others. But a state, a condition. A symbol.

It is life, quite simply. The very fact of rejuvenation; almost of return.

And the preciousness in the least stalk and stem and leaf—brings humility, devotion. And then when it passes over into the play of colors—the patterning of the May meadows now! On the one hand we human beings culminate in "the angel"; on the other we start from "the flower"; or that is what I want to call it when the blissful feeling overwhelms us that what we bear as our corporeal nature is simply too constricting.

I am sure that every year, and in earlier days, and at home, and each year whose book we open, delights have been given to us—and always different ones! Different in our youth—childhood—love and pain or—also renunciation—or—or… (There are other names, too, for the moments of life.) Yet an "awakening" in spring after life has given us months of arrest—and of hesitancy—may be incomparable. Whether it be called—death or the other thing. The other thing? The astonishing. A life—released into life. You were not surprised that to begin with I did not wish to let go of the "rope" or was unable to. You were—the only one—not to be astonished and to help to look the change in the eye and to take it as seriously (and happiness almost as hard)—as it actually was at the time.

Today this is a state I can already "look back upon" but to which I must still, nevertheless, accord validity.

These are, of course, "human" experiences, not just those of Maria K.—, aren't they? And it is this very thing that makes them such that one—almost senses them to be "symbols" within one.

~

Limonest, May 23, 1942
To Toni Schwarz

The recurring theme of our confessional phrase is not yet clear to you?

"Sacrificing one's thoughts to the divine" means neither to "agonize over them" nor to "vaunt" them. Here again is the trap of swinging between Ahriman and Lucifer, which sometimes keeps us in comfortless regret about sinful thoughts and errors, or otherwise makes us proudly rejoice and "paint pictures" showing how we can ascend the empyrean on the lightest of wings. "When I praise myself, then I wish to praise my weakness," is how the apostle Paul expresses it.

And "when I am weak, then I am strong."

Only the idea of surrender is able to help us out of these ambivalent situations. The moment we "give way," the tense, constricted nature of events that plague us usually also fades. Space arises as if something has been emptied, cleansed. We are no longer setting up barricades of resistance but instead allowing "it" to happen, hoping to cope with things with *the help of God*.

The "I" living in our thoughts surrenders to the outspread, most finely and infinitely dispersed cosmic "I." With it, and through this transparent I, it returns, transformed as will received from God. It has immersed itself *in* will, received strength "to act."

This is nothing other than a consciously undertaken "outbreath and inbreath"; through *gratitude.* For just as we can eat without praying, we can also of course think—practice: without praying. And this strange "state of unblessedness" in thinking is something that also always "pursues" you. Because you are afraid to "give up the last vestige of logical thinking." But if you do this properly (in praying) the world of angels descends further in you, and your thinking is no arduous earthly realm but—something quite different.

"And your soul will feel peace."

Pentecost did this: it extinguished the disciples' resistance, their own fixed position, and they became pure. They were able to pour themselves into their surrendered, upward-transformed (emptied) thinking, which since then is passed ever onward. Hearkening to the revelations from eras of time to cycles of time.

~

Limonest, May 28, 1942
To Rudolf Zeitler

The letter intended to thank you, and permitted, as you say, to give you pleasure—has to be shortened into this postcard. But I can't resist sending you a picture of this land of abode of mine. St. Cyr is close by. The photos on postcards today are so true to life that nothing is left in them of the gently "unreal" intimation of reality.

And so I hope this little picture of the landscape "a hundred years ago"—but largely unchanged—gives you pleasure that speaks to the heart. Goethe's drawings have a kind of enchantment (somewhat apparent here) by being simultaneously a glimpse of the real landscape and also something "ideal."... Which one finds where the self touches nature.

Your fine, even airy brush lines that touch your present-day land as if with knowledge: they helped me to see what you see. And how you do it.... Yes, it's certainly true that "northern and southern lands" are different—yet rest "in the shadow of His hands."

This certainty is present too and has grandeur. Time, like a terrible illness, passes across the world; but, where it "alone" remains, it offers endless insight into infinities. A change is passing through the world and all our paths are dictated by it. And the chance glimpse of each other in a distant—unpremeditated country, becomes a wonderful mutual extending of hands that happens in order to—change us.

My situation here in L[imonest] is still not one I am "used to," and this is as it should be. My love and duty have been left behind too much with the living. And this means that all delight at my immediate surroundings mediates pain. This is what gives the "picture" its depth, leaves it fresh; for its symbolic power does not wane. It seems, you know, as though nothing is "surface" but profound, is etched relief. Is carved, sculpted. A different art from the lightly drawn and quietly applied. The other is cut and incised, hammered and carved. (And is also, if you like, a scourging.*)

This comparison derives from a verse play that Dehmels regarded highly: "Life that unrelenting scourges, while God my soul engraves and purges."

As I write and reflect, and consider you in thoughts—the words in your letter tell me much, and engender the close resonance of authentic music—the park rises before my window in all its green glory, impatient in its lush yearning for summer.

In Claudel's five great "Odes" there is a line that engraved itself on my mind an inconceivable age ago. I was young then (and will be fifty in June). "This is the hour that sunders summer from spring; this is the hour that no one names." I can't remember how it continues. But isn't this very beautiful? The long springtime passes over into the decisive hour—around which spreads a secret, proud pain.

Rilke once said, "In transformation go out and in. If you find drinking bitter, then be wine."

---

* A play on the similarity in sound between *meisseln* (carve) and *geisseln* (scourge). —TR.

The fluctuating play of light and shade in today's wild South wind keeps changing my view from the window. Like going out and in. The coolness and distance of shadow intensifies one's love for the closeness and warmth of sunshine.

The great old chestnut trees have finished flowering, now it's the turn of the honeysuckle, the lilac and acacia. (There are places in the woods that are molten with acacia fragrance.) But this "moment" is most informed by—the elder. From my bed I can see its bushes that don't come into flower at home until a month later. (You can make little cakes, pastries, with their umbels and then really "eat" poetry! At Pentecost we even had *baignets d'accacias* here in Limonest!)

The elder flower blossoms float like white, flat faces against the rustling grass. The green is still May-fresh and light. This makes what we regard, at home, as an earnest blossom, always connected in folktales with enchantment and premature death—into something that feels quite different here. The little white faces dance gleefully against their green's bright ground, and since they are abundant and exuberant as they never are at home, they make a fine companion to the mayflower. And my little vase contains this cheerful froth—the starry heaven of an elder umbel—next to a full, strong rose. (That would make a good little May story.)

When you discovered the bellflower: I can almost know how this was—isn't it a fine shiver of cold that strokes the length of your back: "you are overwhelmed by alien feeling."*

Your "alarm" reached all the way here, to my French room and its wealth of green outside, and made itself felt. I, too, got a sense of—cold. I felt similar to you on Reichenau; one experiences these moments almost as—stolen. Because insight accompanies them, like lightning—inexpressible. One becomes "aware" of something. My teacher Rudolf St once said, "becoming aware of the idea within reality is true human communion." This communion is continually within reach of lips and eyes, is the manifest secret and our divine discovery. I thank you for such gifts. Thanks too for another two

---

* quote from a poem by Goethe

poems. Although—I have another view of the bellflower that you saw. My teacher once intimated that the bellflower "contains the unborn child." I just tell you this without explanation.... For me, too, this flower embodies a still, confiding delicacy and simple loveliness. So far there are no campanulas among our meadow flora here, whose waves of sweet color rise as high as your knees. But we make up for this with wild columbines by the woods, here called *clochettes* [little bells]. But these, I think, are deeply bowed little melancholias, burdened with knowledge....

Next time I'll add a text I've copied out. (The Carossa poem "Secrets" is a text I've appended to various letters.) Can you get hold of the wonderful booklet by Kierkegaard, *At the Foot of the Altar?* Published in German by Beck-Verlag in Munich. And H. Hesse's *Journey to the East.* I would gladly "share" this with you since I love it. And you would love both these, though so different.

You remain in my thoughts. I am so pleased that you wish to take a loyal interest! How far life extends, rooting itself and shining in the firmament of friendship. With warm thanks,

Your Maria K.

~

Limonest, June 15, 1942
To the friends in Heidelberg and Mannheim

On festive days such as the one now approaching, it becomes possible to survey the panorama of one's life. I never had a stronger sense of things being incomplete, nor a more wonderful glimpse of extraordinary pain and healing. The grateful wish to enact good, to be able to keep faith, is so strong that it is painful not to be able to set out on the journey. To "stay" is renunciation. Or—staying has to become entirely inner activity. And the limits of mundane life so easily dampen our good spirits, don't they.

As I write, my gaze is plunged in green. For weeks now, this green has been almost star-strewn like the heavens. With elder blossoms.

Whereas the fragrant, lovely and numberless unity fades unfailingly in a vase (almost as soon as picked) it lasts inconceivably long on the branch. And I did not know that the elder flower is so long-lasting? At the very beginning, during winter, I went to see if this park knew of those precious fairytale juniper trees we have at home. And when its branches are bare, of course, it is scarcely possible to find it. And so it surprised me. Yes, here, there, and at last everywhere it was to be found. And is no doubt the most common plant here, alongside the prolific primrose, and the ribbons of iris. Flower clocks are a kind of sundial that artists have discovered: painted them—and learned their language. These transitions through the year from one blossom time to another, and through into fruiting: thus, *prêt à mûrir, prêt à mourir.** That is how I saw a bright cornfield, standing there young and surrendered in the evening. Ranked in its endless, willing rows.

~

Limonest, June 30, 1942
To Rudolf Zeitler

Dear Doctor Zeitler

I have to ask what it is about your letters—and yet know perfectly well.

They come bearing a "mood." A magic. Fine as silk and taut as silk: so firm and—true.

And a shimmer as that around silk. And all comparisons with "silk" want to be used to thank you. The texts you enclose are always a finest essence and a full peal of bells, if you like. Starting with them, the letter swells up and fades. Pure. Clean. For a while still the air carries the tone, sweetened by it. Believe me—this is so.

I ask myself what this is. Yet know. When I was young, I received letters like this from the young man who, a few years later, bound my life to his.

---

*   "Ready to ripen, ready to die." —Tr.

Then my illness and his enchantment with a young lady dissolved our marriage. It did not "break." That is the good thing. So there are no shards and fragments. It was a dissolution. No doubt that was right. And the doors closed—quietly. "And suddenly you know, it has been."

Yes, these letters: I'll gladly tell you because I recognize and love them: they are like a meeting. And the joy they bring is exalted, because they cause me to—"arrange things in my mind."

Your letter on the one hand. The poems on the other:—a work of art.

Each time you also thereby create the possibility of going on giving the poems. And the human being, and those others, stand—yes, almost waiting for and asking for them—ready to receive them. (I myself was the first one awaiting them, and the request: yes, this was granted *me*...)

Do you know that Carossa could easily have written his "Old Fountain" poem here? Below my window in the park. The old fountain only flows in winter, though, to stop the water freezing up. In summer, the water shortage compels it to be silent. Only occasionally, when [they] rinse laundry in the large basins, or spray soft, bright mountains of lettuce to clean them—then it flows and pours. But the same kind of silence and expectancy around the house at night—the Moon, the wanderer and the silence once more—all that is here. And you will understand how delighted I was after G[urs] to be transported here. There is something naturally poetic around this place, around things here, as I have never before experienced. And therefore I keep "realizing" my sense of being here ever anew, perceiving it with inexpressible, inward—care and caution. Do you understand that there are places, times and moments that are so sundered from "the world" that a gentle ecstasy keeps us—as if at arm's length—away from "full realization"?

The butterfly poem also moved me so much because I recently witnessed a tiny drama: a pair. Close together—like "stairs"—leading upward from one to the other: the wonderful white-green spider, very small, delicate, almost like a fashionable summer purse. And lined with silk. But she was stuck firmly to a very small butterfly, a silk-being painted in hues of brown and gold. It seemed drunk with sleep and was—already dead. Both hung on a mallow flower. Sweet it was, and seemed, and pure in nature. And had a quiet composure. It was—so unquestioningly sad and unquestioningly right. I was able to pluck this little butterfly, while the small spider ran hurriedly and prettily off. I wonder if this letter enclosing its butterfly thanks will arrive safely with it intact? I think it possible! The most unlikely things are sustained while the robust ones—that is, self-evident things—often cannot be induced to last. That's so isn't it? For instance, overwintered plants standing there again in spring, after their trials of ice and snow—are wondrous sights. Of course I don't mean things sprouting fresh and new, but what has really endured the winter....

The theme of your thesis is really very wonderful. Does this mean you are an art historian? Or can philologists (or philosophers) study such themes, too, where you live?

The things you say about valuing and even admiring new forms of painting—loving and understanding, engaging and maturing and—continuing to live with the others, the old, or timeless, works—speaks fully to my soul, for I, too, see it like this, recognize and experience it in the same way.

At a very young age, in the fire of the moment, I threw myself into both Impr[essionism] and Expr[essionism] And emerged again. Cleansed. I had been interested. Had been colorful within the most colorful, and "slantwise in traversing" Expr[essionism]. But " beyond" it then, "eternal" art awaited me. In this, I find, one can clearly see what the others offer and—where they fall short. It is like the reference point of the fixed stars, against which we can gauge the motions of the planets. Yet their "fixity" is not stuck or immobile but: in flux...

Do you understand what I mean? I well understand you with your views, and this brings me the warmest pleasure! Thanks!

In our family things are as follows: my sister: a painter. My first brother-in-law: a painter (trained in Paris). My current brother-in-law: an art historian. In California, at the university there.

Aunty is very kind. For my birthday she "arranged" a nest full of the love that springs like balsam, so kind. But I also know what present you gave yourself for your thirtieth birthday!—Thanks. And Aunt received soap.

Warm, heartfelt greetings to you.

Your M.K.

French bellflower with butterfly. They do not stay "blue" when pressed, sadly, but your campanula vision in that church "moved" me (in both senses) to enclose this little *envoi-anime*.[*]

~

Limonest, July 4, 1942
To Maria Gnädinger

Yesterday I had a walk that is worth mentioning. My heart was in my mouth, and the glorious, summer-bright landscape wrested from me feelings of helpless perplexity. It seemed to me like a—horse, that has run well, heavily burdened and spurred on. This emaciated, faithful old hack has now been disburdened, and given a farewell slap on the back, then sent to a peaceful meadow to graze. But the horse doesn't take so kindly to this: sad, its head sways about, and it does not know what to do without the bridle it is used to, and the familiar burden. Yes, that's what happens to us. I stood for a long while under a tree and looked at "my meadow"—an especially peaceful, gently inclining slope of grass.

Suddenly I heard—the wind. The summer wind above me. In the tree. And the loving knowledge came to me that God was not in the fire but in this dulcet whispering. It prompted me to sense God in "felicity." And so I took this with me, to share with you.

My sense of helplessness before what is beautiful, buoyant and good, the quiet of a summer day, may also be connected with being a

---

[*]   "Live dispatch." —Tr.

sensitive "thing of time" that does not trust. It is like a seismograph tuned to earthquakes—rather than stability.

~

Limonest, July 13, 1942
To Anneliese Herweck and family

You should not conclude from my "melancholias" that I am not well, or that I'm fading sadly away because I have nothing to do here and no real "contact." Firstly, I have fine books—a magical landscape around me—and my letters. And my thoughts. Loneliness has always been my preferred companion—but it's to do with the time we live in. The times and their task and their indictment. Not only that one has to wait before a closed curtain. And who knows what scene will open up before us, signifying our distant fate? The great unknown: I always try to transform it into something of grandeur in order to survive it.

One has so many different forms of waiting; from impatient nail-chewing through to serious meditation on acceptance of all that may come. Waiting is a discipline, in fact a matter "of taking the long view." Godhead has a long cycle of breath. A phrase from the Mysteries. If we observe ourselves we can be alarmed to see how short of breath we are—the best evidence of nervousness, lack and fear.

There is a phrase about fear in the Gospels that always helps me to lengthen and broaden my breath.

1 John 4:16–19:

And so we know and rely on the love God has for us.

God is love. Whoever lives in love lives in God, and God in them. This is how love is made complete among us so that we will have confidence on the day of judgment: In this world we are like Jesus. There is no fear in love. But perfect love drives out fear, because fear has to do with punishment. The one who fears is not made perfect in love.

We love because he first loved us.

~

Limonest, July 16, 1942
To Alice and Rosi Ruprecht

Dear Ruprecht sisters

You're no doubt back home again now in Bern? When the Swiss "travel to Switzerland" it's a special drama. To us others it appears as if the Swiss are "more elevated" than the rest of the world. Sometimes Switzerland seemed—and I think, almost, never more than *now*—to have a special mission and place, so that it might be the heart of Europe.

Do you know the works of Adalbert Stifter well? What he is for the German world, isn't Switzerland also? This extraordinarily composed, meaningful sense of confirmation (though no "stuckness" in it; Switzerland's weight is neither heavy nor lazy; but healthy, good and earthy, and pure). The foreword to the *Studies* contains these words: "We seek to identify the gentle law that governs the world." You may know it. Reading Stifter, whose background is Austria and above all the Bavarian forests—you are changed.

Even today still, hoping and believing.

That incomparable book about education, *Late Summer*—has given my grown-up, beloved godson—who is a soldier fighting precisely where he must live and act—the strength to live and act. Now. And in the war.

"Switzerland" as idea and embodiment also equips us with essential strength. By its stance, its land and being, its island nature not "untouched," though, by the terrors of the times—but rather most profoundly "moved" by them and today nothing other than—symbol of the Great Cross (the Red Cross if you like): it serves by its awareness. Knowledge through empathy. A fine tradition, don't you think?

I, too, have once again been a "child of Switzerland" and specifically your child—could you tell Frau Gnäd[inger] that the Chr. Community parcel arrived today, and yesterday the money transfer! Wonderfully good deeds—where money is no longer "money" and food no longer "material" substance.

But here, as there, almost a healing medicine, almost a sacrament. Because it is "provisions for the journey." The inwardness of giving must find the inwardness of receiving. Then it comes as an emissary who "knocks on the door." And you feel like spreading a white tablecloth in welcome.

Thank you. Thanks for the two letters (and the fine reply token). They really carried the fragrance of resin and blueberries. And they lit up a sense of alpine roses, too! A delight how these grow amid the damp moss. Many years ago I saw them, too. And the blueish cyclamens in spring. There's a little color-print volume on identifying alpine flowers. A lovely little book. How I wish I could send it to you. They're all there, and in colors. The first page shows a gentian. Did you know that we often found a type of gentian—the meadow gentian of course—in Gurs, along with the most delicate bell heather, and a variety of edelweiss. Yes, we had comforters. Not only the colors of the sky, the shapes of clouds, the far glory of the Pyrenees. When you went outside, at the margins of the camp, flowers awaited you. And their power of solace was no mean thing. It will be the same on the battlefield, too, for the soldiers: the comforts of grass and flower. It is often the last thing they see, and represents all love.

How our Earth is afflicted, what thousands of seeds sown. What *letters*, later, will be bestowed on us and tell us this? Don't you already get a sense that you can hear them? The rhythm of the long summer days—their wind. (Here, almost daily, we have just as much wind and its variations as we had rain in G[urs].) This accompanies us in soughing and silence, in rushing thunder and whispers.

And the human soul a stage for all this in the tiniest confine of one's own destiny, that grants it nothing but what our two eyes see and—are able to notice. I feel "myself" so often to be nothing but "two wide-open eyes." Such limitation. Why, I wonder, did the old masters, mystical visionaries, cover angels in eyes? Their wings like those of peacocks, but much more thickly strewn with eyes. Because an angel lives in vision, whereas we only "see," for which two eyes are sufficient. The gaze of spirit beings penetrates everywhere, perceiving in breadths and depths.

My thanks once again for all the great, heartfelt kindnesses you have done, and many good wishes for the work and life starting again at home!

Your Maria K.

You will no doubt be pleased to hear that twenty-five Protestant friends from the camp reached a *maison d'accueil protestante** yesterday, in Haute-Loire. It's high up in a beautiful position (and well provided) where they can work—each in his own job—and find their feet again. These are mainly young and middle-aged people, including many from my group. Many good friends and my cousin. Good news, isn't it?

~

Limonest, July 18, 1942
To Toni Schwarz

My dearest Toni, I did, didn't I, copy out the beautiful meditation by Runge? Where he says that contemplating a flower is something he loves to do more with every passing day? I remembered this phrase after I'd finished reading your letter. "Loves...more with each passing day"—it is true. An intimate kind of familiarity has grown up between us, and to you, I think, I can express myself most freely. You also perhaps find a certain "pathos" in my letters? I'd be interested to get a reply to that question. (Someone recently wrote to me about this, saying that people today feel somewhat uncomfortable with it.) You are unable to write in any other than an honest, beautiful—good (that is, "beautifully good") and factual way. When your door opens, the envelope of your letter opens, then I know what I hold in my hand. What you said about the flutter-cloth and flag mast was a brilliantly funny perception. And not a "truth" (but a game). No. When your door opens, I'm

---

* Protestant refugee house. —Tr.

"at home"—*Bethlehem* means "bread house"—this is innocent simplicity in the duplicity of our time. Fragrance of home and bread in your presence, my dear. And so I divest myself. Take off my shield and cloak, hat and even shoes. And you make things homely. Or like the evenings in G[urs], when you arrived like an ray of evening light and settled by my camp bed. Time for leisure with—angelus. Don't let this unsettle you nor object to it. A person does not know what he "presents" to the other if the other doesn't tell him.

And my family in Beaulieu forms a remarkable bridge from the old days to now—also a color bridge by the way. And you're the one who paints it, tumbling around like an elemental being on its various struts, and casting images, and knowing what it was like back home. Not in the "melancholy of home." But with us in the "rooms" and—at the altars. We have each other. And go together to the altar. I was so pleased to pass on the epistle of John to you. Both of us know that this should not be "written down." Nor do we wish to take it and embalm it, however much we might like to "possess" it. Instead we will commit it to memory and then destroy it, if you wish.

The same happens to all that has been written; and especially with a particular type of text. We take it, rejoice or suffer with it; thus consume it. Thus destroy it!—Passing on things taken from other writings, from letters for example, has to be done with thought and care. Here there really is an appeal to our "freedom." It is up to us to decide here between what is right and what is not. And a certain "pure circulation," a pure reproducing of soul processes: may be permissible. Even if—seen in this way—something questionable remains. There are letters that, however personal they may be, acquire greater universality. Then we can say that they are generally valid because they release themselves from the "personality." You understand me. Letters never ought otherwise to be "published," yet even the most intimate are. When the necessary time has passed and this therefore becomes permissible. Maybe so that they ripen enough to fall from the tree of life and be harvested? True letters intrinsically bear a personal tinge as their color, the nuance of their landscape and origin.

But then they can pass beyond this and be more. Because "it" speaks through them.

I'd like to copy down two things (once again!) from the last issue, which will bring you pleasure. And are related to what I'm saying. Only if things are also good for others (apart from the one directly addressed) or worth knowing by them because they do not merely expose the writer but elevate him; and the recipient does not preen himself by—truly a reality—decking himself out in alien feathers (autograph collection may relate to this "vaunting of friends"—which I am very familiar with. I mean this kind of vanity!)—only then can one risk passing on letters that were not originally intended for this. Thus one takes the responsibility on one's own shoulders, almost takes "destiny in hand." For oneself, asked the question as you ask—one can, one must of course, be able to acknowledge that letters likewise (though perhaps not all) can be shown to others.

And—just as I do not show yours to others because they are "secret," belong to me and only give out their aroma of bread when I hold them in the way that is fitting for them—so, Toni, I would like to—release—my letters.

They are riddled with errors, they're imprecise, sentimental and often self-congratulatory. They are, however, true reflections of my striving and learning I. And may serve others through acknowledgement both of what is too much in them; and too little.

So you may do with them what you will. For they really belong to you, dear one, my dear Toni.

Do you know that I write on the big, grey notebook that René brought with him? And so, you could say, upon many, many faces and so almost on beings themselves...? But the underlay does me good, even if in a more material sense—its size and everything is so agreeable. Forgive me—if this troubles you of course I'll put the notebook back. Your permission is still awaited for René to visit you once more, who will then bring me your new things. In particular the painting book and the—little visions. The judgments you wish for I will give in good faith, but then you can erase them again. For I cannot be sure that my imagination about them: should be any kind of judgment. Something like that is much easier to discuss than to write down, as you so rightly feel. For this I would need you, that is, your living presence. Looking at them together is what first renders explicable forms such as this to which you give "passage," as one might say! But I will try. (They do not like being approached in a "neutral" or "prosaic" fashion. Because then, often, one is without love: a touch, a breath of love. And then the spirit—is lacking).

Thank you for your replies. I love it always that you see nothing as too insignificant to answer. The people above you, the fleas around you—come into focus. And Ben[feys] with the bath. And the eye-cup that Mother thought was no use. I have a white porcelain one. Given me by my young French woman, let's call her Marguerite. For that's her name, and she is there too in the little photo, did you know? Dear Aunt Berthe asked whether she was "a Child of God." (I think she assumed this because of her rather *triste* expression!) And my Marguerite thought this very amusing. For, like a great many people here, she is "enlightened." (It seems to me, more of such folk here than at home?) Nevertheless she said: "We are really all 'God's children'!" Ah, I find what Peguy said so important—so glorious. (He was talking about a Jewish friend whom he loved.) He wrote:

C'est un athée, tout ruisselant de Dieu.[*] Surely R[udolf] St[einer] could have said the same thing. In his magnificent way he not only said it but taught us that, since the Mystery of Golgotha, every human being "overflows with God"—because the Earth itself drank the sacred blood, and so received communion in pepertuity. Mother Earth bequeaths this to us, doesn't she, in our blood.

"Earth, my love, I want, I will… I've long since endlessly bound myself to you."[**] Rilke.

Thus we are just as much at home wherever we find ourselves on Earth. Suddenly finding ourselves, each other, as we do here now. 'To

---

[*]   "He's an atheist in whom God overflows." —Tr.

[**]   M. K-D. here slightly misquotes Rilke. The original (Elegy 9 of the *Duino Elegies)* is: "*Namenlos bin ich zu dir entschlossen*"—i.e., "Namelessly bound to you." —Tr.

live like God in France"* is a phrase of contentment, it's true. And one that takes wing. Yes: *takes wing*. That is, a secret angel-phrase in all its innocent visibility. But many have grasped God here. He permitted himself to be grasped....

This time I'm sending Stifter's wonderful "Solar Eclipse." Even if you already know it. For me it is always a cause of inmost elation. Read it, then read it to Mother—then return it, please!

I hold you in my arms.

~

Limonest, August 1, 1942
To Toni Schwarz

*Il ne faut pas savoir le matin où l'on couchera le soir.*** This is nothing other than the path to truth and life, the intrinsic nature of initiation. To possess as if one possesses nothing. To regard everything one has and is as only being lent; and what does this require other than to take wing, to lift the sole of your foot from the ground...shake off the dust when the spiritual journey begins? You may think my words a riddle. And—there's no more I can say to you....

We will be transformed from one clarity into another. And "wandering" from one pain into the next we are the people of God whose path is, as ever, the path to God. Cast out and willing to suffer, we are victorious in pursuing a devotional obedience. The lamb is the symbol of a willingness to follow a path that is *essential* if we are to prevail. Without violence, speechless—pervaded only by the strength of gentleness, the strength of the path to be followed. The love of God passes all understanding—is this true? It *is* true. It equips us to be children, and to fulfil our sacrifice "in the Father." ...

I am starting to realize what a wonderfully healing meditation we possess in the profession of faith—"Christ's birth on Earth is enacted by the Holy Spirit, who, to spiritually heal the original sin in the body

---

*   A German saying, meaning "to live in luxury." —TR.
**   "One should not know in the morning where one will lay one's head at night."
      —TR.

of humanity, prepared the son of Mary to be the vessel of Christ." The healing of corporeal nature occurs through the spirit. And the same likewise causes injury to corporeal nature. We are subject to influences and effects. And we may receive these ourselves from the highest hands. Our own hands are such powerful tools for wounding or healing.

~

Limonest, August 3, 1942
To the friends in Heidelberg and Mannheim

Yes, my dear ones—

After a long silence I come very close to you once again. "And approaching closely" is roughly how such a beginning continues in the Buddha's discourses.

Today is a gift of beauty and silence. A long-awaited storm and unceasing rain at night gave birth to it: blue—pure—no longer hot. An August day to lie upon harvested fields, encompass woods and dwell upon mountain heights. There's the fragrance of fruit in the air. And in the human breast a feeling rises of the year coming full circle. Of what a year contains.

Today it seems to me as though something were leading me toward you with loving compulsion. The beautiful, clear day (one that Stifter would know) is almost asking to be dedicated to you. Although it will soon end, its full, proven beauty only begins where I connect with you....

The time has almost arrived for me to start again [in Gurs]. With others who likewise had their leave extended, and with many who carried on working there.

After the break it will not be so easy to begin with. The weak and human part of me has its fears. What helps me to energetically overcome such pitfalls is the thought that today every place must be filled. And that there are places of work and suffering, but really none for leisure or rest. If you try nevertheless to creep away quietly to a backwater of peace, bad conscience will pursue you, it seems. From far and near one soon spies the neighbor whom one should love as oneself who fills that place: to work and (as so often when we were nursing)—to suffer.

Thus one allows the other to take up burdens, while choosing the easier path, and the excuse of "well-earned" rest. But you see, this rest, this tranquility, does not exist for our kind. Not until we draw our last breath. For our vocation has committed us to suffering and adversity—and—we are no doubt only whole when we stand in the very midst of sacrifice and of being sacrificed. (And understand this as service to humanity and—as meaning and purpose.)

Ready willingness is a quality of opening, unfolding and enlarging the self.

An expansion that brings our arms into the horizontal and our whole being into the form of a cross. But tensing up makes your arms sink, paralyses, accentuates the "I" at the cost of the not-"I"; and instead of gain it works to further our loss.

We have many lovely songs whose words and melodies can arm and fortify us. One of my favorite such *cantiques* is this:

> *Ah, donne à mon âme*
> *Plus de sainteté,*
> *Plus d'ardente flamme,*
> *De sérénité.*
> *Plus de confiance*
> *Pour rester debout;*
> *Plus de patience*
> *Pour supporter tout.*˙

That's only the first verse—all four are helpful, like chorales....

Such faith alone makes us invulnerable nowadays. It stands us in good stead in every situation. It is the only possible defence—is both attack and resistance simultaneously.

Inmost greetings to each and every one of you.

M.

---

* Ah, give to my soul / More sanctity, / A flame more bright and full / Of serenity. / More confidence / To stand up tall; / More patience / To endure all.

~

Limonest, August 5, 1942
To Toni Schwarz

My very dear Toni—

Do you know what would be lovely? To lie side by side in a corn-field. In August when the corn has been cut but the fields haven't yet been ploughed. I no longer remember when or where my feet last wandered thoughtlessly across a harvested field. And still less do I know why they suddenly remember it—now, this year: recall the jolting furrows and the painfulness, almost, of walking over them. Perhaps it's the fitful nature of a stubble field that attracts me? You see the feet of all the stalks. And since the waving corn has gone, instead there is evidence of each single support. However unsettling and "left over" the whole thing is, it offers greater clarity; there's a soberness in it. And do you know? Adoration, too. There's harvest thanks in all thanking. The harvested fields bequeath this to us. In contrast to mown hay fields when all "flowering"s gone," these fields have borne their fruit and the harvest has "come home." For human beings. The hay is brought home, too. But it is light and fragrant, and belongs to the cattle. And as it says in the Psalm—the flowering grass brings forth pain of transience. But blessing issues from the fruit of the grain. And shall stay with us when evening draws nigh. And winter.*

To lie beside you looking up into the skies of August, which are "loftier" than those of July. Already less dense with sun glare. Oh, they are already drawing away from us again. Which gives our upward gaze more strength to seek them. And what is more urgently needed than the search that, on its quest, unravels confusion—growing freer and more blessed...? This seeking is not one that noisily beats its wings, but instead rises in wafting equilibrium. But would that not be floating? And once again the phrase assails us, and the memory of him who spoke it: "A wanderer between two worlds."** For those of

---

* I could not discover which psalm this refers to. —Tr.
** Reference is to a book by Walter Flex, who died in World War I. It became

us in the full, conscious flower of our youth in 1914, "August" since then has no doubt embodied the experience of war. The beginning of a new epoch, unlike any other apart from the one given us in October '40. An era went under. And—another went under again. Yet such up-rush of tumultuous events hurls us in directions we do not wish to go in. And girdles us in chains and challenges that long, long out-match us before we have grasped them. Usually, even, we die of this. Or do we take flight beyond it? A strange thing to find yourself in the abyss of events. There, high above, you glimpse a light. As in a chasm, the danger is as great as the light that is unearthly, hovering high above. Married to the depths! Do you know *The Chymical Wedding*? The huge trial of pulling yourself upward out of a kind of: artesian well? Unforgettable. (It must be an "August experience.")

~

Limonest, August 6, 1942
To her sister

For many, many months now I have been keeping watch in vain for some news from you. Franz likewise. Gradually one loses heart and starts to believe that we've lost touch. That one is now quite alone. No further steps are taken to speed up the immigration application, and everything seems to falter.

Then comes a sign of life again, after such long silence and privation; and with what fervor I take it up, turn it and revolve it, enhance it even and embroider it. And eventually have taken possession again of a sense of connection and belonging, of the hope of seeing each other again at last.

And I feel like laughing and crying simultaneously; and with endless eagerness want to write reams and volumes, words tumbling out in full spate. Yet nothing but all too sober letters result from so many feelings and desires and so much love....

---

very popular but its romantic idealism was later exploited by the Nazis. —Tr.

I have been so greatly subject to the present moment that I had almost ceased to wish for anything, instead staring ahead fixedly at what may come, as if under a spell. Prey to events as we all are. None wrestle themselves free from their place in the contemporary fabric, that is, all sharing a common fate.

Happy are they who can take the small steps of each day and hour in earnest faith and loving warmth. That's how I understand the mysterious phrase, "Except ye become as little children"—looking with faith and devotion only upon the next and closest things. Acting out of untroubled will.

~

Limonest, August 10, 1942
To Marie Baum

Owing to much wind and aridity of the somewhat cool summer, our high-lying meadows are not lush but more sparse. They have a grayish-green color, strewn today with thousands of wild flowers. From afar it looks as though spring has returned with a host of anemones, without winter ever having arrived. Light-brown cows graze this drifting pasture. And its colorless quality seems to conceal a wealth of all colors. And—be patient.... Yesterday—it was Sunday—I sat a long time by the side of the road. My gaze was drawn by hills, raised up to them. My hand rested on the field that had been ploughed and awaited new seed. The plough stood there festively. It was like sitting—waiting—by the world's path.

~

Limonest, around August 13, 1942
To Alice and Rosi Ruprecht

My dear Ruprecht sisters
My warm thanks to you. The cheerful squirrels have somewhat hopped over the pain in your words.

Nevertheless I clearly hear your woe and lament—we who belong together—for you know we have only had a short reprieve and at any time can be conscripted back into the old phalanx—we experience these new events most intensely. And though for now they rush by us: none will be forgotten. They will catch up with all of us, fetch us...but not home. Instead driving us ever onward.

If only this "onward" could be in a higher sense, so that we succeeded in spreading wide the skin of our poor body to follow the flight of the soul, the peace of the spirit....

For these, you know, hover in the blue during trials and tribulations. Nothing better, more vigorous and fitting can happen to them than for us to enlist them in high deeds. Yet this corporeal fabric is earthly, and fear, fear creeps up on it and paralyses it. These days pass between hope and fear, and in deep, all-consuming compassion. Each day that passes without a summons is a victory. But only the night remains for relief. And in the morning it all starts again. One almost feels like turning night into day, so inward is the brief respite of dark and stillness, and so threatening the new, shimmering morning!

We—as yet still here and alive—almost feel we have survived. And are overwhelmed by gratitude, when we are not overwhelmed by fear!

I have a feeling that our rightful place both day and night is at altars: where the unceasing prayer of love should surround those who have passed on and withdrawn. And whom we must serve at the altar with all our strength. The sense of forsakenness one finds oneself in at such moments (for we know it well)—is indescribable. Really it lifts you away from the Earth into a distant vacuum of exposed existence. Serving powers have to hurry by to help: to gather up the souls to make them of use again.

I have the Gethsemane picture in front of me. By Rembrandt.

The angel who supports Christ in this picture is very grave, a warrior entirely. And the Comforter is entirely human. Entirely impoverished. The warrior angel is the messenger of mercy. But nothing indicates this. His supporting gesture is affirmation of tribulation. Only the wings are so mighty! Wide as the world. Nothing today helps us but—to overpower our weakness!

We acknowledge it—and may go under perhaps. But we celebrate that Christ has become our familiar.

Our fate is—*irréparable*. For what power can free us from the mysterious seal of relatedness? And so: we are fearful in the world. But in the world overcome, we have peace. In the Christ world—there lies our peace. There.

Please accept my thanks for all your care and concern of yesterday. And your concern for all of us. And go on giving us much, inexhaustible help through your love. Please....

Your Maria.

~

Limonest, mid-August 1942
To Rudolf Zeitler

My dear friend. Several times I started to reply to your last letter. It was no good. I am too restless. But at the same time one leans with an unspeakable eagerness over something as beautiful as your letter succeeded in being, imparting; and even: in dispensing. Telling of the northern summer: work—people—landscape. So much in it is strong. So that it asks for something. Gratitude and response. And strength.

If only I could! But the present seems to hold us pressed up against the bars—of a grating—of a balustrade. What is beyond is—all that others call life...

Tomorrow perhaps we will give it up again. And may face the new straitjacket of difficult circumstances, more difficult even than those at G[urs]. Some of the others have already reached their new destination. All I know for now is that G.[urs] is empty, and I hope that you have received Aunt's address before I have (and can therefore be reassured).

We know nothing.

Love, says the apostle, is patient and hopeful in all things. Has faith in all things. I am sure this love is also quite fearless. Even in uncertainty it creates its space of peace. In fear we are not within love. I always knew that I, that we, lack the capacity to stand the test of *coming* things. But we suddenly—simply—can cope with what *is*. And this enormous daring of "trust"—this: living under threat as in the greatest safety: gently. If only we could do this.

The enclosed passage from *Faust:* the figure of worries and cares so subtly and surely revealing our magical potency: it can do nothing other than shake us deeply. The unspeakable companion of our days—journeys. Journeys and nights and days.

God bless you for living up there so well protected and in loving awareness.

Your M.

If—if you receive no further letters, you have Margot's address. She will get messages from the Lyon friends, for their son is convalescing with her.

~

Limonest, August 18, 1942
To her brother

I think you are with me in thoughts a great deal, and with inner, heartfelt pleas. These days are difficult and painful. I sit at my desk in an indescribable state of uncertainty. I have lost my connection with almost all my friends from G[urs], whose lives have been suddenly transformed, and thus torn from me.

Will we meet again tomorrow? It may only be a brief separation, and writing is superfluous—

For now, though, I stupidly hold onto the habit of many months, and if no letters come with news, if everything remains so empty, and there is nothing to do all day long—than—wait for tomorrow and *hope*: then this is a trial that sucks the heart dry.

Naturally one seeks some occupation, darns a little, does a bit of laundry, tidies one's room—looks through books—thinks about what one—would leave here if—what one would let go of—and so prepares oneself, though without really being able to do so, and without managing—the authentic, great, tranquil matter of a preparation that has been firmly resolved—which means: accepting what is to be.

But in this way one weakens oneself by weakness! The breakthrough to sanctified acceptance of an unknown departure (which in turn means only passing through to a higher level of suffering and thus insight) is not successful. Not yet.

Groaning with relief I hurl myself into the arms of the night—sink into its protective embrace and the nightly silence. You wish you could make the quiet night into day, and wake and live as long as night prevails—because you would so gladly sleep through the feared day with all it might bring, and so remove yourself from its grasp.

But in turn, what indescribable, high, luminous summer days are passing over the Earth. A summer without rain, without blazing heat. Bad for yield—but a series of festive days for us celebrants. (Trembling, praying for *duration*) And these weeks, long weeks, months of beauty—they last! Interrupted by no rain. This afternoon a southerly wind is blowing, mild and warm; and one feels astonished that the blue of the sky seems streaked now. Will it rain? We're living in drought. And the meadows are hard and grey.

Yet all is renewed again during the night, in the blessed, still "eventless" night. Dew falls, and in the morning renewal has arrived, serene equanimity. And I have learned—to fear—such a beautiful morning.

I'm writing to you in the open air. A little way from the house and room that so long were so dear to me but today are oppressive. And the park begins at the door of the house, with its old ladies and their unendurable gestures, expressive of comfort, health and meals. Harmless chatter—but I cannot cope with it. And flee...

~

Limonest, August 21, 1942
To Toni Schwarz

My good friend. Thank God for your letter. For if the Gurs contingent of my poor friends fall silent—all that remains is panic. And you know how familiar this is to us. It's either the wail of sirens or SOS or the kind of breathlessness that forgets God has inscribed his name in every soul. Therefore one need do nothing other, really, than—breathe. Out and in. In moments of danger, this sole remaining rhythm gives an answer to everything: "Practice spirit awareness in soul composure where surging deeds of worlds" evolving unite our own I with the I of worlds; and you will truly feel within the human working of the soul. For the will of Christ holds sway to all horizons bestowing grace on souls in rhythms of worlds: you spirits of light, let flame up from the East what through the West takes form. This speaks, "In Christ, death becomes: life." ...

How fortunate to be able to take refuge in such wisdom—breathing, perceiving. Receiving soul certainty. And I gaze full of admiration and love at how you can do this: it is wondrous—you heart-tone.[*]

Things seem to be moving again around us. The day spins like a carousel round questions, fear, fear of evil. Who knows? What has our name on it will catch up with all of us—whether joy or suffering. And since what happens to us, against us, so much exceeds the strength of us poor creatures, us weak ones, mighty powers of adversity may well be at work. These are powers of the highest hierarchy who seek to display God's omnipotence again upon the People of God. Once again a super-earthly element descends upon us as woe. And the battle with the angel begins. In order—to end in new dawn if God allows.

But we do not yet know what part it is we must play: whether we belong to posterity, to those who have been spared or rescued, those whose part it is to pray, to serve at altars so that their pleas and compassion can *take effect* both day and night. Heart-rending grief gives rise to a disquiet that is not of this world. No, such things can never

---

[*]   This is a play on the name of the addressee, Toni. —Tr.

have been known before—and those who have been scattered and sent to oblivion—seem to have been torn from us. We who remain for the moment, who are still here, have a mission of mercy toward these torments, and must seek to "mend" the harrowing wounds that have been left. (The image of the deserted camp and tents has a vehemence we have to counter. It's true: guardians of thresholds.) And so the whirlwind spins us in its circle of fear and compassion: real, ancient tragedies climb upon stages the world turns away from. The ear of spirit desires to hear, yearns inexpressibly. "But the dew falls on the grass when the night is most deeply silent." ...

Tell me, Toni, what is still being asked of us "in the spirit," for the sake of the spirit—and for God? Must we have learned to suffer death in the spirit in order to survive in the material world and pursue our path? Does Goethe mean this when he points to this wisdom: "To exist you must relinquish your existence"? The zero point—is a resonant shell. (I'm enclosing—can you see it?—the tiniest snail house as symbol that I came upon yesterday on a spreading, withered meadow: so fine, so whole, so "void." Wrapped in a rose petal.) Are we lacking in seriousness if we can "still" send such messages to each other even as the horn summons us?—departure and dying away.

In Switzerland they know [what's happening]. The R[uprecht] sisters just wrote me a desolate card. We have been sundered from our benefactors. And this time the worst of it is: that—ultimate silence descends. It is therefore best for separated families to gather there and search. But everything outside then remains: outside. Being clear about this gives rise to a state of finality that in fact—intensified again—expresses no-longer-being-of-this-world. "In the world you have fear." So may we hope to encounter peace in this world that has been overcome? You know it is the time of Christ's return.

R[ittelmeyer]'s last, great sermon was in St[uttgart] at New Year '37. (In March '38, he was taken from us.) Unforgettable the huge, candlelit hall. The text was: Christ walking on the waters. "Fear not. I *am*."

Do you know that it wasn't a sermon? Just a stammering. His voice broke with agitation as he exhorted us to believe, to believe him that it was true—for he himself had experienced this—that "where one takes Christ on board the ship, there is land." The unforgettable voice full of truth, of great, great grief about an intimated future. I felt the presence of his death that evening—yes, it seemed he was suffering it in the very midst of these sacred admonitions and "for the sake of faith." Love is the greatest good, is free of fear, for it loves what happens—whatever happens, is emanation; and our highest freedom lies in the triumph of having "chosen" what is asked for, that is, to love it! "Becoming aware of the idea within reality is true human communion." It is here that the most contradictory things correspond. Differences cease. Surrender culminates in the Last Supper. Substance becomes spirit. Do you remember? "We all approach you with our soul, O Christ, so that you may sacrifice us with yourself. And so your light may shine in our daylight. And you may take our part."

Thanks again for all your being and your words. And stay safe in God.

~

Limonest, August 24, 1942
To Toni Schwarz

I find this the most perplexing of all (repeatedly): How almost simultaneously the mass fate (of a race?) is occurring and—nevertheless a person's individual fate can detach itself from it. I don't mean escape, being spared or suchlike. No: amidst collective existence, soul existence arises victorious in so consoling a way—sings. As a dove finds peaceful, almost heavy uplift, and soon disappears. In this way the soul, as soon as it comes to wakeful awareness, senses the spirit of all existence and is able to sustain itself eternally there. As one, and other than all: alongside it.

The effect of all that is happening deepens pain in an extraordinary way, and initiates a new dedication to "life within death."

I saw a graceful, prayerful scene a while back. Four butterflies rose up like paper cut-outs—suddenly white against the green background to my window. They lifted and sank in the interlacing and interplay of their light, spiritual joy, vanished and reappeared: never loosing their bond they fluttered ever further in joyous union, and ever higher—so high at last that they floated over the high chestnut trees and seemed to fade away into green depths and heavenly blue. Do you remember that wonderful moment at the end of Goethe's *Fragments*—the brother, waking early, spies white-robed youths bearing torches in the garden, is woken by their song, sees them absorbed into one as they "vanish into the distance"? It was like that for me when this "sign" seemed to detach itself from the painful devastation (and—eclipse and fear) of the first few days.

So many warm thanks to you again for the strength you poured out to me in your letter, and the strong sign of goodness that it conveyed: in truth, everything is dream and unfolding reality and the "onefold" simplicity of life.

And so let me tell you what I can manage. For instance, this: to take a rest from piercing pain! Set aside moments: of devotion! But also: order my life. Fall asleep into nothing but devotion to the sleep of peace. For you see, "we" are quite unable to "stem" the overwhelming burden—we are only mothers beside it, nursing to ward off despair, and servants, attendants in loving veneration.

Because our own condition is, after all, entirely ungrounded, is lightweight and rootless in the earthly—we do not have the corporeal weight to *expect* of ourselves what we would otherwise wish to *take upon* ourselves.

~

Limonest, September 3, 1942
To Toni Schwarz

Here is that—now already "old"—poem ["Pale Bouquet," page 171] with a word of greeting, Toni, to thank you. How restlessly I await post. And today to see "none" come instead of the usual pile: is each day a signal for the most painful states. Like a hard, reverberating gong beat on my heart. Right in the middle of it. And the painful place remains there all day. Leaving as much agitation as plea. The plea is this: "Soul, do not forget them, soul do not forget the dead. Look, they hover round you, anxiously, forsaken"—I can't remember how it continues, [Friedrich] Hebbel's "All Souls" song. When my fiancé died in '18, these tones first resounded, penetrating everything. They are infinitely beseeching, and have the right to stir the heart. The stirring has to somehow go right down into firm solidity (where things happen too "solidly"), don't you think?

Not only because we—momentarily spared—will tomorrow share in the suffering for which, today, we feel compassion. What you say is so true: "The world" will carry on. But that is only apparently so. The thought that we think, merely "think," can move worlds, and its impression will one day grow to be expression. And should deeds bring about less transformation? "In transformation go out and in. If you find drinking bitter, then be wine"—Friend Sokal bequeathed a greeting. A really wonderful "picture book" by Waetzoldt, a guide for understanding art and its development. It is a big, thick volume. How can I ever take it with me? And I so much wanted to show it to you and—leave it with you because you would find so much, so much there to engage you.

Verrons [let us see]. The good thing is that when—sooner or later—I leave things behind, everything can be kept by the friends in Lyon, and so eventually find its way to Margot or others as legacy.

At present my life is a matter of just getting by.

Very remarkably (alongside the pain and troubles), my health is better. I get up for a few hours, then slip back exhausted under the blankets—exhausted by everything. Eating is difficult—I only want to drink coffee, which for moments at a time—eases my breathing and allows me to think less tormented thoughts.

Your garland of roses arrived safely. It is different from before, isn't it—the roses are paler, too, or rather, they are no longer earthly roses.

They shine sweetly in the spirit's reflection and have drunk tears like dew. "By your gracious gesture now, God and humanity are allied," Steffen wrote once on the occasion of St[einer]'s death.

To the black wood has come a higher fusion.* And at night recently, as I was sitting by the window for a long time, wedged against the window cross, I looked for the cross next door with the ivory Christ—but it did not "help" as I had hoped. And the reality of the roses (instead of the corpse, the return of life) then came very close to me. The next day I attached my three dried roses around the cross. Today your greeting strengthens my longing for victory over death.

Dear Toni, you see we are intimately connected with each other. And—let us hope—that we will find one another as latecomers when the last of us are ferried home (as in a "late train"). It would be infinitely good to be together again. And yet—who can find the other in these conditions? My consolation for the shut-in travelers is that they are accompanied either by accustomed comrades or true friends. Erica wrote to her acquaintances here about the farewell Sunday greeting. I haven't heard any news from our Ch[ambon] friends either. Aunt Berthe no longer replies—and there were a couple more to whom I sent letters and parcels... Even Merle [d'Aubigné] is silent. In accounts of mining accidents, you hear how the weak pulse fades. A brief card arrived from Luise Schw[arz] today. Living outside of all context. Questioning. As we are.... In the end all this will be generally decided by decrees, and ultimately it is Heaven's providence that preserves us. I pray, "Decide thou for me. And give me strength: for this." There is no other course. If I should no longer reply to you, herewith the address of the friends in Lyon who will always know what has happened: Hilda Lagrange, rue Garibaldi 72. But—if I do not reply, no doubt you will likewise not ask. But what will happen to our letters? When my sister traveled to the United States, it was unbearable for me to think of her "over the oceans." But I gained some tranquility from reflecting that all our connections with people

---

* Maria Krehbiel-Darmstädter is referring to the Rose Cross meditation—an image of a black, wooden cross from which roses spring. —Tr.

should become increasingly *spiritualized* (even while we're still alive). Our bonds (that lighten us) loosen and cease to be visible; and "now the high realm of the beyond begins to be populous."

In their place, unknown "strangers" approach our hearts. And we begin to "adopt." It is so isn't it. Didn't you and I find each other "here" in place of so much that we left behind "there"? And so it continues. No substitute, this, but higher development—Toni.

"Now, though, faith, hope and love *remain*."

I too rejoice at your lonely discovery in the middle of the riverbed. Ah, that we can still rejoice. One thing made me weep: all these days we heard only a kind of humming; and then the inner roar of the swarm of unquiet thoughts—and suddenly it happened: the cheeps of nestlings became audible. The sweet chirrup and satisfied sounds of the last brood of the season—"hearing" this, and *forming* the word *nest*. It was like a stream of tears flowing inward.

For us. This word alone.

Gathered and dulcet: young birds in their nest. And it is nearly fall. On the eighth, it is "the birth of Mary. And then the swallows set out on their journey."

Yes, so it is. Adieu. Whatever happens. Wherever it should be. In the fitting harmony of final notes.

M.

~

Limonest, around September 10, 1942
To Rudolf Zeitler

Dear friend, both your letters arrived at the same time, several days ago now.

I was only able to read them today.

I know you will understand.

Before I read the letters I took out the poems enclosed with them (all "prayers"). They were addressed to "all humankind." And there are times, days, times of day, when we are to such a degree nothing but human that we dismiss the personal. As being too difficult. As too seductive. As too awakening. Of the past, and feeling. And at odds with greater compassion. It's this: compassion has been accorded the most complete place alongside the severe anxiety we have about our own life. You may likewise grasp this.

"Meanwhile" I lay ill. A heart condition; I suffer from blood pressure problems that sometimes become risky. (And on this occasion led me close to a great yearning to reach the ultimate ending.) Weak and incapacitated as I am, I am forbidden to write more about myself and all this. Especially as I know nothing at all about Aunt. And by now you will have received my last letter.

For a long time now these replies have no longer been a proper reply to your unspeakably beautiful letters, that are so precious to me. And yet each letter of yours contains a medicine. The tales of your upbringing—that re-encounter—the reflections you elaborate from this, how you depict the figures and essential being of your parents—this is: do you know what it is for me? A gathering together. I take back into me all the fear and pain that has flowed out. As possession. And a new core of crystal forms—accrual. But from "far off." As the Duino Elegies put it: "Every angel is terrible." But every "messenger" is an angel—if he comes from Him who weighs life in the balance. Rembrandt's Gethsemane picture is so right because the angel supporting the Christ who is giving himself entirely to what is human, does not—how can I put this—does not offer him solace in his super-earthly form. No, this angel is a grave, stalwart warrior. And his countenance is almost hard. But not with the obduracy of stone. The tempered hardness of knowledge shines from this armed figure's golden severity. It is a Michael. The vanquisher—will we be able to do what we must? And here endurance is almost the hardest. Waiting—and suffering. Forgive me (but you will)—that this is no letter. It is only—grasping your hand in thought through your being. You are close to me—especially in shared anxiety about the dear, dear person of your aunt.* Do you know these poems (from an earlier time)

---

* Marie Kühn, deported from Gurs to Auschwitz in August 1942.

that she once copied out for me? How moving they are now. And resonant. From far off.

Do reread Goethe's *Mysteries*. In thanks for what you have guided toward me. Then let us also keep this in mind: "Nothing of the transient, howe'er it may be—we are here, after all, to embrace eternity."

This is very much the meaning, the art of life, that your aunt embodied. I myself saw it in her. And since you describe your mother, I have the sense that—it is true of her, too. Don't you think they resembled each other...like the sisters they were?

Your card arrived as I was writing this. Before you got my letter, of course. Do not write to me. But send all questions and good words in future to my Margot since I do not yet know my new address. And if you speak of her friend Maria, the dear one will always know whom you are asking after.

There are an endless number of things I'd like to tell you, convey to you. In gratitude for your inestimable support and encouragement; and these last letters, especially, will remain with me forever. Just imagine, at this moment the great pain came: that the mother of my godson was suddenly torn from us. In fear and anxiety about him—she slipped away from us...

Good bye Rudolf.

THE GATE OF ETERNITY

You portal high, behind which is concealed
The peace we seek but only dimly sense.
Why I wonder do we fear the moment
When open gates invite us to approach?

It is but coming home again, to find
The land where nothing binds us any more:
A last, deep sleep, release from suffering,
Where your soul, too, will find its place of rest.

M. Kühn

THE ANGEL OF DEATH

A day will come when no bird sings to me
When flowers no longer bloom. When Sun
no longer shines upon my face:
But peacefully I'll smile then.

Tended upon an angel's lap
I'll lie in festive, silent calm.
And in his white coracle he'll bear me
Back to my last and greatest home.

M. Kühn

~

Limonest, September 12, 1942
To Toni Schwarz

Dear Toni, and lovely soul. I tried to reply yesterday to yesterday's glorious letter from you, by starting to copy something out; its purpose, you see, was to show the true connection of love with light.

Of course your experience was not "wrong"—as you will see. No, you did the right thing. Absolutely.

And how capable you are of it today (with the aid of what we try to enliven in us)—is something, Toni, that I can never tire of telling you. I can only thank you, and just as you say that my letters or words or messages are the most important ones for you—so the same is utterly true of yours for me: I hang upon your words. Trusting when you speak. And I hearken to their resonance.

Their fine echo hangs in the air like—incense after the act of worship.

For in prayer you elevate us all, and this being-creating love engenders timeless existence. In which the good endures, and in which the "I" can sustain itself.

Last night I half-slept again—but toward morning I felt the urge to look out of the window. Now we're living beneath the stars of fall.

Their wide-eyed beauty was turned toward my fearful human face—that was seeking peace without finding how to enliven it.

I have become very aware of how, in "good times" we live (and draw sustenance) from sustaining grace and from our "apple stores" of knowledge. And behold, among the well-stored apples (even protected against bruising with straw!) there are a fair few that have no taste and just—lie there still, without life.

What we truly possess is extraordinarily and so disappointingly small that this accounts for a great deal of the hardship of these days we pass in the torment of hunger. There is no doubt, surely, that these are times of initiation. And—you're about to see; what I discovered early this morning (after I had "read" it) is really true: we are close to allowing ourselves to be deprived of our I while we are still alive. And—what is left for the second death, of the physical body, if "I"-consciousness is already extinguished in spiritual death—and the Christ impulse does not mightily and overpoweringly encircle and storm round us?

After this I fell asleep again. Bright morning had long since arrived. (And the glorious stars that streamed through the foliage and had wrapped the empty, yearning soul in almost tangible jewelry, had quietly withdrawn. Had bowed out like servants before the light of the Sun. (Are our friends stars like this?)) My brief sleep seemed to have been a deep rest, for I awoke feeling stronger and nourished by the feeling and content of those three words: Christ in us.

Like you coming upon your helpful Bible words, I stumbled then upon this St. Paul poem (which appeared this winter). I'm copying it out for you. And then at last today's letter arrived from you, which is nothing other than—in complete, pure consecration—your: "Christ in us."

~

Limonest, September 15, 1942
To Maria Gnädinger and the friends in Bern

The second address (no. 72) was the right one, and so I came into possession of your letters, their loving breath and protecting love.

The importance of such things (as spiritual raiment, protecting angels and beings) cannot be expressed even though one wishes to.

My heart isn't really *in* my body any more—that is, between my ribs and under my skin. It is quite naked and free. And utterly vulnerable and utterly—curable at the same time. "Practice spirit awareness in soul equilibrium"—that is what one should do, finally, and after so many trials, *ought* to be able to. And when the time arrives (a time so difficult, for now I see that I have only so far climbed the lower slopes)—then, when this God time has arrived: how unfit one is.

All my strength it seems has been blown away. And I cling tight as if in fear of going under. I cling on: to fear. For me this has been the most evil and terrible torment: to know the great phrase, "Fear not, I am"—and yet to let myself be driven as if I did not.

The indescribable misery in this sense of loneliness, the caving in to fear and helplessness and compassion, and the pure fear of death: was terrible and—remains so.

It seems to me that to daily and hourly face "decisions" is one of the cruelest kinds of torture. Only now do I really know what "night" is. When nothing happens—except stillness and starlight. And the trees blow in the wind. But when you sit at the window the departed emerge in mourning from the depths of the park—pleading that we think of them and bless them. They draw you after. And leave you quaking. It is hard to go on living with others who are not suffering. You yourself are "somewhere else." And you stare upon this peace that inhabits the world in almost harmonious accord with strife.

Yes, if life were not a path of initiation, how could one ever dare to go on?

These past days I had to involuntarily reach for Karl Hilty (as well as other things), his books about happiness. Back then in the—camp

I had the great fortune to receive these as a real gift: their help was inestimable. You may know him since you're Swiss—but do you also know *Pilgrim's Progress* by Bunyan, an Englishman writing in the seventeenth century? Although it's a very famous book I only became acquainted with it shortly before I left (I mean from home still). I read it then in English. And this book too fell into my hands again in the camp. In an old, illustrated edition and—with a sense of much gratitude I'm reading it again now. If you don't know it, do borrow it.

Perhaps, like us, one must have been "*cast* upon the road" to fully understand the nature of suffering. Yet its stages are "I" mysteries, and if one knows *The Chymical Wedding*, some of these experiences come close to it.

Now I've complained enough to you, and must hold on to myself if I am to be worthy of your confidence. I understand so well your laments about being robbed, your empty hands, people who were your "children" being torn from your heart. The same thing more or less is true for all who are caught up in these events. And, thank God, much honest compassion has arisen. But—the world forgets very quickly. We know ourselves how unable we are to sustain, to endure things for a long time in a deep and thorough way. "Pain says, 'begone.'" Habit, the track of our life, entices us back. And if we only rediscover "ourselves," we abandon the other. We pass through all these disillusionments in our own, weary soul. And so can only lament—without laying the blame at another door. Willing sacrifice is more difficult than anything. You live in a trembling that is prayer for—preservation. But if this cannot be, one would wish it to come *soon,* for these days are like a secret, violent theft one snatches hold of and with which one—cannot flee.

Yes, I had to take to my bed with a *crise cardiaque.* I am almost better. But as I said, a driven, rustling heartbeat, and right on the surface of the skin! (You do really jump out of your skin with terror and affliction.)

I had Rembrandt's Gethsemane picture in front of me. And the Emmaus picture by Vermeer van Delft—which is little known and is indescribably mild, wretched and so "present with us." I so much wish I could show it to you—or can you find a reproduction? The Altdorfer arrived today. From you. It is the other side of the grave when morning is dawning. Where the Resurrection is at work—and this help is glorious in its loveliness. I am so deeply captivated by the work that I have seen by Altdorf—which brings me the gift of the experience of the rainbow. And the way the light gathers and shimmers around the lofty resurrected one fills one with bliss and releases the soul from horror. Free of ropes, chains, grave and death.

I trust you feel how my thanks and thoughts hurry to unite with your prayers and loving deeds.

Maria.

~

Limonest, September 19, 1942
To her brother and his family

What shall I write to you that you do not know better than I? My portion, continually, is the same kind of harried and hard-pressed state. But uncertainty is slowly turning to certainty. No one escapes the fate that is assigned him in such a general, all-encompassing way. And since fear and anxiety make us ill and still more ill, and ever less suited for the future, a person resolves after all to be courageous again

I once read something that is very true—that courage is not lack of fear, but a quality that we can have despite our weakness because courage wishes it. Because it decides to augment itself with what it lacks. And does so, my dear ones, from a higher armory. The extra inches one adds to one's imperfect form are not drawn from earthly repositories.

And it's true. When one stretches this hand out toward strength, we do also receive it.

What is in reality so terrible if an individual human being of fifty, who has had a good portion of life, has seen and learned things, has loved, suffered, been chastised and blessed—if he reaches the point of saying, simply: this is where he has got to—and he wishes to now try what is new.

Others, so many others, have done this before me. Had to do so, exposed themselves to it painfully, and some also willingly and in acceptance.

As long as we live, we cannot be anywhere other than here upon the dear Earth and under the mighty heavens. And the terror and splendor of life will keep reappearing, making us human and permitting us to find love and solace and mercy. The fact that a place awaits one again where one can serve, and is expected, is not the least comfort but the first and best. And therefore? I have always had an inmost doubt about whether we would see one another on Earth again. Sundered from Lulu, separated from you, from my ones at home by death and life, I have long been living just "somewhere"; in exile only. And the only thing one would be leaving now, again, is the improvement in one's outer life and circumstances. But from the beginning I had scruples about this, enjoying it only with half my soul, which no longer had the custom of it. I could never get the afflicted ones out of my mind. And even belonging again to these afflicted ones horrifies the body, of course, which has grown to like its comforts, but not the soul, that will feel itself freer. "At home in misfortune," the soul is now and forever *unable* to enjoy "good fortune."

When I thought, at first, that I would be spared, I resolved to devote the rest of my life to service, nothing but service. To all. I do not wish to choose but to "let myself be chosen." Standing and falling in this way will surely be the right thing. And one gives this to one's own people as legacy for the time when one has vanished altogether (but is not lost).

Henceforth every stranger is my "brother" or "sister." And because this is done in *your* name, this far-off love will intimately and tenderly serve you. I hope so much that you will find solace when events take their course. Please tell me it is so, since it will give me great peace of mind.

Since Karol[ine] has left us, I feel something has changed. The Earth holds for me one less great, faithful love. But the world of spirit has been enriched by it.

How glad I am that you, Annie, find inward and perhaps lasting interest in what is most important to me [Anthroposophy]. The lectures will give you an initial stimulus to seek further. My good heart, you have true beginnings. Please greet Frau Lew[is] from me; she will grieve for Lore.

By the way, when you go to Dornach again, please tell Herr Bühler—who sent the precious journals—how much his poem moved us, and that we thank him; and how in every other way too, all that is essential to life contracts around this island. As one continually senses meaning and blessing emanating from *here*. A home in the spirit! How wonderful that it is embodied somewhere upon the Earth. Please greet everything there from me: the path, the house.

"One who sees time as eternity, and eternity in temporal life, is free of every strife." Jakob Böhme said this once, for all time, and I hold to it. What else? Love to you all and to Lulu.

M.

~

Limonest, September 23, 1942
To Toni Schwarz

My favorite occupation at present: gathering horse chestnuts as winter fodder for the goats. The beautiful conkers gleam and sparkle in sun and rain, rattle down delightfully from the trees in their hedgehog shells. Endless shells everywhere, for we have many ancient park trees.

The loveliest thing is to pick them out of their shell: to open the wondrous moist interior of their nursery chamber, silken and protected. And have the fruit fall into your hand. Gathering fruit. The year has come full circle and the noble rounding of the conker fills you with a strange tranquility. Perfection can be "plucked."

~

Limonest, September 26, 1942
To Maria Gnädinger

Michaelmas is here now, and spreads its hand over our whole age. Its dragon, however, at the same time signifies initiation for us. Just as Advent knows in *advance* that victory has been achieved, and that this was an angel's victory. As fall approaches we grow firmer and more tranquil. We return from blazing into cosmic realms, as it were, to the Earth, and to all that Earth means to us. This requires exertion. And fear. And renunciation. Do you know Doldinger's words about the colors? I'll copy them here. As Michaelmas gift.

But now I can't find them: arranging (and disposing) of my possessions in recent days has now disrupted their order. These pages must have been packed already—since I did not wish to do without them.

And with this "confession," I suddenly remembered where they were. And so here they are after all:

> Amid the colors of the soul
> inner life weaves.
> Red is love
> orange is enthusiasm
> yellow the joy of wisdom
> blue is devotion
> indigo the sense of peace
> at sacred thresholds
> violet colors the austerity
> of insight—
> and in their midst the human being discovers
> blessed enactment of the good
> enlivened in red
> growing in orange
> hovering in yellow
> grown selfless in blue
> tested in indigo.
> Released to take effect
> in violet—
> the green of all presence

in action and rest.
Bliss through the Seraphims'
soul-endowing
spirit of colors.

I am sure, my dear Marie, that these rainbow words will also joyfully enliven you. Once absorbed, they have an unforgettable rhythm; and even if you do not learn them by heart, they become an inner possession that can lead you into the colors' joys and sufferings. And into life itself, which of course also has its colors—not just grey affliction and black death.

On the twenty-ninth, I will think my way to your room and the altar. It should be like a lifting of hands and heart. In petition. For the grace *to be* what one ought to be.

~

Limonest, October 29, 1942
To Franz Darmstädter

Bright moon-night and dark morning
are the authors of my day.
Vain wrestling to find utterance.
The wax of words has grown rigid.
Howl of a tone that is not music
and not human.
Nature goes its way...
when awareness sleeps.
And waiting stands baffled at the fork in the road.
There is no sign.
In the mist—"where from?" is gone from sight.
And "where to?" fades in dull twilight.

My dear ones—the butterfly has fallen still. The second thumbtack must finally have rid it of the habit of trembling and whirring. But it is still alive. Though sad. Everywhere there's a battle of fall between uncomplaining surrender of wilting and fading or a last gleaming and rebellious flaming. The bunch of dahlias that started as a delicate play of colors has left me with only two white flowers. And has become like All Saints. Or the graver All Souls. I look in vain upon your Sunday table.

When we were little, mother used to sing this—a song that suited her: "Place sweet mignonettes upon the table."* Her voice had the timbre—and experience—of pain. We have still more such experiences. Yet live still.

Thank you for the newspapers. And for all you have done—or will do. Please discuss with faithful Margot how to arrange the money transfer in future. I have reached the end, you see. And she will tell you some important things relating to Hilda that are painful in themselves—and, alongside this, also have serious implications for me.

To be alone now—you know or can sense what this means: loneliness as winter approaches. The endless "threat" eventually turns to a kind of weary habit. It seems to me that a heart (not in the metaphorical but the medical sense) could die as a result. And might wish to do so.

This week, at all events, I was permitted to go to town—not a happy outing. As I used to be allowed. (Every now and then one has had, after all, beautiful islands in the black ocean of one's time.) No. I was required to go to see an official doctor who has to write a report on my health. Endless hours of waiting. And I almost sank into unconsciousness. The lovely book I wished to read had no power over me—there is a kind of tension that simply extinguishes the best in us. And *that* is the most terrible thing.

I think that things improved after that. When I got outside, my feet did not easily find their way. Tears darkened my gaze. What a *single* kind gesture can do for us. Oh, the unstoppable collapse of barriers, walls and caverns. One is still quite soft after all. And receptive. And has faith in kindness and goodness

When things got so bad for our parents, due to their illness and poverty (and also their isolation) I felt for years that I might not properly put my feet down anywhere on the earth. You see, there *was* no

---

* A song for All Souls by Richard Strauss. —Tr.

earth. The ground beneath me felt like cold steel. A knife edge. I'm not speaking metaphorically. At the time I experienced the fact that there is such a thing as a knife-edge on which feet must stand; and must walk with endless caution so as not to fall off or bleed to death

This is why I know today about this realm under my feet.

At the time no help was forthcoming from anyone. (Although some help did come *through* people!) The same is true again now. True forsakenness must have begun, people must have vanished with their help, which seemed like that of good spirits.

Then God rises amidst the great silence with his lonely Word. And then the Sun rises. And the seas part. And a path *appears.* Where there is none.

Has Herr Bach[mann], cousin of my dear little Kühn, heard where she may be, and the nephew in Sweden? How are Ellen, Anneliese.... I have had no sign of life from our sister.

Farewell. If all stays as it is, I will get a *colis suisse* [Red Cross parcel] again and notebooks and paper? Nothing left at present.

Kisses and all love, quietness, closeness.

M.

~

Limonest, October 29, 1942
To Margot Junod

In the autumnal whirl of storm, leaves and cloudscapes—one understands neither the noises in the house nor one's own voice. Everything seems submerged in hurricane and ferocity. Failures and relinquishment. New trials, new threats. Something inhuman has seized power. And we ourselves are offered up like prey to the fall, to storm, decay—to fading and disappearance. Going on living is a strange sensation. In profound inaction. In an emptiness that stands unprotected in the full glare of the desolate world—and for that reason may not yet have caved in?

I fetched a large, round stone in from the garden. It goes in the oven in the evening, and then at night into my bed, emitting a steady, tranquil warmth more reliable than hot water bottles and compresses. And it's solid. Heavily it rests at my heart, and when I place my hands upon it, it becomes an ancient, eternal mountain.

There's a song that goes something like this:

> Shine into time, eternity—
> so that what's little may little seem
> and what's great may great appear:
> Lofty eternity—

We have such need of anchorage. Everything, everything is giving way, crumbling, vanishing. Human help is such a "chance" and fragile thing.

When the bright moon nights lie in your room as if on the prowl to see if, perhaps, you are either "fat or dead" (isn't that the phrase in a fairytale?) and when the morning dawns in gloom: you can so easily shiver and ask what you are—waiting for really. How long for, for what?

Until a strong gust of wind again shakes the rafters and you just enjoy lying there once more in your own (borrowed) bed: beside, on, with the tranquil, hot stone. Buried, burrowed. Saved. How long for? How fearful.

~

Limonest, October 31, 1942
To Toni Schwarz

My dear Toni. In the past I gladly wrote long letters, and was able to. Time was such that you felt you were in a safe, protected "cradle."

This sense of protection may have been constricting—not reaching further than one's own nose and nearest surroundings. But the best thing about a "sense of protection" is that it offers a boundary or "wall." And now things are so different. All torn down. The wind and rain, the fall and swirl of leaves—everything gains entry, pulling down fences and exposing summer nests. It makes hearts shiver and burrow into themselves.

To become speechless. To wish to become so—that is the nature of this change. All Saints and All Souls, this time they bring more saints and souls to seek us and flow round us. You cannot defend yourself. And the day, when you reflect, is almost, is certainly more unreal than the night when you dream. Since it rides roughshod over sleepers so that the forgotten past becomes *real* . . .

There is little that *remains* clear in these shaken days and nights. You almost step back from your life—you have seen it too often, clothed in too many garments. The body of our life is lost to us. In the past, Toni, unfolding events always made me more aware and versatile; today, though, a prayer for tranquility is wrung from what is. A prayer for wholeness remains. But actually nothing "remains." Every soul-spiritual possession is nothing but an "eternal call for renewal." And—we cannot do or achieve this, cannot will it, enact it, resurrect it. We have become begging creatures, pleading for love and clinging to the "cradle"—the brief, transient roof over our fluctuating condition.

And meanwhile the days are grey and long and monotone. Just as a tone become unbearable when it is held too long. No end or out-breath in utterance. Nothing that hovers.

But always, instead, a breaking off. What will this daily existence cease with? And the inaction?

Now I have let all this out (please don't catch it in a matchbox) I feel better. It is also Saturday evening and Sunday will come into the world tomorrow, bringing All Souls. And—hopefully—non-egoism.

The park, which so long preserved its dry, grey green, is now giving way to the old colors of fall. But red is lacking. Though yellow makes up for it. Instead of sunlight, a kind of reflected glow on my table. Brightening it with that quiet attempt at a golden ground that the thrifty world uses today instead of true gold. Yet I, too, greedily embrace this illusion, because it is gentle.

~

Limonest, All Saints Day
To her brother and his family

It is still an early, godly hour and the house sleeps or is just waking. The Sunday angelus is ringing through the dark, damp, time-
burdened dawn.

Sleeping: a blessing because it releases you from the body and opens
paths and vistas that reality has long since threateningly shut off; but
sleeping ceases when morning approaches. And waking around four
in the morning is an arduous thing. I endured it for an hour, but then,
quiet as a mouse, I fetched what I needed to make myself a coffee. The
moonlight gave a helping hand, and so all my preparations took place
in the darkness of this strange morning brightness—and—loveliness.
In these difficult days Hilda was still able to send me a small tin
with her last store of c[offee]. And was aware what a redemptive gift
this was. My thoughts and hopes are also most directed toward these
hard-pressed friends. But then repeatedly return—as if compelled to
do so by the tug of deceived hope—to circle around their own concerns, which, more frail than ever, seem to tremble in their own win-
ter-naked loneliness. My small cupful was accompanied by a morning
reading in the pages of the leaves, which tell such harrowing tales of
winter and poverty and forsakenness. Holding this cup of coffee quiet
and warm under the blankets, it eases and releases me, conveying to
my senses something like strength and light. I know you would send
me more if you could. And so it is almost a "coffee morning," a circle
of my dearest ones, whom I invite to sit here with me as I drink.

I feel your protecting love more strongly than ever, and the strength
of your care and efforts.

~

Limonest, November 4, 1942
To Toni Schwarz

The most beautiful, stillest day, golden and blue [Sunday, All Saints, November 1]. I picked dandelions at around midday, standing up at the top of the park where there is a far, open view: to the church firstly and in the distance the Lyon mountain ranges—my tightly armored heart cast off a few weights that hour and confided in itself—as you, as your intrinsic being, the love rooted in Him, counselled me.

Yes. As all "human aid" fell away, I [realized I] had long sensed, as a premonition, that it was not the right thing (for me) to place not only all hope but also all "faith," really, on this [her flight]. This grew gradually for me. We so easily submit to the influence of beloved people, raising them to "divine" status; my conscience *knew* this, but "Maria" did not wish to believe it.

But when things collapsed, in one way and another, really more than I can tell: all that had been constructed—I had the clear sense of coming closer to truth, the source, my real home. My deep feeling of forsakenness was precisely what created a home for me in grace and mercy. And within me formed the words of a prayer to Christ: *"C'est toi maintenant qui doit tout te charger de moi."**—You understand this....

Not that I was close enough to feel Him within me—no doubt that would require still many renunciations and—catastrophes perhaps. But I knew where I stood once more. The sole clear orientation. It seemed to me that I was able to make one more choice, almost without my will. As one finds the way home again, quite naturally, after getting lost, without thinking about it. The path was there all the time and waiting. It is not for nothing that our feet are a sacred symbol. Wiser than our thoughts, they follow their creator's path.

But how pierced by woe and illusion as soon as knowledge bends down and touches its own "feet." Only the revelation that feet once bore the holiest wounds, that they hearkened with such such

---

* It is you now who must take sole charge of me

unspeakable obedience—can let us hope that love is greater than death, than aberration and atrocity....

Poverty is the necessary gift today. And so I offer only that. Of myself.

And spread my arms yearning and thanking around you—a daughter and sister—

Your Maria.

~

Drancy, February 6, 1943
To Toni Schwarz

Dear friend, whom my heart seeks unceasingly in the hours of these decisive days! My return from the hospital came all of a sudden. Barely four weeks. More weakened than anything by the treatment, which kept me in bed the whole time; and then this weakness of soul, you know. And for the first time I feel myself growing weak, both physically and spiritually. Erika and her fate fill me with agitation for good reason. You understand what I mean, and that these words are for you. Addressed to you so as to thank you once more for this whole friendship, deep support in these hours when the light seems extinguished...the trials—will one endure them? With the help of the Lord who has unlimited power: I know this. But I still lack it. Back there [in Limonest] I had started to let myself go. At present I feel agitated, more so than words can tell. Forgive me my friends, please believe nevertheless that your Maria will get a grip again on herself. These loving, loving messages. The two latest, enclosed with a cross and roses. My thanks. You know that I am permitted to write only one card every two weeks. Please give Marguerite my pressing greetings, my thanks for the clothes parcel that will again prove especially useful to me; the honey was missing from the small parcel from friend Doy. One ought to have a tin [for it] (for next time?...) Mme Beysson at the *Vieux Logis* wrote so warmly. Thanks. And please tell Margot about the latest turn of events and ask her to pass this on also to Dr. Marie. How disappointing. In writing I feel my strength returning because you will read this, and because you wish to preserve my memory intact. The thought that you will read my old letters moves me infinitely. From afar I will add to them, won't I, what I have to experience at first hand, and you will know this through the super-natural means that God allows us: prayer. Thus if she can, Marguerite should inform Margot, and she in turn tell my brother and Dr. Marie. Send my thanks to Toureille (who has also written) for his good card. And ask him above all to send my greetings to Merle and Freudenberg. Here below we have no peace. But future peace we seek. Adieu, Maria. Who is yours.

Figure 76: Maria Krehbiel-Darmstädter in Limonest, springtime, 1942

Notes

1 Maria Krehbiel-Darmstädter, *Briefe aus Gurs und Limonest 1940–1943* (Walter Schmitthenner, ed.). Heidelberg, 1970.

2 In a letter to Margot Junod on September 15, 1942. Only date or recipient will be cited for quotes from Maria Krehbiel-Darnstaedter's letters within the text or notes. Where no other indication is given they are contained in the edition of her letters edited by Walter Schmitthenner (see note 1). Quotations from unpublished letters by Maria Krehbiel-Darmstädter as well as other documents in Mannheim City Archive will be referenced separately in the notes.

3 To Tony Schwarz, 7/18/1942.

4 Margarete Susman, *Hiob und das Schicksal des jüdischen Volkes*. Zurich, 1946.

5 Paul Celan, *Gesammelte Werke in fünf Bänden* (Beda Alleman and Stefan Reichert, eds.). Frankfurt a.M. 1983, vol. 1, p. 214 (all poems and quotations from poems retranslated for this volume by Matthew Barton).

6 To Toni Schwarz, 2/5/1943; originally in French as follows: *"L'idée de relire mes anciennes letters me touche infiniment. J'y penserai. J'ajouterai de loin ce qu'il me faut vivre de près, n'est-ce pas."*

7 Most of the letters that Maria Krehbiel-Darmstädter wrote in 1942 during her (police-monitored) sick leave in Limonest were addressed to her companions at Gurs internment camp. For seven months until the camp was vacated in August, she sent 2 or 3 letters there each day— probably more than 400 letters, few of which survived, however, since their recipients died at Auschwitz. However, letters are extant from Maria Krehbiel-Darmstädter to her friend Toni Schwarz, who escaped deportation, survived World War II, and later helped found The Christian Community in Paris. Five months before Maria's death, September 3, 1942, in relation to their possible shared fate of deportation to Auschwitz, Maria asked Toni Schwarz, "But what will happen to our letters?"—already knowing that this special correspondence would remain of lasting value.

8 To Toni Schwarz, 7/18/1942.

9 "The letters strike one as bewildering initially, owing to their syntactical and semantic deviations from normal language, their idiosyncratic neologisms and metaphors. Phrases such as 'Oh—different. Floating. Free. Without—without wishes,' which translate the process of reflection into speech and do not adhere to grammatical convention. Likewise by leaving out definite articles, personalizing substantives ('Sun sparkles round everything, strokes tenderness from us') and creating neologisms by transforming substantives into verbs, an idiosyncratic rhythm arises. The frequent hyphenating separation of compound German words and of their prefixes demonstrates an intentionally wilful mode of language" (Gabriele Mittag: *"Es gibt Verdammte nur in Gurs." Literatur, Kultur und Alltag in*

einem südfranzösischen Internierungslager 1940–1942. Tübingen. 1996, p. 57.

10 Ibid, p. 59.

11 Ibid, p. 61.

12 In: Martha and Else Liefmann: *Helle Lichter auf dunklem Grund. Die "Abschiebung" aus Freiburg nach Gurs 1940–1942* (Erhard Roy, ed.). Vienna and Konstanz 1995, p. 91.

13 Viktor E. Frankl: *...trotzdem Ja zum Leben sagen. Ein Psychologe erlebt das Konzentrationslager.* Munichc 1997, p. 111 (in English as *Man's Search for Meaning.* Beacon Press, 2006).

14 Ibid, p. 162 f.

15 To Franz Darmstädter, 3/11/1941. Unpublished. Mannheim City Archive

16 Unpublished. Mannheim City Archive

17 Marie Baum, *Rückblick auf mein Leben.* Heidelberg, 1950, p. 282.

18 Cf. p. [249].

19 Letter from Hilde Besag to Walter Schmitthenner, 11/19/1947. Unpublished, Mannheim City Archive.

20 Hanna Schramm, *Menschen in Gurs. Erinnerungen an ein französisches Internierungslager (1940–1941).* With documentation of French emigration policy (1933–1944) by Barbara Vormeier. Worms, 1977, p. 2.

21 To Franz Darmstädter, 11/1/1941.

22 Friedrich Schiller, *Briefe über die ästhetische Erziehung des Menschen* ("Letters on the Aesthetic Education of Man"), in Collected Works in 5 vols. (Peter-André Alt, Albert Meier and Wolfgang Riedel, eds.). Munich, Vienna, 2004. vol. 5, p. 577.

23 Cf. "Die Wiederkunft Christi im Ätherischen," in Peter Selg, *Michael und Christus. Studien zur Anthroposophie Rudolf Steiners.* Arlesheim, 2010, p. 331.

24 To Toni Schwarz.

25 To Margot Junod, 10/11/1941.

26 To Alice and Rosi Ruprecht.

27 To Toni Schwarz.

28 Quoted by Walter Schmitthenner, in Maria Krehbiel-Darmstädter, *Briefe aus Gurs und Limonest 1940–1943,* p. 339.

29 Maria Krehbiel-Darmstädter's style of writing and Walter Schmitthenner's mode of transcription (see his explanations in Maria Krehbiel-Darmstädter, *Briefe aus Gurs und Limonest 1940–1943,* p. 15) have been retained (see also the translator's preface on page ix f). However, I have included only Schmitthenner's parentheses where the context absolutely requires an explanation. Numerous abbreviations used by Maria Krehbiel-Darmstädter (such as *&* for *and*) are easily understood and intrinsic to her style—even in letters from Limonest which were no longer subject to camp-imposed page limits.

30 Although Walter Schmitthenner's edition of the letters in 1970 met with a very positive response, the *Frankfurter Allgemeine Zeitung* [newspaper] refused to print a selection of the letters, as Schmitthenner invited them to do, partly because of references to Anthroposophy. On behalf of the newspaper's editors, Dr. Peter Jochen Winters wrote to Walter Schmitthenner on 11/11/1970: "These letters are too personal and too informed by the anthroposophic worldview, and it is therefore certain

that only a very small number of our readers would gain anything from reading them. Only very few passages offer anything of general interest; and such things have also already been stated elsewhere" (unpublished, Mannheim City Archive). Walter Schmitthenner himself had no connection with Anthroposophy or The Christian Community. But, as a professor of ancient history at Freiburg University, he was academically fair and meticulous enough to reference in the notes to his edition all allusions to anthroposophic contexts in Maria Krehbiel-Darmstädter's letters— knowing of course how important such matters were to her. At the same time, however, Schmitthenner's edition omits various things that are of great contextual importance but decidedly anthroposophic in nature—such as long quotations from Rudolf Steiner's works which Maria Krehbiel-Darmstädter appended to her last letter to Toni Schwarz (see pp. 209ff) and that are fundamental to her thoughts and feelings—in other words, they form an integral part of her letters.

31   In Maria Krehbiel-Darmstädter, *Briefe aus Gurs und Limonest 1940–1943*, p. 28.

32   At the beginning of the 17th century, Elector Friedrich IV of Pfalz laid out Mannheim's horseshoe-shaped center in a grid or lattice of streets. The parallel roads of the two main thoroughfares bear no names while the quadrates between them are designated with a letter and number.

33   Regarding Rudolf Tillessen, cf. Ralf Reith: "Rudolf Tillessen—Mannheims Villenbauer." In: *Jugendstil-Architektur um 1900 in Mannheim.* Mannheim, 1985, pp. 65–99.

34   In Maria Krehbiel-Darmstädter, *Brief aus Gurs und Limonest 1940–1943,* p. 28.

35   Ibid.

36   To Margot Junod, 5/2/1942. Unpublished. Mannheim City Archive.

37   Nelly Sachs, *Briefe aus der Nacht.* Unpublished typescript, p. 22. Marbach German Literature Archive. Cf. Peter Selg, *"Alles ist unvergessen". Paul Celan und Nelly Sachs.* Dornach, 2008, pp. 25ff.

38   To Anneliese Herweck, 7/13/1942.

39   To Toni Schwarz, 8/1/1942.

40   In the 1920 and 30s, Maria was already translating the Breton Grail story, "Perronik the Simple," into German, and Emil Franz Krehbiel published this with Elpis Verlag after World War II.

41   In relation to Luise Kayser-Darmstaeder, see Petra Weckel, "Light from our past"—Rückbesinnung auf jüdische Traditionen im amerikanischen Exil am Beispiel der Künstlerin Lulu Kayser-Darmstädter," in Helga Schreckenberger (ed.), *Ästhetiken des Exils.* Amsterdam/New York, 2003, pp. 187–208.

42   Letter to Toni Schwarz, 8/5/1942.

43   To Magda von Hattingberg, in Rainer Maria Rilke, *Briefe zur Politik* (Joachim W. Storck, ed.). Frankfurt a.M and Leipzig, 1992. Cf. also Peter Selg, *Rainer Maria Rilke und Franz Kafka. Lebensweg und Krankheitschicksal im 20. Jahrhundert.* Dornach, 2007.

44   In Rainer Maria Rilke, *Die Gedichte.* Frankfurt a.M. 1986, p. 1,010.

45   Cf. Peter Selg, *Rainer Maria Rilke und Franz Kafka. Lebensweg und Krankheitsschicksal im 20. Jahrhundert,* pp. 38 ff. Two years after World War I ended, on 7/23/1920 Rilke wrote as follows to Princess Marie

of Thurn and Taxis about radical changes relating to art and travel: "Everything is altered, and the nature of art trips, with their unsuspecting and somewhat leisurely approach, which one could sum up as travel for the "cultured" classes, is really at an end now. We are driving "on empty" into the future—which naturally doesn't stop many people continuing in the old ways, without for a moment considering that their enterprise is outmoded. What I mean is that esthetic viewing, with no direct exertion involved, will in future be impossible. Basically it will be impossible to admire an image or fresco in a church—unless, opening to it through absolute necessity or exaltation, one is drawn right out of oneself before it, terrified and blessed by it. Princess, you have no idea how different the world has become. This is something we have to understand." (In: *Rainer Maria Rilke/Marie Von Thurn und Taxis: Briefwechsel*. Frankfurt a.M. 1986, vol. 2, p. 611).

46   To Toni Schwarz, 4/5/1942.

47   This portrait, entitled "Maria Darmstädter," is reproduced in Petra Weckel, "Light from our past"—"Rückbesinnung auf jüdische Traditionen im amerikanischen Exil am Beispiel der Künstlerin Lulu Kayser-Darmstädter." in Helga Schreckenberger (ed.), *Ästhetiken des Exils*. Amsterdam/New York, 2003, p. 190 (picture 2). Walter Schmitthenner gave the painting on permanent loan in his bequest to Mannheim Art Gallery (Sign. SO Inv. 65).

48   It is not recorded when Maria Darmstädter began studying Steiner's works systematically. Walter Schmitthenner, who knew a great deal about Maria Darmstädter's inner path from his parents—especially his mother—only referred as follows to her membership of The Christian Community: "As a member of the congregation of D. Paul Klein, whose work ranged widely, she later joined The Christian Community, which was oriented to Rudolf Steiner's Anthroposophy" (in Maria Krehbiel-Darmstädter, *Briefe aus Gurs und Limonest 1940–1943*, p. 14). Schmitthenner provides no information about her first connection or encounter with Anthroposophy itself.

49   Rudolf Steiner, *Vier Mysteriendramen*. Collected Works (CW) 14, Dornach, 1998, p. 39 (*Four Mystery Dramas*. Great Barrington, MA: SteinerBooks, 2007).

50   Cf. Wolfgang H. Vögele: *Rudolf Steiner in Mannheim. Briefe—Dokumente—Chronik*. Supplements to the Complete Works of Rudolf Steiner, no. 120, Forrest Row, UK, 2009.

51   The "August Lamey Lodge" was founded in Mannheim in 1896 as part of the "Independent Order Bnei-Brith, and was named after the creator of the law for equal status of Jews in Baden. According to its statutes, the lodge's aim was to "promote the purest principles of human love, to collaborate in the cultural tasks of our German fatherland, and, through cultivation of the eternal ideals of Judaism, to seek its preservation and invigoration" (cited in Volker Keller, *Jüdisches Leben in Mannheim*. Mannheim 1995, p. 159 f.). The Bnei-Brith Order was prohibited by the Nazis in 1937, and the premises at C4, 12 were closed.

52   Wolfgang H. Vögele, *Rudolf Steiner in Mannheim. Briefe—Dokumente—Chronik*, p. 7f.

53   In relation to the history of the founding of The Christian Community, see Alfred Heidenreich, *Aufbruch. Die Gründungsgeschichte der*

Christengemeinschaft. Stuttgart 2000; and Rudolf F. Gaedeke, *Die Gründer der Christengemeinschaft. Ein Schicksalsnetz.* Dornach, 1992.

54 We do not know exactly when Maria Krehbiel-Darmstädter became a member of the Society, since many documents belonging to the Anthroposophical Society were confiscated by the Nazis after it was proscribed in November 1938. The list of members of the General Anthroposophical Society in Dornach includes Maria Krehbiel-Darmstädter as a member in 1924 (Archive at the Goetheanum, Dornach).

55 To Gertrud Spörri, end of May 1942. Spörri's striking account of the days following Rudolf Steiner's death appeared in the internal newsletter of the priests of The Christian Community.

56 Albert Steffen: "To the friend of God and leader of humanity," *In memoriam Rudolf Steiner.* Basel, 1927, p. 5.

57 Published in Albert Steffen, *Geistesschulung und Gemeinschaftsbildung.* Dornach, 1974, pp. 217–239.

58 To Franz Darmstädter, 9/19/1942.

59 Cf. Peter Selg: *The Figure of Christ. Rudolf Steiner and the Spiritual Intention behind the Goetheanum's Central Work of Art* (London: Temple Lodge, 2009).

60 Rudolf Steiner, *Vorstufen zum Mysterium von Golgotha.* CW 152. Dornach, 1990, p. 46 (*Approaching the Mystery of Golgotha,* Great Barrington, MA: SteinerBooks, 2006).

61 Cf. Gundhild Kacer-Bock, *Die Christengemeinschaft in Stuttgart. Chronik 1922–2005.* Stuttgart, 2007, pp. 35 ff.

62 To Margot Junod, 2/16/1942.

63 "Then my illness and his enchantment with a young lady dissolved our marriage. It did not 'break.' That is the good thing. So there are no shards and fragments. It was a dissolution" (letter to Rudolf Zeitler, 6/30/1942).

64 To Walter Schmitthenner, 10/2/1942.

65 To Franz Darmstädter, 6/19/1942. Unpublished. Mannheim City Archive

66 Quoted in Paul Sauer, *Die Schicksale der jüdischen Bürger Baden-Württembergs während der nationalsozialistischen Verfolgungszeit 1933–1945.* Stuttgart, 1969, p. 212.

67 To Margot Junod, beginning of September 1941.

68 To Franz Darmstädter, 10/29/42.

69 To Wilhelm and Walter Schmitthenner, 9/5/42.

70 In Maria Krehbiel-Darmstädter, *Briefe aus Gurs und Limonest 1940–1943,* p. 29.

71 Rudolf Steiner, *Die Grundimpulse des weltgeschichtlichen Werdens der Menschheit.* CW 216. Dornach, 1988, p. 97f. (*Supersensible Influences in the History of Mankind,* London: Rudolf Steiner Press, 1956).

72 Ibid, p. 100.

73 Unpublished. Mannheim City Archive

74 Biographical notes (Gurs). In Maria Krehbiel-Darmstädter, *Briefe aus Gurs und Limonest 1940–1943,* p. 28.

75 To Franz Darmstädter, 8/2/1942. Unpublished. Mannheim City Archive

76 Marie Baum: *Rückblick auf mein Leben.* Heidelberg, 1950, p. 282 f.

77 Cf. Peter Selg: *Die Kultur der Selbstlosigkeit. Rudolf Steiner, das Fünfte Evangelium und das Zeitalter der Extreme.* Dornach, 2006. (*The Culture*

of Selflessness: Rudolf Steiner, the Fifth Gospel, and the Time of Extremes,
Great Barrington, MA: SteinerBooks, 2013).

78   Cf. Peter Selg, *Rudolf Steiner. Zur Gestalt eines geistigen Lehrers.*
Dornach, 2010. (*Rudolf Steiner as a Spiritual Teacher: From Recollections of Those Who Knew Him,* Great Barrington, MA: SteinerBooks, 2009).

79   To Toni Schwarz, 8/21/1942.

80   7/28–8/21/1938. According to a note in his own handwriting in his literary estate (Mannheim City Archive), Walter Schmitthenner destroyed Maria Krehbiel-Darmstädter's journal of these conferences.

81   Sister Aloysia Butz had helped Maria nurse her parents on their deathbeds. They became friends and later she invited Maria to join her for a short recuperative trip to Lake Constance, where Butz came from. She would also gladly have offered her refuge in her religious community, but this was not possible there (letter from Aloysia Butz to Margot Junod, 11/16/1947. Unpublished. Mannheim City Archive).

82   To Rudolf Zeitler, 5/3/1942. Three weeks later Maria Krehbiel-Darmstädter again briefly described her experiences at Reichenau to Zeitler, writing, "I felt similar to you on Reichenau; one experiences these moments almost as—stolen. Because insight accompanies them, like lightning—inexpressible. One becomes 'aware' of something. My teacher Rudolf St once said, 'Becoming aware of the idea within reality is true human communion.' This communion is continually within reach of lips and eyes, is the manifest secret and our divine discovery" (5/28/1942).

83   Cited in Paul Sauer, *Die Schicksale der jüdischen Bürger Baden-Württembergs während der nationalsozialistischen Verfolgungszeit 1933–1945.* Stuttgart, 1969, p. 177.

84   Quoted in Dorothea Freudenberg-Hübner and Erhard Roy Wiehn, *Abgeschoben. Jüdische Schicksale aus Freiburg 1940–1942. Briefe der Geschwister Liefmann aus Gurs und Morlaas an Adolf Freudenberg in Genf.* Konstanz, 1993, p. 111f.

85   Volker Reinhardt, *Geschichte der Schweiz.* Munich, 2008, p. 112f.

86   To Alice and Rosi Ruprecht, 7/16/1942.

87   To Toni Schwarz, 9/3/1942.

88   Kläre Herrmann: "Die Maria Briefe." Unpublished typescript, circa 1970, p. 1.

89   Quoted in Erhard Roy Wiehn (ed.), *Oktoberdeportation 1940.* Konstanz, 1990, p. 256.

90   In: Paul Sauer: *Dokumente über die Verfolgung der jüdischen Bürger Baden-Württembergs durch das Nationalsozialistische Regime 1933–1945.* vol. 2, p. 2

91   Irmgard Herrmann, in Maria Krehbiel-Darmstädter, *Briefe aus Gurs und Limonest 1940–1943,* p. 18.

92   To Anneliese Herweck, 3/24/1941. Unpublished. Mannheim City Archive

93   In Paul Sauer, *Dokumente über die Verfolgung der jüdischen Bürger in Baden-Württemberg durch das Nationalsozialistische Regime 1933–1945,* vol. 2, p. 2.

94   Erhard Roy Wiehn, in Martha and Else Liefmann, *Helle Lichter auf dunklem Grund. Die "Abschiebung" aus Freiburg nach Gurs 1940–1942.* Erhard Roy Wiehn (ed.). Konstanz, 1995, p. 11.

95   Hanna Schramm, *Menschen in Gurs. Erinnerungen an ein französisches Internierungslager (1940–1941)*, p. 69 f.

96   Quoted in Michael Philipp (ed.), *Gurs—ein Internierungslager in Südfrankreich 1939–1943. Literarische Zeugnisse, Briefe, Berichte.* Hamburg, 1991, p. 34.

97   Erhard Roy Wiehn (ed.), *Oktoberdeportation 1940*, p. 118.

98   Quoted by Barbara Vormeier, in Hanna Schramm, *Menschen in Gurs. Erinnerungen an ein französisches Internierungslager (1940–1941)*, with a documented commentary on French emigration policy (1933–1944) by Barbara Vormeier, p. 239.

99   Quoted in Erhard Roy Wiehn (ed.), *Oktoberdeportation 1940*, p. 253.

100 Hanna Schramm, *Menschen in Gurs. Erinnerungen an ein französisches Internierungslager (1940-1941)*, p. 72.

101 Ibid, p. 74.

102 In Erhard Roy Wiehn (ed.), *Oktoberdeportation 1940*, p. 187.

103 Hanna Schramm, *Menschen in Gurs. Erinnerungen an ein französisches Internierungslager (1940–1941)*, p. 79.

104 Quoted in Gabriele Mittag, "Frauen von Gurs. Stationen des Überlebens." In Gabriele Mittag (ed.), *Gurs. Deutsche Emigrantinnen im französischen Exil.* Berlin 1991, p. 47.

105 To Margot Junod, 6/27/1942.

106 To Franz Darmstädter, 12/12/1940.

107 Cf. Rudolf Steiner: *Vorträge und Kurse über christlich-religiöses Wirken II.* CW 343. Dornach 1993, p. 471

108 To Alice and Rosi Ruprecht, around 4/11/1942.

109 On Nov. 10 ,1940, Margot Junod wrote as follows to Franz Darmstädter: "Dear Mr.Darmstädter, I am extremely worried about your sister Marie. I know only that she had to leave very suddenly. Please let me know by return of post whether you have any news of her, and what has happened. Marie is very dear to me, and you would be setting my mind at rest. Yours sincerely, Margot Junod (daughter of Felix Meyer)." Unpublished. Mannheim City Archive.

110 To Anneliese Herweck, 11/27/1940.

111 To Margot Junod, 5/28/1942.

112 To Margot Junod, 11/12/1940.

113 To Luise Kayser, 6/25/1941.

114 To Margot Junod, 3/5/1941.

115 To Margot Junod, 11/12–13/1941.

116 Quoted in Erhard Roy Wiehn (ed.), *Oktoberdeportation 1940*, p. 285.

117 To Franz Darmstädter, 11/19/1940.

118 Martha Besag, in Maria Krehbiel-Darmstädter: *Briefe aus Gurs und Limonest 1940–1943*, p. 118.

119 To Maria Gnädinger, 5/22/1941. Unpublished. Mannheim City Archive.

120 To Margot Junod, 12/7/1940.

121 Ibid., 12/5/1940.

122 Ibid., 10/30/1941.

123 Ibid.

124 Sayings of Solomon, 24:11–12 (Zurich Bible).

125 Cf. Jeanne Merle d'Aubigné, "Lager Gurs," in Adolf Freudenberg, *Rettet sie doch! Franzosen und die Genfer Ökumene im Dienste der Verfolgten*

des Dritten Reichs. Zürich, 1969, p. 88–122; and Madeleine Barot, "Die Cimade: Bereitschaft, Gemeinschaft, Aktion," ibid, pp. 77–87.

126 Quoted in Elsbeth Kasser Stiftung (ed.), *Gurs—ein Internierungslager. Südfrankreich 1939–1943. Aquarelle, Zeichnungen, Fotographien*. Elsbeth Kasser Collection. Basel 2009, p. 15.

127 Ibid, p. 16.

128 To Margot Junod, May 1941. Unpublished. Mannheim City Archive.

129 Biographical notes (Gurs), in Maria Krehbiel-Darmstädter, *Briefe aus Gurs und Limonest 1940–1943*, p. 29.

130 To Franz Darmstädter, 12/12/1940.

131 To Margot Junod, 12/15/1940.

132 Ibid., 12/22/1940.

133 Rudolf Steiner, *Vorträge und Kurse über christlich-religiöses Wirken II*. CW 343. Dornach 1993, p. 511.

134 "The first snow surprised us, and then frost came again. We live in dependency on the elements and have priorities that others would not recognize," wrote Maria Krehbiel-Darmstädter at the beginning of Jan. 1941 to Margot Junod. Unpublished. Mannheim City Archive.

135 To Margot Junod, 12/15/1940.

136 Ibid.

137 Letter from Martha Besag to Kläre Hennig, 12/14/1947. Unpublished. Mannheim City Archive.

138 Unpublished. Mannheim City Archive.

139 To Franz Darmstädter, 12/28/1940.

140 To Anneliese Herweck, 1/1/1941.

141 To Margot Junod, 1/10/1941. Unpublished. Mannheim City Archive.

142 Ibid.

143 To friends in Heidelberg and Mannheim, 1/7/1941. Unpublished. Mannheim City Archive.

144 Unpublished. Mannheim City Archive.

145 To Margot Junod, 3/5/1941.

146 To Luise Kayser, 4/11/1941.

147 To Anneliese Herweck, 2/13/1941. Unpublished. Mannheim City Archive.

148 Cf. Peter Selg, *Die Arbeit des Einzelnen und der Geist der Gemeinschaft. Rudolf Steiner und das "Soziale Hauptgesetz."* Dornach, 2007. (*The Fundamental Social Law: Rudolf Steiner on the Work of the Individual and the Spirit of Community*, Great Barrington, MA: SteinerBooks, 2011).

149 Cf. Peter Selg, *Das Vaterunser in der Darstellung Rudolf Steiners*. Stuttgart, 2009, p. 110 f.

150 To Maria Gnädinger, 1/10/1941.

151 On hearing that Spörri had distanced herself from The Christian Community (cf. Rudolf Gaedeke, *Die Gründer der Christengemeinschaft*, pp. 98–109), Maria Krehbiel-Darmstädter wrote a few succinct words in a letter from Gurs: "I heard of her decision only later on, by hearsay. I could not grasp much of it, but I have no wish to pass judgment, and this does not affect our bond. I trust you, hearing you, sensing you" (end of May 1941).

152 Unpublished. Mannheim City Archive. However, on 1/17/1948, Gertrud Spörri told Margot Junod (who thanked her for visiting Gurs) that she had

never been there. She had only "sent her greetings," and Maria must have experienced this as a "visit" ("For her it was like a visit.").

153 To Maria Gnädinger, circa 2/13/1941.

154 To Margot Junod, 3/5/1941.

155 To Anneliese Herweck, 2/20/1941. Unpublished. Mannheim City Archive.

156 To Gertrud Spörri, end of May 1941.

157 To Margot Junod and Kläre Hennig, circa 4/25/1941.

158 2/5/1941. Unpublished. Mannheim City Archive.

159 To friends in Heidelberg and Mannheim, 3/7/1941.

160 In Martha and Else Liefmann, *Helle Lichter auf dunklem Grund. Die "Abschiebung" aus Freiburg nach Gurs 1940–1942*, p. 117.

161 To Luise Kayser, 3/20/1941.

162 To Laure Wagner, Margot Junod and the friends in Heidelberg and Mannheim, 3/19/1941.

163 2/5/1941. Unpublished. Mannheim City Archive.

164 To Anneliese Herweck, 3/24/1941. Unpublished. Mannheim City Archive.

165 Ibid.

166 To Margot Junod, 4/22/1941.

167 To Maria Gnädinger, 4/16/1941.

168 To friends in Mannheim and Heidelberg, 6/23/1941.

169 Ibid., 3/7/1941.

170 To Luise Kayser, 4/11/1941.

171 To Maria Gnädinger, 4/16/1941.

172 Rudolf Steiner, *Vorträge und Kurse über christlich-religiöses Wirken IV* CW 345. Dornach 1994, p. 101.

173 Unpublished. Mannheim City Archive.

174 Rudolf Steiner, *Die Evolution vom Gesichtspunkte des Wahrhaftigen.* CW 132. Dornach 1999, p. 44. (*Inner Experiences of Evolution,* Great Barrington, MA: SteinerBooks, 2009).

175 The letters Franz Darmstädter sent to Gurs, preserved in Mannheim City Archive in carbon copies, show both his tireless efforts on behalf of his sister and also his discontent. Franz Darmstädter always wrote in a neutral and factual style, occasionally complaining about Maria's handwriting and also about the lack of real information in her letters, her passivity about emigration, and related things. On Jan. 21, 1941, he wrote in a letter to Gurs: "Please be so kind as to answer my various questions fully so that one can form an idea of how you fare." Even before deportation, there was not a great deal of contact between Maria and her brother; "I last spoke to her in Mannheim in 1936," wrote Franz to Margot Junod Nov. 16, 1940. Unpublished Mannheim City Archive.

176 Unpublished. Mannheim City Archive.

177 Rudolf Steiner, *Wahrspruchworte.* CW 40. Dornach, 2005, p. 21. (*Truth-Wrought-Words: And Other Verses and Prose Passages,* Hudson, NY: Anthroposophic Press, 1979).

178 Rudolf Steiner, *Der irdische und der kosmische Mensch.* CW 133. Dornach, 1989, p. 61. (*Earthly and Cosmic Man,* Blauvelt, NY: Garber, 1986).

179 Rudolf Steiner, *Erfahrungen des Übersinnlichen. Die drei Wege der Seele zu Christus.* CW 143. Dornach, 1994, p. 164.

180 Ibid

181 To Maria Gnädinger, 5/22/1941. Unpublished. Mannheim City Archive.

182 Unpublished. Mannheim City Archive.
183 Rainer Maria Rilke, *Gedichte aus den späteren Jahren*. Frankfurt a.M. 1990, p. 41.
184 To Maria Gnädinger, 6/12/1941. Mannheim City Archive.
185 To Maria Gnädinger, 10/14/1941.
186 To friends in Mannheim and Heidelberg, 6/23/1941.
187 "Since no room was available, we met together each Sunday at 10 in the open air to celebrate the Act of Consecration by speaking its words. To start with there were seven of us, sitting on a bench in the hospital gardens. I spoke the words softly, for people kept going past. But this hardly disturbed us—we didn't notice what was happening around us. Of course we would have preferred a room indoors, but we found none. We held this service even in rain and wind, and once while standing, as it was too cold to sit. We always kept this hour free, whatever happened, preferring to catch up with our work afterward by doing extra. After a couple of weeks we had to find a different spot, because the hospital gardens were placed out of bounds. Then we sat on the little stools common at the camp by the road alongside the hospital; later we met for a few Sundays by a slope behind a barrack. We forgot that we were behind barbed wire, under guard, and surrounded by deadly enemies. 'You spread for me a table in the presence of my enemies.' We felt that helping powers were with us. Under no circumstances did we wish to give up these gatherings when the weather grew cold—we had to find space indoors. In the fall of 1943, therefore, we gathered many times in the attic of the home for blind people, in the wings of an old theater stage. It was cold up there, dusty and dirty, and in the end we had to give up meeting there too.... But in the winter of 1943–44 we were at last granted indoor premises; Professor K from Berlin was able to make a room available to us until she died. In the spring and summer of 1944, we again met outside; we would wander around with our little stools until we found somewhere.

"All of us found it wonderful to experience such community during these years. None of us were alone. Sometimes it seemed to me that we were living on an island in the midst of a sea of destruction" (Martha Haarburger, "Erinnerungen aus dem Konzentrationslager Theresienstadt," in *Die Christengemeinschaft* 1978, no. 5, p. 159f.).
188 To Margot Junod, May 1941. Unpublished. Mannheim City Archive.
189 To Marie Baum, 5/22/1941.
190 Cf. Rudolf Steiner, *Das Ereignis der Christus-Erscheinung in der aetherischen Welt*. CW 118 (*The Reappearance of Christ in the Etheric*, Great Barrington, MA: SteinerBooks, 2003); and Peter Selg, "Die Wiederkunft des Christus im Ätherischen," in Peter Selg: *Michael und Christus. Studien zur Anthroposophie Rudolf Steiners*. Arlesheim, 2010.
191 To friends in Heidelberg and Mannheim, 6/1/1941.
192 Cf. Rudolf Steiner, *Menschenwesen, Menschenschicksal und Welt-Entwicklung*. CW 226. Dornach, 1988, p. 96f. and p. 128f. (*Man's Being, His Destiny, and World Evolution*, New York: Anthroposophic Press, 1966); also Peter Selg, *Christus und die Jünger. Vom Schicksal der inneren Gemeinschaft*. Arlesheim, 2009, pp. 125 ff. (*Christ and the Disciples: The Destiny of an Inner Community*, Great Barrington, MA: SteinerBooks, 2011).

193 To the friends in Heidelberg and Mannheim, 6/1/1941.

194 Report by the Reich Security Head Office (RHSA) in June 1941; quoted in Michael Heidenreich, "Briefe und Erlasse. Verbot der Christengemeinschaft vor 50 Jahren." in *Die Christengemeinschaft* 1991, no. 6, p. 291.

195 To Maria Gnädinger, 6/13/1941. Unpublished. Mannheim City Archive. Besides articles by Emil Bock ("Whitsun, the cosmic mission"); Friedrich Rittelmeyer ("Sun of grace"); Eberhard Kurras ("The new world: An apocalyptic reflection"); Wilhelm Salewski ("Christ as physician: The healing cosmic word"); and others, Maria Krehbiel-Darmstädter also found in this issue a little reflection by the priest Rudolf Frieling—whom she esteemed highly—on *the seasonal colors of the priest's raiment*. In this essay ("Casula Planeta") Frieling wrote: "In 1922, when the priests of the newly founded Christian Community overlaid the black robe with the white of the Alba and the colorfulness of the Casula, they certainly did not do this because they wished to rejuvenate an old tradition going back to a time preceding four centuries of Protestantism. They dressed themselves in these priestly garments again in earnest awareness of the specific 'rightness' of this religious custom. New consciousness had arisen concerning the fact that the human beings have subtler aspects of their being. These finer aspects flow around the death-related earthly body (the black robe!) as brightly weaving vitality (alba) and as surging play of colors (casula). The Catholic Church allows only five colors for the casula (as originally laid down by Pope Innocent III, 1198–1216).These are green, red, white, black, and purple; the casula of The Christian Community by contrast is accorded a far wider range and wealth of colors—twelve possible colors distributed across ten different festive garments. Our members may not all be fully aware of a fact that they should, by rights, know, and rejoice that a fully equipped Christian Community has ten casulas! These are for Advent, Christmas, Epiphany, Passiontide, Easter, Ascension, Pentecost, St. Johns, Michaelmas, and for intervening times between the festivals. This breaks open the narrowness of former tradition, with its traces of olden times when the human being had not yet grown into an experience of the full range of soul qualities in the color spectrum. This traditional view, therefore, regards purple as just a variant of black (in the fourteenth century, still, an *Ordo romanus* declared, 'Some consider black and purple to be the same'). It expressly excludes blue. The patterns on our casula have already been discussed in our newsletter. The double circle in front (lemniscate, 'eight'), among other things, also depicts the trajectory of planetary movements in the heavens. Now, the planets with their motion—as the world of *astra*—have an intimate connection with impulses of the soul, and are therefore rightly called 'astral.' From there, a surprising light falls on the remarkable fact that, besides the word *casula* (*casa* = hut), another name has also been retained in Church tradition for the garment worn by the priest at mass. It is called 'planeta'! Rhabanus Maurus (died 856) first used this word, as far as we can tell from the extant literature: 'This [casula] is called *'planeta'* by the Greeks. We do know, in fact, that the word *planeta* was used in early centuries to refer to a supposedly 'secular' article of clothing. It was worn as a completely enclosing cloak. But in ancient times, 'secular' clothing was in fact not as secular as today.

Mundane concerns did not mean that pictorial, religious consciousness was forgotten. This cloak was no doubt called 'planet' because it encompassed the human being, as a planet encompasses the Earth with its vibrant sphere. It therefore makes absolute sense to develop the priest's casula from this 'planetary cloak'—'*planeta*'! In former Church tradition, people did not know what to make of this designation; but today it can become very meaningful for us" (Ibid, p. 45f.).

196 To Maria Gnädinger, around 7/17/1941: "In what is lost let loss find itself, / And in gain, let gain be lost, /In what is grasped may grasping seek itself / And uphold itself in what is upheld./ Raised through becoming to existence, /Through existence inwoven with becoming, /May loss be its own gain!" (Rudolf Steiner, "Twelve moods. Fishes," in Steiner, *Wahrspruchworte*. CW 40. Dornach 2005, p. 60 (*Truth-Wrought-Words*. Hudson, NY: Anthroposophic Press, 1979).

197 To Maria Gnädinger, 10/14/1941.

198 To Franz Darmstädter, 7/1/1941; regarding the verse on the cross of lilies see also the letter to Luise Kayser on 6/25/1941.

199 To friends in Mannheim and Heidelberg, 10/14/1941. (The quote is from a poem by Novalis—TR.)

200 To Margot Junod, circa 7/16/1941.

201 To Luise Kayser, 10/2/1941.

202 To Margot Junod, beginning of July 1941.

203 Martha Besag, in Maria Krehbiel-Darmstädter, *Briefe aus Gurs und Limonest 1940–1943*, p. 117.

204 To Maria Gnädinger, 8/26/1941.

205 To Margot Junod, 8/28/1941.

206 To Margot Junod, beginning of September 1941.

207 To Anneliese Herweck, 9/27/1940. Unpublished. Mannheim City Archive.

208 Ibid.

209 To Luise Kayser, end of September 1941.

210 To Margot Junod, October 11 1941.

211 To Margot Junod, beginning of September 1941.

212 Rudolf Steiner, *Anthroposophische Leitsätze*. CW 26. Dornach, 1998, pp. 59ff. (*Anthroposophical Leading Thoughts: Anthroposophy as a Path of Knowledge: The Michael Mystery*, London: Rudolf Steiner Press, 1999)

213 Rudolf Steiner: *Vorträge und Kurse über christlich-religiöses Wirken IV*. CW 345. Dornach 1994, p. 125.

214 To Maria Gnädinger, 10/14/1941.

215 Unpublished. Mannheim City Archive

216 Jeanne Merle d'Aubigné: "Lager Gurs" in: Adolf Freudenberg: *Rettet sie doch! Franzosen und die Genfer Ökumene im Dienste der verfolgten des Dritten Reichs*, p. 92.

217 In a letter to Margot Junod written at the end of April 1942, Maria Krehbiel-Darmstädter accentuated Merle d'Aubigné's largesse of spirit and stressed that she came from a very old Huegenot family in France. She called her a "distinguished historical individual." Unpublished. Mannheim City Archive.

218 Unpublished. Mannheim City Archive.

219 To Anneliese Herweck, 10/16/1941. Unpublished. Mannheim City Archive.

220 To Luise Kayser, 10/2/1941.

221 To Margot Junod, 11/15/1941.
222 To Maria Gnädinger, 10/14/1941.
223 To Margot Junod, 11/15/1941.
224 In: Maria Krehbiel-Darmstädter: *Briefe aus Gurs und Limonest 1940–1943*, p. 117.
225 Unpublished. Mannheim City Archive.
226 11/9/1941. Unpublished. Mannheim City Archive.
227 Cf. Elsbeth Kasser: "Im Lager Gurs 1940–1943," in *Oktoberdeportation 1940*, pp. 567–572.
228 To Franz Darmstädter, 11/1/1941.
229 Ibid.
230 11/6/1941. Unpublished. Mannheim City Archive.
231 At the beginning of September, Maria had written as follows to her sister Luise about the catechumen sessions on the Old Testament—as introduction to the world of Judaism: "Naturally I am pleased to start on the New Test. but the Old strikes me as so venerable. I learn to respect my past, to 'see' my forefathers and parents. And to understand your nature and the inspiration of your art." Unpublished. Mannheim City Archive. For more on Luise and Stefan Kayser's intensifying preoccupation with Judaism, cf. Petra Weckel: "Light from our past—Rückbesinnung auf jüdische Traditionen im amerikanischen Exil am Beispiel der Künstlerin Lulu Kayser-Darmstädter." In: Helga Schreckenberger (ed.), *Ästhetiken des Exils*. Amsterdam/New York, 2003, pp. 187–208.
232 Six months later, on July 18 1942, after sending parts of the St. John's Epistle to Toni Schwarz, she wrote in justification of this: "Both of us know that this should not be 'written down.' Nor do we wish to take it and embalm it, however much we might like to 'possess' it. Instead we will commit it to memory and then destroy it, if you wish. The same happens to all that has been written; and especially with a particular type of text. We take it, rejoice or suffer with it; thus consume it. Thus destroy it!"
233 Rudolf Steiner, *Vorträge und Kurse über christlich-religiöses Wirken IV*. CW 345. Dornach, 1994, p. 77.
234 To Maria Gnädinger, beginning of December 1941.
235 To Rudolf Zeitler, 1/23/1942.
236 To the friends in Mannheim and Heidelberg, 1/18/1942.
237 Ibid.
238 To Margot Junod, second week in Advent 1941.
239 12/12/1941. Unpublished. Mannheim City Archive
240 To Rudolf Zeitler, 5/3/1942.
241 To Margot Junod, 12/17/1941.
242 To Maria Gnädinger, 1/31/1942.
243 In: Maria Krehbiel-Darmstädter, *Briefe aus Gurs und Limonest 1940–1943*, p. 119.
244 Ibid, p. 20.
245 To the friends in Heidelberg and Mannheim, 1/18/1940.
246 To Toni Schwarz, 12/31/1941.
247 To Rudolf Zeitler, 1/23/1942.
248 "Why? Because it is inexpressible. And it can only be experienced, and retrospectively experienced by those who are willing to suffer. To suffer from it truly. Not saying *"Oh, quelle Horreur."* And glad that they got

off lightly. I meet few people who have truly asked with a desire to know. 'Knowledge through compassion'—the path of the Grail: which today is still—and particularly today—the path for enquiring into suffering in the world. Do you recall the saying about the spear of Amfortas? 'Only the spear that caused the wound can heal it.'—Something has to 'fight back,' be strong enough. The love that heals an injury must be as strong as that injury. And usually one encounters only moderate interest. And this is why—speaking metaphorically—the wound one has received should not heal until it is 'healed in all.' This is 'mysticism' you may think, though perhaps without smiling. I hope so, The fact that I love you all proves that you are included in my monologue, in what my being speaks to itself" (to Anneliese Herweck, 7/2/1942).

249 To Maria Gnädinger, 1/31/1942.
250 To Anneliese Herweck, 1/6/1942.
251 To Margot Junod, 2/6/1942. Unpublished. Mannheim City Archive.
252 To Rudolf Zeitler, 5/3/1942.
253 In: Maria Krehbiel-Darmstädter, *Briefe aus Gurs und Limonest 1940–1943*, p. 120.
254 To Maria Gnädinger, 1/31/1942.
255 To Margot Junod, 1/14/1942.
256 To Franz Darmstädter, 1/15/1942.
257 To Kläre Hennig and Margot Junod,1/15/1942.
258 To Margot Junod, 1/14/1942.
259 To Margot Junod, 1/15/1942. In this letter Maria Krehbiel-Darmstädter described her impressions on reading the book *Le grand Meaulnes,* by Alain-Fournier, which Hilda Lagrange had given to her to read in Limonest. Maria knew that Margot Junod thought very highly of this novel, and she wrote to her about it after finishing it. Among other things she said: "I know that you love the book which Hilda gave me to read here. It is the first novel I have read for inconceivable ages. Down there [in Gurs] I never managed to 'read' as normally understood. I mean, as *'une occupation suivie, pleine d'abandon et semée de joie'* [a dedicated occupation, full of abandon and imbued with joy]. No: there was only a piecemeal grasping of ideas or texts that had to be great enough for one to rediscover the whole in a small part of them. And the whole text had to have eternal value to count in any way in our life there. In our little, worn out existence it had to give us a harsh, vigorous 'blow.' But 'books' that were novelistic or dreamlike were scarcely endurable for us—apart from the young children and elderly women, who may indeed have enjoyed them. Some of these wanted an epic, adventuresome quality, and liked an ongoing narrative; whereas others only wished to take flight from the state that was 'unbearable' for them. We, as I'll say again, the younger ones, that is, really the "bearers and fellows" of our time's destiny, we could not endure 'books'" (author's emphasis).

260 1/29/1942. Unpublished. Mannheim City Archive.
261 Unpublished. Mannheim City Archive.
262 To Anneliese Herweck, 1/29/1942. Unpublished. Mannheim City Archive.
263 To Margot Junod, 1/23/1942.
264 To Rudolf Zeitler, 5/3/1942.
265 To Margot Junod, 2/16/1942.

266 5/3/1942. Unpublished. Mannheim City Archive.
267 To Kläre Hennig and Margot Junod, 3/10/1942.
268 To Margot Junod, 2/6/1942. Unpublished, Mannheim City Archive.
269 To Toni Schwarz, 2/17/1942. Unpublished. Mannheim City Archive.
270 Cf. Peter Selg: *Rudolf Steiners Toten-Gedenken. Die Verstorbenen, der Dornacher Bau und die Anthroposophische Gesellschaft*. Arlesheim 2008. (*The Path of the Soul after Death: The Community of the Living and the Dead as Witnessed by Rudolf Steiner in his Eulogies and Farewell Addresses*, Great Barrington, MA: SteinerBooks, 2010).
271 To Toni Schwarz, 2/17/1941[1942?]
272 Unpublished. Mannheim City Archive.
273 Unpublished. Mannheim City Archive.
274 3/2/1942.
275 To Franz Darmstädter, 6/18/1942.
276 Ibid.
277 To Toni Schwarz, 2/17/1941.
278 To friends in Heidelberg and Mannheim, 3/13/1942.
279 To Franz Darmstädter, 3/2/1942.
280 To Kläre Hennig, 3/10/1942.
281 To Toni Schwarz, 3/11/1942.
282 Ibid.
283 To Margot Junod, 3/18/1942.
284 To Rudolf Zeitler, 5/3/1942.
285 Cf. Maria Krehbiel-Darmstädter's explanatory comments on learning to "surrender your thoughts to the divine" in her letter to Toni Schwarz of 5/23/1942, pp. 278f.
286 Cf. Peter Selg: *Die letzten drei Jahre. Ita Wegman in Ascona 1940–1943*. Dornach, 2004.
287 To Rudolf Zeitler, 5/3/1942.
288 To Anneliese Herweck, 7/13/1942.
289 7/25/1942.
290 To Anneliese Herweck, 7/13/1942.
291 To Rudolf Zeitler, 3/5/1942.
292 Rudolf Steiner: *Wahrspruchworte*. CW 40. Dornach, 2005, p. 24 (tr. Christopher Bamford, in *Start Now! A Book of Soul and Spiritual Exercises*. Great Barrington, MA: SteinerBooks, 2004, p. 148).
293 5/28/1942.
294 5/30/1942.
295 To Margot Junod, 6/10/1942.
296 To friends in Heidelberg and Mannheim, 6/15/1942.
297 6/10/1942.
298 To Toni Schwarz, 6/26/1942.
299 To Anneliese Herweck, 7/2/1942.
300 Unpublished. Mannheim City Archive.
301 Rudolf Steiner, *Vorträge und Kurse über christlich-religiöses Wirken IV*. CW 345. Dornach, 1994, p. 117.
302 To Anneliese Herweck, 7/2/1942.
303 To Maria Gnädinger, 7/4/1942.
304 To Margot Junod, 7/7/1942.

305 Quoted in Walther Hofer (ed.), *Der Nationalsozialismus. Dokumente (1933–1945)*. Frankfurt a.M. 1957, pp. 304 f.

306 Quoted in Michael Philipp (ed.), *Gurs—ein Internierungslager in Südfrankreich 1939–1943. Literarische Zeugnisse, Briefe, Berichte*, p. 78.

307 In Hanna Schramm, *Menschen in Gurs. Erinnerungen an ein französisches Internierungslager 1940–1943*, p. 143.

308 Weinstock, quoted in Michael Philipp (ed.), *Gurs—ein Internierungslager in Südfrankreich 1939–1943. Literarische Zeugnisse, Briefe, Berichte*, p. 78.

309 Ibid, p. 76f.

310 To Franz Darmstädter, 8/2/1942. Unpublished. Mannheim City Archive.

311 "In the first week of August 1942, when the terrible death trains were rolling eastward from France, I received a despairing letter from Maria. This was the only time she fell apart. And I remember that at the end of the letter she apologized and said that she had allowed herself to be weak this once with me. This was the last time I heard from her, for we fled to the woods the same day" (letter from Martha Besag to Kläre Hennig, 12/14/1947). Unpublished. Mannheim City Archive.

312 "Each time a sense of compassion or shared joy is developed in the soul, this creates a power of attraction for the Christ impulse, and, through compassion and love, Christ connects with the human soul. Compassion and love are the powers from which Christ forms his ether body through to the end of earthly evolution" (Rudolf Steiner, *Erfahrungen des Übersinnlichen*. CW 143. Dornach, 143, pp. 183f.).

313 To Toni Schwarz.

314 The "Reflections on Rudolf Steiner's mystery plays" from the literary estate of Mathilde Scholl, edited by Hugo Reimann, appeared from July 19, 1942, onward in the "members-only" section of the Dornach weekly *Das Goetheanum*.

315 To Rudolf Zeitler, 8/11/1942.

316 To Alice and Rosi Ruprecht, around 8/13/1942.

317 To Luise Schwarz, 8/14/1942.

318 Friedrich Hölderlin, "Patmos," in *Sämtliche Werke und Briefe. Münchener Ausgabe*, Michael Knaupp (ed.). Munich, 1992, vol. 1, pp. 447f. Cf. Peter Selg, "'But pure on untethered ground St. John endured.' Christ hymns in hard-pressed times," in *Friedrich Hölderlin. Die Linien des Lebens*. Stuttgart, 2009, p. 293–348.

319 Rudolf Steiner, *Anthroposophische Leitsätze*. CW 26. Dornach, 1998, p. 118. (*Anthroposophical Leading Thoughts*, London: Rudolf Steiner Press, 1999).

320 To Rudolf Zeitler, mid-August 1942.

321 To Franz Darmstädter, 8/22/1942.

322 Ibid.

323 Cf. Rudolf Steiner, *Die Konstitution der Allgemeinen Anthroposophischen Gesellschaft und der Freien Hochschule für Geistewissenschaft*. CW 260a. Dornach 1987, pp. 34ff. (*The Foundation Stone / The Life, Nature & Cultivation of Anthroposophy*, London: Rudolf Steiner Press, 1998); cf. also Willem Zeylmans van Emmichoven, *The Foundation Stone*, London: Temple Lodge, 2002.

324 To Toni Schwarz, 8/24/1942.

325   To Alice and Rosi Ruprecht, around 8/13/1942.

326   To Toni Schwarz, August 21 1942.

327   To Toni Schwarz, 8/21/1942 (author's emphasis).

328   To Franz Darmstädter, 8/22/1942.

329   Nelly Sachs, "Leben unter Bedrohung" (1956), in Walter A. Berendsohn, *Nelly Sachs. Einführung in das Werk der Dichterin jüdischen Schicksals.* Darmstadt, 1974, pp. 9 ff.

330   To Franz Darmstädter, 8/22/1942.

331   Cf. Richard Zahlten: *Dr. Johanna Geissmar. Von Mannheim nach Heidelberg und über den Schwarzwald durch Gurs nach Auschwitz-Birkenau. 1877–1942.* Konstanz, 1991.

332   To Toni Schwarz, 8/24/1942. Cf. Rudolf Steiner, *Das Geheimnis der Wunde. Aufzeichnungen zum "Samariterkurs,"* CW 108, 1992.

333   To Toni Schwarz, 8/29/1942.

334   Ibid.

335   To Margot Junod, around 9/15/1942.

336   To Franz Darmstädter, 8/28/1942.

337   Ibid.

338   She wrote this on September 3, 1942, in relation to the deportation that they both were very likely to face; but also added: "And—let us hope—that we will find one another as latecomers when the last of us are ferried home (as in a 'late train'). It would be infinitely good to be together again. And yet—who can find the other in these conditions? My consolation for the shut-in travelers is that they are accompanied either by accustomed comrades or true friends."

339   Cf. the letter on pp. 278f.

340   To Wilhelm and Walter Schmitthenner, 9/5/1942.

341   To Franz Darmstädter.

342   Unpublished. Mannheim City Archive.

343   Cf. Peter Selg, *Christian Morgenstern. Sein Weg mit Rudolf Steiner.* Stuttgart, 2008.

344   Quoted in Thomas Bertram: *Chronik 1942.* Dortmund 1991, p. 158.

345   To Franz Darmstädter, 10/9/1942.

346   On October 10, 1942, Franz Darmstädter had written to the local authorities in Binningen (unpublished, Mannheim City Archive): "I hereby apply for a residence permit in Binningen, and an entry visa to Switzerland, for my sister Maria Krehbiel, currently living in Limonest, Dept. Rhone, France. I beg you most kindly to carefully examine this request, the reasons for which follow below, and, together with your endorsement, to pass it on to the cantonal police department for aliens in Liestal so that this office can in turn forward it to the immigration office of the Swiss police department for aliens in Bern. Frau Maria Krehbiel, no children and divorced, is of German nationality, fifty years of age and presently stateless, having been deported in October 1941 from Germany to Gurs as a Jew of Christian confession. Frau Krehbiel has a severe heart condition and since the beginning of the year has been granted sick leave from the internment camp. Current circumstances in France make it seem highly probable that my sister will shortly face further deportation to Poland, which she would be unlikely to survive for health reasons. I therefore submit the above application and would be willing to have my sister live with us

here, and would myself pay for her board and accommodation. Her stay in Switzerland would last only until approval is granted for her onward journey to the United States, since my other sister [Frau Dr. Luise Kayser, Berkely City, California] has lodged all necessary applications for Frau Krehbiel's immigration there. [The visa to be lodged with the US Consul in Lyon]. I also append here the names of the following referees: Frau Dr. Margot Junod, Lausanne-La Rosiaz, Bd. De la Forêt 11, a relative of Frau Krehbiel and of Swiss nationality. Father Dr. Franz Gnädinger, Bern, Bellevuestrasse 136, Frl. Rosa Ruprecht, Muri near Bern, Reinweg 10. I look forward to receiving your esteemed reply, and thank you warmly in advance for your kind efforts. Yours sincerely, Franz Darmstädter."

347 To Franz Darmstädter, 10/29/1942.
348 To Toni Schwarz, 10/28/1942.
349 To Franz Darmstädter, All Souls 1942.
350 Ibid.
351 Ibid.
352 10/31/1942.
353 Rudolf Steiner, *Die geistigen Wesenheiten in den Himmelskörpern und Naturrreichen.* CW 136. Dornach, 1996, pp. 38ff. (*Spiritual Beings in the Heavenly Bodies and in the Kingdoms of Nature,* Great Barrington, MA: SteinerBooks, 2011).
354 Rudolf Steiner, *Von Jesus zu Christ.* Dornach, 1988. CW 131, p.80. (*From Jesus to Christ,* London: Rudolf Steiner Press, 2005).
355 Rudolf Steiner, *Der übersinnliche Mensch, anthroposophisch erfasst.* CW 231. Dornach, 1999, p. 76. (*At Home in the Universe: Exploring Our Suprasensory Nature,* Hudson, NY: Anthroposophic Press, 2000).
356 Rudolf Steiner, *Von der Initiation.* CW 138. Dornach, 1986, p. 112. (*Initiation, Eternity, and the Passing Moment,* Spring Valley, NY: Anthroposophic Press, 1980).
357 See the section "The flight" and the account given there by Françoise Labouverie, a 21-year-old cousin of Jacques Lagrange, who accompanied Maria to Lons-le-Saunier and saw her there again. In: Maria Krehbiel-Darmstädter: *Briefe aus Gurs und Limonest 1940–1943,* pp. 324ff.
358 Words of Maria Krehbiel-Darmstädter to Walter Schmitthenner, Drancy, 1/6/1943. Transcribed by Walter Schmitthenmner. Ibid, p. 334.
359 Ibid.
360 Unpublished. Mannheim City Archive.
361 Words of Maria Krehbiel-Darmstädter to Walter Schmitthenner, Drancy, 1/6/1943. Transcribed by Walter Schmitthenner, in Maria Krehbiel-Darmstädter, *Briefe aus Gurs und Limonest 1940–1943,* p. 334.

"If Maria Krehbiel-Darmstädter had stayed put in Limonest, she might possibly have survived the war as her friend Toni Schwarz and her mother did, avoiding the deportation due to their 'sick leave' in Beaulieu (Dordogne)—at Pension Ste. Marie. With this in mind, Maria Gnädinger wrote to Walter Schmitthenner in 1948: 'I am still preoccupied with this strange fact: that Toni Schwarz was able to save herself by staying put, and that Maria also wished to do this—but that she was persuaded to flee across the border'" (letter of 9/1/1948. Unpublished. Mannheim City Archive).

362 Words of Maria Krehbiel-Darmstädter to Walter Schmitthenner, Drancy, 1/6/1943, transcribed by Walter Schmitthenner. In Maria Krehbiel-Darmstädter, *Briefe aus Gurs und Limonest 1940–1943*, p. 335.

363 Ibid, p. 333.

364 In his letter to Leo Schaeffler on 8/4/1962, Paul Celan described "Jewishness" as a "form of what is human." Years before this, he had likewise written to Jean Starobinski: "What is Judaism if not a form of what is human?" (cf. Peter Selg, *"Alles ist unvergessen." Paul Celan and Nelly Sachs*. Dornach, 2008, pp. 229, 429).

365 Friedrich Rittelmeyer: Unpublished conversation with Dr. Steiner. Typescript (1932). Quoted by Peter Selg in *Michael und Christus. Studien zur Anthroposophie Rudolf Steiners*. Arlesheim, 2010, p. 53.

366 Rudolf Steiner, *Wahrspruchworte*. CW 40. Dornach, 2005, p. 127. (*Truth-Wrought-Words*, Hudson, NY: Anthroposophic Press, 1979).

367 To Toni Schwarz, 8/1/1942.

Bibliography

Baum, Marie. *Rückblick auf mein Leben*. Heidelberg, 1950.

Blattmann, Georg. "Ein Zeichen des Lichts aus dem Dunkel," in *Die Christengemeinschaft*, Christmas 1970, pp. 377–378.

Elsbeth Kasser-Stitftung (ed.). *Gurs—ein Internierungslager. Südfrankreich 1939–1943. Aquarelle, Zeichnungen, Fotographien*. Elsbeth Kasser collection. Basel, 2009.

Fliedner, Hans-Joachim. *Die Judenverfolgung in Mannheim 1933–1945*, 2 vols. Stuttgart, 1971.

Freudenberg, Adolf (ed.). *Rettet sie doch! Franzosen und die Genfer Ökumene im Dienste der Verfolgten des Dritten Reichs*. Zurich, 1969.

Freudenberg-Hübner, Dorothea und Wiehn, Eberhard Roy. *Abgeschoben. Jüdische Schicksale aus Freiburg 1940–1942. Briefe der Geschwister Liefmann aus Gurs und Morlas an Adolf Freudenberg in Genf*. Konstanz, 1993.

Gädeke, Rudolf. *Die Gründer der Christengemeinschaft. Ein Schicksalsnetz*. Dornach, 1992.

Heidenreich, Michael. "Jüdische Schicksale und die Ausbreitung der Christengemeinschaft," in *Die Christengemeinschaft*, no. 3, 1998, pp. 130–132.

Hofer, Walther. *Der Nationalozialismus. Dokumente (1933–1945)*. Frankfurt a.M. 1957.

Kacer-Bock, Gundhild. *Die Christengemeinschaft in Stuttgart. Chronik 1922–2005*. Stuttgart, 2007.

Keller, Volker. *Bilder vom jüdischen Leben in Mannheim*. Mannheim, 1988.

Klarsfeld, Serge. *Vichy-Auschwitz. Die Zusammenarbeit der deutschen und französischen Behörden bei der "Endlösung der Judenfrage" in Frankreich*. Hamburg, 1989.

Krehbiel-Darmstädter, Maria. *Briefe aus Gurs und Limonest 1940–1943* (Walter Schmitthenner, ed.). Heidelberg, 1970.

Liefmann, Martha and Else. *Helle Lichter auf dunklem Grund. Die "Abschiebung" aus Freiburg nach Gurs 1940–1942* (Erhard Roy Wiehn, ed.). Konstanz, 1995.

Mittag, Gabriele (ed.). *Gurs. Deutsche Emigrantinnen im französischen Exil*. Berlin, 1991; *"Es gibt Verdammte nur in Gurs." Literatur, Kultur und Alltag in einem südfranzösischen Internierungslager 1940–1942*. Tübingen, 1996.

Obst, Johannes. *Gurs. Deportation und Schicksal der badisch-pfälzischen Juden.* Mannheim 1986.

Philipp, Michael (ed.). *Gurs—ein Internierungslager in Südfrankreich 1939–1943. Literarische Zeugnisse, Briefe, Berichte.* Hamburg 1991.

Sauer, Paul, *Dokumente über die Verfolgung der jüdischen Bürger in Baden-Württemberg durch das nationalsozialistische Regime, 1933–1945.* Stuttgart 1966; *Die Schicksale der jüdischen Bürger Baden-Württembergs während der nationalsozialistischen Verfolgungszeit 1933–1945.* Stuttgart, 1969.

Schadt, Jörg and Caroli. Michael (ed.), *Mannheim unter der Diktatur.* Mannheim, 1997.

Schmitthenner, Walter. Literary estate in Mannheim City Archive.

Schramm, Hanna. *Menschen in Gurs. Erinnerungen an ein französisches Internierungslager (1940–1941);* with a documentary essay on French immigration policies between 1933 and 1944 by Barbara Vormeier. Worms, 1977.

Schreckenberger, Helga (ed.). *Ästhetiken des Exils.* Amsterdam/New York, 2003.

Mannheim youth welfare office (ed.). *"Auf einmal da waren sie weg."* Jüdische Spuren in Mannheim. Mannheim, 1995.

Steiner, Rudolf. Collected Works [CW] (Gesamtausgabe [GA]). Dornach, 1956 ff.

Vormeier, Barbara. *Die Deportierungen deutscher und österreichischer Juden aus Frankreich.* Paris, 1980.

Weinstock, Rolf. *Das wahre Gesicht Hitler-Deutschlands.* Singen, 1948.

Wiehn, Erhard Roy (ed.). *Oktoberdeportation 1940.* Konstanz, 1990.

Picture credits

Mannheim City Archive: 1, 3, 4, 6, 9, 10, 11, 12, 13, 14, 16, 21, 25, 26, 27, 29, 33, 37, 38, 39, 42, 43, 44, 45, 46, 47, 48, 51, 55, 56, 59, 60, 65, 67, 69, 70, 73, 75, 76

Elsbeth Kasser collection, Zurich: 23, 24, 32, 48, 61

Rudolf Steiner Archive, Dornach: 2, 72

Archive of The Christian Community, Berlin: 8, 15, 31, 35

Archive at the Goetheanum, Dornach: 52, 61

Ita Wegman Institute, Arlesheim: 5, 49

National Gallery, London: 34

The Vatican, Rome: 36

From Volker Keller. *Bilder vom jüdischen Leben in Mannheim*: 16

From Philipp Michael (ed.), *Gurs—ein Internierungslager in Südfrankreich*: 18, 19, 20, 22, 30, 37, 41

From Paul Sauer, *Dokumente über die Verfolgung der jüdischen Bürger in Baden-Württemberg durch das nationalsozialistische Regime, 1933–1945*: 17

Michael Schnur, Dresden: 7, 65

Walter Schneider, Stuttgart: 58, 68

Books in English Translation by Peter Selg

ON RUDOLF STEINER:

Rudolf Steiner and Christian Rosenkreutz (2012)

Rudolf Steiner as a Spiritual Teacher: From Recollections of Those Who Knew Him (2010)

ON CHRISTOLOGY:

The Creative Power of Anthroposophical Christology: An Outline of Occult Science · The First Goetheanum · The Fifth Gospel · The Christmas Conference (with Sergei O. Prokofieff) (2012)

Christ and the Disciples: The Destiny of an Inner Community (2012)

The Figure of Christ: Rudolf Steiner and the Spiritual Intention behind the Goetheanum's Central Work of Art (2009)

Rudolf Steiner and the Fifth Gospel: Insights into a New Understanding of the Christ Mystery (2010)

Seeing Christ in Sickness and Healing (2005)

ON GENERAL ANTHROPOSOPHY:

Crisis in the Anthroposophical Society: And Pathways to the Future (with Sergei O. Prokofieff) (2013)

The Culture of Selflessness: Rudolf Steiner, the Fifth Gospel, and the Time of Extremes (2012)

The Fundamental Social Law: Rudolf Steiner on the Work of the Individual and the Spirit of Community (2011)

The Path of the Soul after Death: The Community of the Living and the Dead as Witnessed by Rudolf Steiner in his Eulogies and Farewell Addresses (2011)

Rudolf Steiner and the School for Spiritual Science: The Foundation of the "First Class" (2012)

Rudolf Steiner's Foundation Stone Meditation: And the Destruction of the Twentieth Century (2012)

Rudolf Steiner's Intentions for the Anthroposophical Society: The Executive Council, the School for Spiritual Science, and the Sections (2011)

The Agriculture Course, Koberwitz, Whitsun 1924: Rudolf Steiner and the Beginnings of Biodynamics (2010)

ON ANTHROPOSOPHICAL MEDICINE AND CURATIVE EDUCATION:

The Mystery of the Heart: The Sacramental Physiology of the Heart in Aristotle, Thomas Aquinas, and Rudolf Steiner (2012)

I Am for Going Ahead: Ita Wegman's Work for the Social Ideals of Anthroposophy (2012)

Ita Wegman and Karl König: Letters and Documents Karl König's Path to Anthroposophy (2009)

Karl König: *My Task: Autobiography and Biographies.* Peter Selg, ed. (2008)

Karl König: *The Child with Special Needs: Letters and Essays on Curative Education.* Peter Selg, ed. (2009)

ON CHILD DEVELOPMENT AND WALDORF EDUCATION:

The Essence of Waldorf Education (2010)

A Grand Metamorphosis: Contributions to the Spiritual-Scientific Anthropology and Education of Adolescents (2008)

I Am Different from You: How Children Experience Themselves and the World in the Middle of Childhood (2011)

Karl König's Path to Anthroposophy (2008)

The Therapeutic Eye: How Rudolf Steiner Observed Children (2008)

Unbornness: Human Preexistence and the Journey toward Birth (2010)

Ita Wegman Institute
for Basic Research into Anthroposophy

PFEFFINGER WEG 1 A CH 4144 ARLESHEIM, SWITZERLAND
www.wegmaninstitute.ch
e-mail: sekretariat@wegmaninstitute.ch

The Ita Wegman Institute for Basic Research into Anthroposophy is a non-profit research and teaching organization. It undertakes basic research into the lifework of Dr. Rudolf Steiner (1861–1925) and the application of Anthroposophy in specific areas of life, especially medicine, education, and curative education. Work carried out by the Institute is supported by a number of foundations and organizations and an international group of friends and supporters. The Director of the Institute is Prof. Dr. Peter Selg.

CPSIA information can be obtained at www.ICGtesting.com
Printed in the USA
LVOW08s1608031013

355309LV00007B/999/P